Teaching in the universities

Teaching in the universities

no one way

edited by
EDWARD F. SHEFFIELD

McGill-Queen's University Press
Montreal and London 1974

International Standard Book Number 0-7735-0193-2 (cloth)
International Standard Book Number 0-7735-0235-1 (paper)
Library of Congress Catalog Card Number 74-75974
Legal Deposit fourth quarter 1974
Bibliothèque nationale du Québec

Design by Hjordis P. Wills
Printed in Canada by The Hunter Rose Company

Contents

Acknowledgements

Funds for this project were provided by the Varsity Fund of the University of Toronto and by the Canada Council. Neither is responsible for what is said; both are to be thanked for their aid. I am grateful to the university officials who made participation by their institutions possible, the graduates who responded to my request for their assistance, and the essayists, who had no easy task. I relied heavily on the help of my wife, Nora, who did much of the work on the analyses of data and acted as my chief critic. I am in debt also to Ruth Corbin, Arlene Tinkler, Jean Cunningham, Susan Ruiter, and Muriel Kinney for secretarial services; J. A. d'Oliveira of Glendon College, York University, who bolstered my shaky French; John C. Ogilvie, Director of the University of Toronto Institute of Applied Statistics, for statistical advice; and Stan Cabay who told the computer what to do.

E.F.S.

Contributors

FREDERICK A. ALDRICH, Professor of Biology and Dean of Graduate Studies, Memorial University of Newfoundland

MURIEL ARMSTRONG, Professor of Economics, Sir George Williams University

EARL W. BUXTON, Professor, Department of Secondary Education, University of Alberta

MARGARET E. COCKSHUTT, Associate Professor of Library Science, University of Toronto

WILLIAM H. FOWLER, Associate Professor of Physical Education, McMaster University

GEORGE GALAVARIS, Professor of Art History, McGill University

LEON GETZ, Professor of Law, University of Toronto

J. C. GILSON, Professor of Agricultural Economics and Vice-President (Research, Graduate Studies, and Special Assignments), University of Manitoba

JAROSLAV HAVELKA, Professor of Psychology, King's College, University of Western Ontario

A. W. JOLLIFFE, Emeritus Professor of Geological Sciences, Queen's University

PAUL L'ARCHEVÊQUE, Professeur titulaire de docimologie, Département de pédagogie, Université Laval

JEAN-LOUIS MAJOR, Professeur titulaire, Département de Lettres françaises, Université d'Ottawa

G. G. MEYERHOF, Professor and Head of the Department of Civil Engineering, Nova Scotia Technical College

Z. MÉZL, Professeur émérite de pathologie buccale, Université de Montréal

JACQUES-YVAN MORIN, Professeur titulaire à la Faculté de Droit, Université de Montréal

BRENDAN O'GRADY, Professor of English, University of Prince Edward Island

R. W. PACKER, Professor, Department of Geography, University of Western Ontario

GEORGE SETTERFIELD, Professor, Department of Biology, Carleton University

JAN W. STEINER, Professor of Pathology and Associate Dean of Medicine, University of Toronto

JACK L. SUMMERS, Professor of Pharmacy, University of Saskatchewan

ELEANORE VAINES, Assistant Professor, School of Home Economics, University of British Columbia

ZDENEK VALENTA, Professor of Chemistry, University of New Brunswick

DOUGLAS WAUGH, Dean of Medicine, Queen's University

Introduction

This project was undertaken in the hope that it might contribute to the improvement of teaching in the universities.

It seemed reasonable to assume that among the most appropriate people to consult about the characteristics of effective university teaching were students. So the assistance of students, or rather former students, was sought. Deans and alumni directors provided the names and addresses of roughly seven thousand graduates of twenty-four faculties and schools in nineteen Canadian universities—members of the classes of 1968 (the most recent then available), 1963 (five years earlier), and 1958 (ten years earlier). Among them they represented the fourteen top faculties in terms of numbers of first degrees awarded in 1966–67, the latest year for which data were published at the time—four of arts, three of science, two each of education, engineering, commerce/administration, law, and medicine, and one each of nursing, physical education, agriculture, home economics, pharmacy, dentistry, and library science. Some were in large universities, some in small. Five of the twenty-four were French-language faculties, and the list included at least one university in every province, from Memorial University of Newfoundland to the University of British Columbia.

Letters were sent to these seven thousand graduates inviting them to name professors they had known as excellent teachers, and to say what there was about these professors and their teaching which made them effective. It was explained that of the teachers so identified a score or more would be invited to write essays on the teaching of undergraduate students, reflecting their own beliefs and practices, and that these would be published. (Copies of the letters and attachments—in English and in French—which were sent to the graduates are appended.) Replies were received from just over a thousand. (This is a low rate of response but it would appear to have been representative, because, as is pointed out below, the pattern of comments received from the respondents is like that found in other studies.) On the average each named two professors; some named as many as six. Forty-one graduates took the trouble to send back the response form saying that, unfortunately, they had had no professor whom they would classify as an excellent teacher.

Among those mentioned were men who were or later became well known in other roles. Arts graduates of McGill named the late F. Cyril James, principal of McGill; F. Kenneth Hare, later president of the University of British Columbia; R. Cranford Pratt, who was to serve as principal of the University College in Dar es Salaam; Hugh MacLennan, novelist; Louis Dudek, poet; Stanley Gray, revolutionary; and Eric Kierans, later a minister in the government of the Province of Quebec and then in the government of Canada. John W. O'Brien, who was to be principal of Sir George Williams University, scored with commerce graduates of that university; Alphonse Riverin, first president of the Université du Québec, was remembered by students of commerce at Laval; and graduates in law of the University of British Columbia drew attention to A. W. R. Carrothers who subsequently became president of the University of Calgary. Identified as having been excellent teachers in the Faculty of Law at the Université de Montréal were Pierre Elliott Trudeau, who became prime minister of Canada; Jean-Guy Cardinal, later a minister in the Union Nationale government of Quebec; and Jacques-Yvan Morin, who became leader of the Parti Québécois in Quebec's National Assembly in 1973. Robert Bourassa, who led the Liberals to victory in that and the previous election, was singled out for his teaching at the Université d'Ottawa. And Arthur Tremblay, Quebec's deputy of education during most of the period of the Quiet Revolution, was remembered by those who studied with him in the Ecole de Pédagogie et d'Orientation de l'Université Laval.

It had been expected that the graduates of each faculty would name a few teachers with marked frequency. There was enough concentration of choices to help identify at least some good teachers in each faculty or school, but many different professors were named by each group of graduates. Of course, not all students had the same teachers and that could account for much of the spread. It seems likely though that another factor was present, what one might call a compatibility factor: some professors are good for some students but not for others. Maybe there is hope for all of us. Somewhere out there. . . .

After applying a simple weighting scale to take account of the differences in class size and the order in which professors' names appeared on the returned forms, in each faculty there was identified at least one, in most cases several, of those mentioned with sufficient frequency to suggest that they were excellent teachers. There was no way of knowing which one was the best nor how many others were excellent too. Because only one was sought in each faculty, the final choice was to some extent arbitrary.

When the choice had been made, the dean or director of the faculty or school was consulted to see if he concurred in the choice or had some essential information which would affect it. In several instances the professor who had been identified was no longer a member of the faculty; that led to another choice. In most cases, though, confirmation was prompt. The editor then sought out the chosen professor—in person—and invited him to write an essay for this collection. "What is wanted," each was told, "is a personal expression of what you believe about teaching undergraduates, and how you go about it." All appeared to be interested and flattered. All accepted the invitation, although one was unable to provide an essay.

Each of the next twenty-three chapters is written by one of those identified as an excellent teacher, followed by a brief outline of his career and a summary of the comments made about him and his teaching by the graduates who named him. As a matter of strategy, the writers were *not* shown the comments made by their former students until after their essays had been sent in. The reader may need to recall this fact from time to time because the correspondence in some cases is striking. It is scarcely necessary to note that the essays differ markedly from one another. They differ not only because they reflect different people with different styles of teaching, but also in the extent to which they succeed in revealing how their authors teach. For many of the chosen professors this turned out to be an extremely difficult assignment. One mark of this diffculty is that some of the writers found that they could not bring themselves to use the first person; they had to say, in effect, "One ought to . . ." when what they meant was "I do . . ." or "I try to . . ." They had other problems as well. Most found it hard to define teaching, let alone creativity in teaching, and some admitted that they really function intuitively. One observed that his performance in the classroom is probably better than his description would indicate, another found that writing about his teaching was painful because he was forced to confront himself, and still another concluded that trying to explain how you teach is like trying to explain how you breathe. These illustrations underscore the complexity of the teaching process and help to prepare the reader for the fact that the essays do not supply magic formulas, packaged for easy consumption.

Following the twenty-three essays, some generalizations and observations about them have been attempted, and a few tentative conclusions are drawn. Next is an analysis of all the responses received from graduates who named professors they thought of as excellent teachers. It too allows for some generalizations and comments about the characteristics of effective university teaching.

Finally there is some indication of what might be done with the results of the study—how they might be used to encourage improvement in the quality of teaching in Canadian universities.

EDWARD F. SHEFFIELD

Higher Education Group
University of Toronto

➣ Teaching Is Giving Yourself

George Galavaris

Freedom, a word of which one hears so much these days, is above all a respect for life and for the value of man. As long as neither of these exists the life of the spirit can never find its proper course. Nevertheless the misery into which we have been thrown in recent times does show some light: the desire seen in the youth of today who flood our universities in search of a better life, a life of the spirit.

Youth is not striving for a life of material comforts devoid of meaning, whose lonely desolate road some of us have trodden with despair, often with an indifference becoming to the dead. The young people have seen our heavy faces and want to take another road. The demands that youth poses for educators (and here I have in mind not professors alone, but all those who have some responsibility both for the new generation and for the demands that the meaning of values places upon us), force those of us who realize and are willing to undertake this responsibility to bring our inner self into sharper focus. We are forced to concentrate upon our "self" to see whether there is anything left there that we can give to the young; something that will help them find an answer to the agonizing problem of our time, the unbalanced situation which youth has recognized: an enormous development of technology on the one hand and the diminishing of human values as well as the meaning of man's life on the other.

These are thoughts which occupy my mind any time I am to prepare a lecture and any time I go to the lecture room to face the eager students. In both instances I realize the problem. I am an ordinary human being like any other, with no exceptional gifts, but I have the great fortune to speak about works of beauty which take man away from the transitory. Nevertheless I feel that an answer to the problem does not depend on the knowledge that I try to impart to the student or on whether my lecture has the sparkle of cleverness and dazzle. My responsibility, as far as this is possible, is to encourage the return of wonder and the holy fear of life in the inner being of the young person who stands next to me. Only if the student becomes aware of these two things will the knowledge he acquires bear fruit for it will become part of his inner self.

My colleagues, if they agree with these thoughts, and not all do, always point out that my intention is not difficult to achieve after all. I am an art historian, dealing with pictures and colours which, by their own nature, exert an intrinsic appeal upon the student. The usual expression of opinion is this: "You show lovely pictures, you talk about the pictures, you have such a nice lecture hall. Surely pictures and a nice auditorium are bound to throw the students or at least some of them under a spell." Some of these statements may be true. All of them, however, sound superficial or reveal ignorance of the real issues involved. Perhaps the student may well agree with my view.

The auditorium is comfortable and deceptively small. It contains exactly one hundred seats, but it is designed in such a way that neither teacher nor students are aware of its exact numbers. Without the ingenuity of the architect this could not have been achieved, particularly since the auditorium is simply a renovated area in the old Arts Building of McGill. It is true that the intimacy of the hall helps the creation of another intimacy which must come into existence if my aim is to be accomplished. This intimacy is felt in the classroom but is by no means revealed in terms of words or any other signs of familiarity between the participants. It is an intimacy that is felt by one and all and which has no need of words. It is an intimacy that goes beyond the comfort of the room and the colour of the lovely pictures shown on the large screen and the semidarkness of the room, necessary since all our art history lectures are illustrated.

This intimacy begins with the preparation of the lecture. I work extremely hard in organizing my material to the utmost detail. I am extremely sensitive to method and to use of words as well. The material takes the form of a formal lecture, in the old-fashioned style, a system which has been considered by some educators as destructive because they claim "it encourages passive receptivity rather than active discovery." The correctness of this view, I think, would very much depend on the intention of the lecturer. My intention is not to fill the mind of the student with a body of dead knowledge found in compendia and encyclopaedias or text books—by the way, something that surprises college text publishers is that I never use text books in my courses—but to help him discover that which exists in himself and of which he is not always aware. In this way one can no longer speak of passive receptivity. In preparing the lecture, in choosing and meditating on the works of art,

I think of the student and of ways in which these works of art, presented in an historical context (since I teach the history of art), could exert an appeal for him; how the works might acquire a different meaning for him, revealing the drama of man in history and, if this is possible at all, man's struggle to unite a divided self. So the works of art cease to be objects, or dissected insects in a laboratory. They become living flowers which guide the spirit from the temporary to the timeless beauty which is the same yesterday and today.

I have not and I do not follow a particular formula in the implementation of these aims. Each time I prepare a lecture I need desperately as much time as possible to think of the ways in which these works first became part of myself. Then, and only then, can they be offered to the students. Sometimes I put works of different periods on the screen right at the outset of the lecture, just after I have said "good morning, everyone," a way of bringing the class to order and of creating the first step for the intimacy of which I spoke earlier. This "good morning" also helps me feel the disposition of the students which varies considerably from day to day just as mine does. Often it depends a good deal on external factors over which none of us has any real control. If I get the feeling of the students right, then I know how to begin and how I must give myself that day; for I can only describe my teaching in terms of giving. This means that the opening of the lecture and the lecture itself can be considerably modified during the process of its delivery. For instance, if I feel that the students are sleepy in the early morning hours, I ask the projectionist to show two slides on the screen and I ask the students to look at them and think about them for a few moments. I receive a few comments. I pick the one which seems to be most apt and use it to begin the lecture. Then I continue as I have planned, seldom using my notes. If, however, I am in a bad mood, I try my best to get out of this state before I begin the lecture. I take a few minutes before the lights are lowered to look into the eyes of the students. Some of them smile and this on a dreadful winter day helps me think of beautiful warm places. This is easy to do since the works I discuss are so often located in beautiful places. So I begin by saying, "now I shall take you to Venice," and as a painting from a Venetian collection comes onto the screen I think of Venice and at once my own disposition changes. I feel then that I can give myself.

In the course of the lecture the students can interrupt and ask any questions they like, or even enter upon a discussion if they think this necessary. But here too I prefer to have anticipated this in preparing the lecture. Purposely I introduce into my text something difficult to understand and bring it to a climax. After I feel I have exhausted the capabilities of the students, I come to a halt. I recognize the difficulty of the question involved and ask the students to discuss it or to give an answer. Here a lot of experience is required to control the limits of this intermezzo in terms of both time and territory. Once this control has been achieved and some answers which often lead to great problems have been given, I resume the lecture. Often the added material leads the students to second thoughts and the discussion continues either between members of the class or between me and the class after the lecture is over in the corridor or in my office.

To supplement the formal lecture with new material, to establish the knowledge of that acquired during the lecture, and to create a more productive intermezzo I have scheduled planned discussions for each class. The course, therefore, consists of two formal lectures and one discussion per week. The topics of the discussion, all chosen in advance as well as readings that are to help the discussion, are printed and given to the students together with a syllabus of the lectures on the first day the course begins. The topics are based on the material of the lectures but are not repetitions of it. They try to open new avenues of thought and perception to the student which, however, stem from the mastered material. They can be very specific or very general. For example, if I discuss during the week the Art of the Catacombs, I can have a topic as broad as the Concept of History of the Early Christians, or as specific as Sources of Symbols. Depending on my experiences the topics change from year to year and once a month the students can choose their own topic, provided that it is related to the discussed material. The "signal" for the discussion may take the form of a question I pose at the beginning, or a picture I show on the screen; the students discuss the theme among themselves while I play the part of the moderator trying to keep the discussion under control. It goes without saying that the success of this "controlled freedom" depends to a large extent upon preparation by the student. It is necessary for him to have familiarized himself with the material and to have completed the reading assignments that are intended to give him a foundation and also some new thoughts. On the whole, the reading is of a controversial nature, not always representing the professor's point of view. If the students do not keep up with the preparation, the discussions are limited to a small number of bright students or lose their liveliness. Although the value of the weekly discussion may be limited in this way, I have been convinced by the reaction of a large number of students that they are of value and an integral part of the course. In the mind of the participants it is the liveliness that counts most and from which the student carries away something.

I should not, however, give the impression that liveliness is a constant feature of my classes in all their aspects. Unfortunately this is not always so. A great deal depends on the standards of the students, their background, and preparation. And here I mean not only the scholastic background that they get in schools before they enter the university, usually without method or system, but the cultural background and a certain cultural sensitivity that one normally acquires in his own home. This is one of the many serious problems that I have to face and for the solution of which I have no formulas to offer. I have only found that in the course of my teaching, and I have been teaching for fourteen years now, one must never yield to lowering of standards. Instead one must set and require the highest standards possible.

Lowering of standards does harm the student (particularly the poor student), the class as a whole, and above all the teacher himself. For I feel, if I give myself so easily (and this is really the meaning of lowering of standards), I would stop questioning myself, I would become complacent, and I am sure I would end up having a set of notes that I repeated unaltered for thirty years, if I were to live that long! It is only if I myself face the challenge of high standards, that I can renew myself and, therefore, that that part of myself which I give to the students will be constantly new.

But to think of standards and of one's own renewal does not mean that one has a formula to give or to follow. A great deal depends on the questions I put to myself in preparing the lectures and on what the student gives back to me. If I am to question myself as a human being, and a teacher, and if I am to improve upon my many failures, I need time. Time is of the essence. Time to reflect upon the material, time to put it together, and above all time to read which opens my mind to other points of view, other possibilities, and enables me never to repeat a lecture.

Reading becomes meaningful and fruitful if one is involved in it. And one gets involved in it if one thinks of a particularly fascinating problem which is pursued for the soul's edification and not always for the benefit of specialized scholarship. In other words an absolute component of teaching is what in general is termed "research." And here I must stress the fact that it is through research that one meets new challenges and is able to put the problems of the classroom in a larger perspective. For this, too, time is of the essence. And here I feel that often neither university administrators nor the general public, who these days tend to govern university policies, programs, and timetables, recognize this. Very often the unpleasant music of these words reaches my ears: "But if he is a good teacher (I do not know if I am), why doesn't he teach more courses and more hours?" Or another comment: "Ah these teachers, they have such an easy profession. Imagine, they have a full summer free and they are paid for the whole year." I do not, of course, mean to say that this is a generally accepted view and that there are no people or administrations aware of time and of the value of research to teaching. I personally have been lucky in this respect and have understanding colleagues. Nevertheless this view exists and it reveals to me the lightness with which some people consider the problems which conscientious teachers face.

I cannot stress enough the fact that time is of the essence. The aware and conscientious teacher cannot give forever without suddenly coming to the realization (if he is aware of himself) that there is nothing left for him to give. The encroaching routine of the years has left the teacher with nothing else but an empty shell. What then? Many of the complaints we hear today on the part of the students may well be explained through this reality. The truth is that we cannot go on giving without replenishing ourselves. Teaching (I speak only of my own field, art history) is not a matter of a tape recorder or a computer.

As I have tried to suggest, teaching is giving yourself. Beyond the facts of knowledge, beyond books or papers or exams, there is something else which is the most important of all. It can only be described as a love affair between the teacher and the students. It is this relationship which creates the necessary climate in which the student grows, and the teacher finds a meaning for what he is trying to do. It is necessary that the students consider their own role in this relationship. Unless they, too, give, unless they share themselves with the teacher, they cannot and must not expect fruits from a one-sided relationship. In this relationship youth comes to find eventually his maturity, but here also the intent and destiny of the mature man, the teacher, reaches its peak. Without this inner relationship and the giving of one to the other, education can easily be reduced to a cold, dry, soulless tradition and mere reception of knowledge. For this type of knowledge neither universities nor professors are needed. The machine in its various forms would serve the purpose beautifully. It is against this type of knowledge that students rebel today. It is only through this relationship that we can constantly be aware of our shortcomings, and strengthen our efforts to go beyond the transitory and reach that which is beyond time. Without this relationship we cannot bring the "self" of the youth that comes to us into a unity and open ways for him through which he can find values whose strength does not lie in what is temporary.

My colleagues, the non-art historians, would say this is easy to accomplish with beautiful pictures and works of art! I believe that this is not so. The form of works of art can often be made to speak only to the senses, and therefore does not feed the hunger that exists in all of us. Forms and colours must be connected with the metaphysical root of life in such a way as to make the student experience with great intensity the antinomy that exists in all of us: the antinomy between necessity and freedom. The unity of the two, which I do not think can be achieved in terms of actual experience, must be sought by a true personality. The work of the teacher is to help the student achieve a synthesis, as much as possible with the elements that comprise the youth's "self." No matter how many educational devices and tests we invent, experiments we carry out, examinations we give, papers we correct, books we publish, my contact with academic youth has convinced me that none of these can be substituted for real education based on an inner relationship between teacher and student.

Today teachers become fewer and fewer. Teachers who value more the living word that comes from the teacher's soul than that written in a book are fewer today, I think, than in the past. On the other hand there are many more books these days than ever before. And as a result education suffers a great deal. As long as, with a certain laziness on our part, we refer the student to the book, to what is written, and do not attempt to resurrect the word that comes from within us, we cut off the student from the creative source of his inner being. This cannot be called education. We must not expect any accomplishments as long as we substitute for the living word the written word or the machine. It is in this spirit that I enter the classroom and face my students. If this old-fashioned "system" and these old-fashioned ideas have led me to a total failure I am willing to reconsider them and go with the times. But I am a poor judge of my work as a teacher. Of this, perhaps, the students who have sat in my classes may be the better judges.

GEORGE GALAVARIS

A native of Greece, George Galavaris studied in Europe and the United States—painting, classics, history, archaeology, fine arts, and philosophy. He is a Master of Arts of the University of Athens and holds the degrees of Master of Fine Arts and Ph.D. from Princeton University.

While a student, he was the recipient of numerous awards, including a Fulbright fellowship. He was at one time a visiting fellow in the Dumbarton Oaks Research Library and Collection of Harvard University and, at another, visiting professor of the history of art at the University of Wisconsin (Madison). He was the founder and first president of the Canadian National Committee of Byzantine Studies (Association internationale des études byzantines).

Dr. Galavaris has published widely on late antique, early Christian and mediaeval art and archaeology, including three books: The Illustrations of the Liturgical Homilies of Gregory Nazianzenus, *Studies in Manuscript Illumination 6 (Princeton University Press, 1969),* Bread and Liturgy: The Symbolism of Early Christian and Byzantine Bread Stamps *(University of Wisconsin Press, 1970), and* Icons from the Elrehjem Art Center *(University of Wisconsin, Madison, 1973). In addition, he has lectured in North America and Europe on various aspects of art.*

He has taught fine arts at McGill since 1959 and has been professor of art history since 1965. He is also a painter whose pictures have been exhibited in Europe as well as Canada, and a writer of short stories: Invocation to a Pagan Divinity *(The Magic Flute Editions, Athens, 1972).*

His former students remembered, above all, his enthusiasm for his subject—his love of and total involvement in art—and his compelling desire to share this with them. They testified to his scholarship, his mastery of the field, and also to his sensitivity, not only to art but to life. "He put feeling and life into his course," said one, "because he cared so much for life, and for transmitting this to us." Another graduate put it this way: ". . . he was so fond of and involved in his fine arts courses that he showed real emotion to the class and made us love and relive the past as he did." He was poetic, even mystical and, according to some, exhibited an extravagant individualism.

His lectures were thoroughly prepared, and liberally illustrated by slides. He had been to see many of the works of art and places studied and added personal touches which heightened interest. One former student referred to his lectures as "a commentary at once rapturous and informative." Seminars too were arranged, and interested students were invited to visit him individually to discuss art. He showed a keen sense of responsibility for his students. He knew them by name and personally read and commented on their essays. He impressed one graduate "as being the rare sort of person who is fitted by temperament to teach rather than having been reduced to it."

Enseigner ou L'égotisme partagé

Jean-Louis Major

> *Empruntant un mot à Stendhal, qui l'a introduit dans notre langue, et le détournant un peu pour mon usage, je dirai que la vraie Méthode de Descartes devrait se nommer* L'EGOTISME, *le développement de la conscience pour les fins de la connaissance.*—VALÉRY.

Plus de dix ans déjà, mais peu de souvenirs. Les années se recouvrent, se superposent, comme l'année scolaire brouille celles du calendrier. Les événements se mêlent à moi-même, et je distingue mal ce que j'ai fait de ce que je suis devenu.

J'ai découvert, avec quelque surprise, que mon comportement en classe accusait une continuité dans le temps. Un étudiant à la maîtrise, qui avait suivi mes cours au baccalauréat quatre ou cinq ans plus tôt, me dit un jour: "On vous reconnaît bien. Vous êtes toujours le même, vous l'êtes plus que jamais." Certain haussement des épaules, qu'accompagne une inclinaison de la tête et une moue bien particulière, se serait même accentué au cours des années. Paraît-il que se sont perpétuées certaines expressions telles que "C'est amusant," pour qualifier une façon de voir, ou "Ce serait amusant," pour engager à l'étude de quelque problème. Ces expressions, je le reconnais aujourd'hui, révèlent une bonne part de ma façon de concevoir et de pratiquer l'enseignement.

La première année, j'enseignai le latin et la philosophie dans un collège de jeunes filles affilié à l'Université d'Ottawa. Le programme et l'examen étaient imposés de l'extérieur, je n'avais qu'à me conformer aux directives. Plus je m'y conformerais, plus mes élèves auraient de chances d'obtenir de bonnes notes. Tout le reste était affaire de pédagogie.

En philosophie, mes premières leçons se firent à partir d'un texte que j'avais rédigé en guise d'introduction. J'avais lu et annoté quelques manuels, mais très tôt je m'aperçus que j'étais incapable de présenter un cours qui se limiterait à suivre un manuel en le commentant. Je demeurais trop astreint au texte imprimé, j'avais tendance à le lire. Je me mis à rédiger mes cours en résumant le manuel mais en bouleversant aussi l'ordre de l'exposé. La phrase était moins parfaite mais elle s'adaptait à mon souffle; les idées s'enchaînaient d'une façon moins absolue mais leur séquence suivait ma pensée. Bientôt, je m'enhardis; à mesure que la rédaction progressa, je fus de moins en moins lié au manuel. C'est alors que je perçus ce qui allait orienter le travail des années à venir.

Je compris que la valeur et l'intérêt d'un cours ne résidaient pas pour moi dans la capacité de bien présenter et bien expliquer les formules d'un manuel mais dans les distances que je prenais à leur égard en les assumant. Le travail s'accomplissait d'abord pour moi-même, puis il marquait ma façon d'enseigner. Peu à peu l'essentiel était déplacé. Il s'agissait moins de faire apprendre à mes élèves un élément particulier du système que de manifester ma compréhension d'une philosophie. Du même coup je mettais en relief le côté systématique d'une philosophie avec ce que cela comporte de cohérence et de rigueur mais aussi de limites. Il devenait inévitable qu'entrât en jeu mon attitude à l'égard d'une philosophie aussi bien qu'à l'égard de la philosophie.

A la fin de l'année, je devins professeur régulier à l'Université. Je savais que je devais tout refaire. Ce travail, repris selon des formes et des moyens divers, se prolongera jusqu'à mon affectation au département de Lettres françaises, où je devrais repartir à zéro. Cette première année m'avait permis d'entrevoir quelques vérités que j'allais découvrir de jour en jour, et d'autres qui me sont demeurées obscures.

Dès les premiers cours je fus aussi en butte à des problèmes moins théoriques. Je m'étais découvert une répugnance à contrôler les présences. On insista un peu, au début seulement. J'oubliais. Dès que je me retrouvais en classe, il me semblait que j'avais bien autre chose à faire que compter des étudiants.

Le refus ou plutôt l'oubli de faire l'appel comporte un avantage sérieux: le professeur n'a pas à tolérer la présence d'individus à l'ennui trop tapageur. Je n'aime pas devoir maintenir la discipline en classe; j'eus rarement à imposer des sanctions ou même à rappeler à l'ordre. Lorsqu'il devient nécessaire d'intervenir, je pratique le sarcasme plutôt cinglant mais je le fais avec répugnance. Il me semble que chacun ne doit venir en classe que parce qu'il le désire ou parce qu'il en perçoit lui-même les raisons.

Puisque j'en suis à l'aveu de mes défauts, aussi bien m'y enfoncer encore un peu. On m'a souvent répété que pour donner un bon cours un professeur doit savoir interroger ses étudiants, faute de quoi il s'installe dans le discours magistral. Or tous les experts, depuis l'élève de pré-universitaire jusqu'aux gouverneurs, découvrent aujourd'hui que le cours magistral est une invention diabolique des professeurs paresseux. Eh bien! je me rends compte que j'ai été magistral plus souvent qu'à mon tour. J'eus toujours des difficultés à poser des questions aux étudiants, et ce, depuis ma première année d'enseignement. J'essayais, j'étais chaque fois découragé par le caractère artificiel du procédé.

Quelle méthode d'enseignement ai-je pratiquée? Je n'en sais rien. Je n'ai jamais su à l'avance de quelle façon je présenterais un cours. D'ailleurs comment le prévoir? Le comportement des groupes varie, leur nombre aussi, qui peut aller d'une dizaine à plus de cent. Il y a, dans le nombre d'étudiants, des lignes de démarcation qui affectent la manière d'enseigner: de dix à vingt, de vingt à quarante, de quarante à soixante. Au delà de soixante, les seuils n'existent plus, aussi bien remplir un amphithéâtre. Seule augmente la pénible sensation d'être physiquement opprimé.

Cours magistral? Séminaire? Je n'ai jamais pratiqué l'un ou l'autre de façon systématique mais selon les circonstances et le sujet, selon ma fantaisie et celle des étudiants, la mienne plus que la leur. Un cours normal me paraît devoir s'organiser par blocs d'une heure ou de quelques heures. Déjà le rythme du cours doit établir un ordre, des articulations, une certaine intelligence de la matière et de la méthode. J'explique et commente d'un seul jet ce qui peut constituer un ensemble. On peut m'interrompre n'importe quand, je ne m'y suis jamais opposé car je préfère laisser aux étudiants l'initiative des questions et des commentaires. Une fois établi le climat nécessaire, tout se déroule allègrement. Toutefois, une consigne tacite ou un certain tempo régissent d'ordinaire l'ordre et le temps des interventions.

Je ne crois pas aux vertus foncières et infaillibles de la discussion; elle n'est souvent que le prétexte à une affirmation outrée de soi-même. Toute discussion en classe doit s'engager à partir d'un travail précis et s'y tenir le plus près possible; elle doit tendre à compléter ce qui est déjà fait. La controverse n'a de sens que si elle ouvre des perspectives nouvelles. Il n'est pas sûr que le séminaire soit la forme d'enseignement idéale pour ceux qui préparent le baccalauréat. Les étudiants du premier cycle peuvent-ils vraiment progresser au moyen d'une série d'exposés? Sont-ils bien préparés pour tirer profit d'une discussion ou pour la rendre profitable? Ne vaut-il pas mieux leur donner d'abord l'élan, les orienter sur des voies nouvelles, s'expliquer longuement s'il le faut? A travers toute matière nouvelle que l'on présente ne vise-t-on pas d'abord à renouveler l'étudiant lui-même? Quoi qu'il en soit, mes préférences vont vers une forme d'enseignement qui oscille entre le cours et le séminaire. En ce domaine, je n'ai d'autre principe que celui de n'en pas avoir. Je m'oppose cependant à ce que les administrateurs de l'éducation, qui se mêlent d'avoir des principes, puissent imposer une formule rigide. Que le professeur soit libre de passer d'une forme d'enseignement à une autre quand bon lui semble.

Les circonstances et mon goût personnel ont fait que j'ai mené sans cesse, à côté de l'enseignement, un travail ou un loisir que j'appellerai, pompeusement sans doute mais aussi en toute humilité, d'écriture. Un aîné, écrivain et professeur, me conseilla un jour de réserver les vacances à l'écriture et de consacrer l'année scolaire aux seuls cours. Le conseil est sage, je ne suis jamais arrivé à le suivre. Je tente, sans toujours y parvenir, de ne pas sacrifier l'une à l'autre écriture et enseignement. Je suis convaincu toutefois que, si l'enseignement m'a permis de vivre tant bien que mal, les travaux d'écriture, en fin de compte, ont contribué à faire vivre mon enseignement. Peu de choses en réalité–je n'en suis qu'à l'apprentissage en ce domaine–mais leur valeur objective importe moins ici que leur rôle dans ma façon d'enseigner.

Préparer un livre, un article, ou un compte rendu, autant de façons de susciter et de maintenir une disponibilité intellectuelle. Un texte publié permet une distance critique à l'égard de soi. J'ai vécu ainsi en perpétuelle tension à l'égard de moi-même. Je n'ai jamais attribué valeur définitive à ce que j'écrivais; je l'ai fait de mon mieux. Cela m'a permis de fixer des étapes et des jalons à mon cheminement. Une partie de ce que j'allais publier a quelquefois passé dans mes cours. Il est arrivé plus rarement que le matériel d'un cours parvînt à l'état de publication. Je constate un fait, je ne sais pourquoi il en est ainsi. Peu m'importe que l'écrit passe comme tel ou non dans le cours; les questions que je me pose, l'activité de l'esprit que cela entraîne, ne peuvent demeurer étrangères à l'enseignement. Ce que je produis ailleurs modifie le ton de mes cours.

Je crois que les étudiants, du moins les meilleurs d'entre eux, perçoivent la différence entre celui qui se contente d'enseigner et celui qui vit de recherche et d'écriture. Les mots et les choses n'ont pas même résonance selon qu'un professeur se borne à répéter des cours ou qu'il tente l'aventure de l'esprit. Je me trompe peut-être, il me semble que l'étudiant éprouve quelque réticence à l'égard d'un esprit amorphe, si bon pédagogue soit-il, parce qu'il perçoit alors chez son professeur une forme subtile du mensonge. La pédagogie peut être un masque vide. A un certain niveau, la différence devient de plus en plus perceptible, la qualité de présence n'est plus la même. Mais, pour qu'en soit modifiée la qualité même de celui qui parle en classe, il faut qu'articles et "recherche" correspondent à autre chose que le souci d'étoffer une bibliographie. Il est question ici d'une qualité d'esprit, non d'une comptabilité. L'écriture est *une libre nécessité personnelle* qui me harcèle comme aucun dictat administratif ne saurait le faire; elle est l'exigence intérieure qui m'a lié à mon métier malgré les obstacles et les dégoûts. Si cette exigence n'existe pas, à quoi bon écrire? A quoi bon enseigner?

Je n'ai jamais accepté de n'être que celui qui transmet: j'aime me reconnaître en ce que je fais, j'y veux une part de moi-même, la plus vraie possible. Chacun des cours que j'ai donnés répond à la volonté d'apprendre quelque chose, au désir de voir un peu plus clair en quelque domaine. Dès la première année j'ai su qu'enseigner pour enseigner n'est qu'une besogne sans intérêt. Ne vaut que le plaisir de la mise en question, de la découverte, de l'invention, à quoi l'on invite les étudiants à participer. L'enseignement n'aura été un stimulant que de façon indirecte. Les étudiants s'imaginent que leurs questions, leurs examens, leurs devoirs sont pour le professeur des sources d'inspiration, des révélations. Moi aussi, j'avais imaginé qu'il en est ainsi. Je dois le reconnaître, ce ne sont pas les étudiants qui ont provoqué en moi le besoin de renouvellement. J'avais cru qu'ils apporteraient chaque année un affrontement nouveau: ce fut l'une de mes premières désillusions. Dans l'ensemble, ils sont réfractaires à toute véritable nouveauté; s'ils sont révolutionnaires, c'est de façon tellement conventionnelle qu'on n'y voit plus que la facilité. Ils pratiquent tout avec si peu d'exigence qu'on en reste déconcerté. L'une des tâches les plus difficiles du professeur consiste à radicaliser les attitudes de ses étudiants, à susciter en eux une certaine lucidité pour les livrer ensuite à leurs propres vérités.

On dit: "Il y a bien des consolations dans l'enseignement." Comme si enseigner était une si triste besogne qu'il y faille ajouter des consolations. Voir une intelligence s'ouvrir, une superbe s'effondrer, des préjugés mis en question, tout cela est bien, mais j'avoue que pour moi ce n'est qu'accessoire. C'est avant tout par rapport à moi que je juge mon enseignement. Et je veux que mes étudiants sachent, lorsque j'entre en classe, que l'essentiel ne dépend pas de leur réprobation ni de leurs applaudissements. Exactement comme je n'attends pas de l'administration universitaire qu'elle me dise quoi penser. Avouons-le, je n'ai toujours travaillé que pour moi, pour mon plaisir. On n'insistera jamais trop sur les valeurs ludiques de l'enseignement. Faire un cours *pour* les étudiants, c'est se rabaisser et les rabaisser avec soi; c'est édulcorer une réflexion et engourdir leur propre sens de la découverte.

D'un Monsieur Gâtier, qui fut son précepteur au séminaire et l'un des modèles du Vicaire Savoyard, Rousseau dit: "Il semblait plutôt étudier avec moi que m'instruire." A condition qu'on l'interprète bien, la formule décrit de façon assez juste le climat qui doit exister à l'université. Cependant, pour éviter de donner aux étudiants l'impression qu'on les instruit, d'aucuns voudraient que l'on se place à leur exact niveau: en d'autres termes, qu'on ne leur apprenne rien qu'ils ne savent déjà ou qu'ils ne trouvent par eux-mêmes. Il faut qu'en son cours le professeur s'instruise et qu'il montre comment il s'instruit. D'accord. Mais il n'est pas du niveau des étudiants et il n'a pas à s'en cacher. Ce que les étudiants doivent retirer de son témoignage, de la démarche exemplaire qu'il accomplit en leur présence, ce sont des connaissances et une méthode, des instruments pour s'instruire eux-mêmes. Je ne veux pas former des imitateurs ni des serviteurs du Régime. En chacun je ne veux qu'éveiller ses propres possibilités. Mon travail est d'alimenter en chacun sa propre recherche, son propre sens critique, sa propre capacité de découvrir et de connaître. Et je n'y arriverai qu'en cherchant à être d'abord moi-même.

Dépourvu de pédagogie, c'est-à-dire d'une *technique* de l'enseignement, je n'ai à livrer que moi-même. Je joue chaque fois quitte ou double. Au début de chaque année j'ai le trac, puis tout se tasse et je recommence à vivre selon mon rythme. Certains jours, les cours ou plutôt l'obligation de donner des cours m'accable. Talonné par tout ce que je veux lire, apprendre, écrire, j'éprouve à devoir me présenter en classe à heures fixes une impatience qui est en même temps de la panique. Une fois en présence de mes étudiants, quelques minutes suffisent: tout le reste est aboli, il n'y a plus que cet espace clos où se joue l'affrontement de moi-même à moi-même. Cette méthode, qui n'en est pas une, permet de moins en moins la production massive et l'horaire bien rempli. Jusqu'où peut-on aller? Combien de temps peut-on tenir? Ces questions viennent parfois hanter les heures où je me sens démuni face à l'avenir.

Si possible, un cours doit être complètement rédigé avant le début de l'année scolaire. C'est rarement possible, mais quelle que soit la situation, chaque leçon doit être rédigée à l'avance. Cela m'est nécessaire, pour mon plaisir et ma liberté. Lorsque je présente une leçon, j'en suis dégagé, je peux la mettre en question, déceler ses faiblesses et ses possibilités. Si je répète un cours, j'ai déjà un texte devant moi; je puis me relire, repenser l'ensemble et le détail. La préparation immédiate d'un cours consiste souvent à m'interroger sur ce que j'ai écrit et à le corriger.

Il m'est arrivé de ne pas donner un cours parce que j'avais oublié mes notes. Si je demeure incapable d'affronter une classe sans mon texte, je puis parler une heure sans m'y reporter, soit que j'ouvre une interminable parenthèse soit que je décide d'abréger ou de résumer une partie du cours. Même lorsque je suis mon texte de près, je ne le lis pas, je le reformule ou le déforme. Le rythme de l'écriture ne concorde pas avec le débit de la présentation en classe. C'est dans cette reformulation du texte écrit que joue aussi la mise en question. De l'écrit à la parole s'accomplit l'espace d'une perspective critique. Parler sans l'appui d'un texte laisse souvent l'impression qu'on a donné un cours excellent. Je me méfie de ce genre d'impressions. N'y a-t-il pas là une part de l'illusion que crée le brio de l'improvisation? Le discours improvisé escamote facilement les problèmes. L'expérience et l'habileté permettent de camoufler les difficultés mais non d'échapper aux pièges de la facilité.

Rédiger un cours oblige d'abord au travail du mot à mot, à la patiente démarche qui laisse peu de place aux illusions. L'écriture m'oblige à aller jusqu'au bout de moi-même, elle m'accule à la découverte de la pensée jusqu'en ses derniers retranchements. Du même coup, l'écrit me situe à distance. Je suis convaincu, si paradoxal que cela paraisse, qu'un cours donné à partir du seul plan ou de quelques notes éparses invite à la répétition. Encore ici il faut se méfier du mythe de la spontanéité. Il me suffit de relire le texte d'une leçon pour commencer à en voir les défauts, pour vouloir tout changer l'année suivante ou avant même de l'avoir présenté en classe.

J'ai mis parfois jusqu'à trente ou quarante heures à préparer fébrilement une heure de cours. J'accumulais les pages d'écriture; je ne préparais pas un cours, j'étudiais, j'écrivais, je me découvrais à moi-même. Aux étudiants, je ne présentais qu'un reflet de tout cela. Dans ces conditions, comment organiser un programme? Maintenant que je suis prévenu, je trace au début du semestre un plan de cours que j'ajuste à measure que l'on avance. Les étudiants voient d'abord comment on pourrait traiter le sujet, ensuite, comment ils devront compléter ce que je fais. D'ailleurs, il me semble que tout ce qui est préparé et que je ne communique pas comme tel pèse sur ce que je dis en classe, y ajoute de quelque façon une présence. J'ai développé là-dessus une théorie, ou un postulat, qui me confirme dans mes habitudes et les justifie peut-être. Par exemple, dans un cours sur la poésie je préfère étudier à fond un poème plutôt qu'un ensemble d'oeuvres. Quelques poèmes bien analysés devraient révéler de l'intérieur et dans leurs particularités les plus significatives toute une œuvre, toute une époque.

J'ai peu de goût pour le survol. Si je consacre des semaines ou des mois à une oeuvre, je demande aux étudiants de présenter des études sur ce qui reste à voir. Cela les intéresse plus que de m'entendre énumérer des titres et des jugements. Cette façon de faire n'est possible qu'à certaines conditions: sujet, nombre d'étudiants, niveau des études, mais j'avoue l'avoir pratiquée dans des circonstances qui défiaient la prudence. Cela réussit parfois, je connus aussi des échecs. Quoi qu'il en soit, les étudiants qui s'étaient soumis à cette épreuve m'ont souvent dit qu'ils en avaient tiré un plus grand profit qu'à prendre des notes en m'écoutant parler. Ils avaient été forcés d'assimiler et d'appliquer une façon de voir et de faire qu'ils croyaient facile ou impossible tant qu'ils la considéraient de l'extérieur. Si les conditions ne s'y prêtent pas, je n'impose à personne ce genre de travail; à ceux qui se portent volontaires, j'accorde l'équivalence d'un devoir ou même d'un examen. Mais l'exemple est communicatif. Il suffit d'un ou deux étudiants qui s'y essaient pour que d'autres soient tentés par l'aventure. A mon étonnement, je n'ai jamais regretté les plus folles entreprises, même quand elles échouaient. Cependant il m'a toujours paru nécessaire de me livrer à un premier travail, afin de provoquer par ma recherche celle de l'étudiant, afin de l'amener d'abord à une nouvelle façon de comprendre. A quoi bon lui faire répéter ce qu'il sait déjà? A quoi bon lui laisser croire que tout est certain? Ma propre façon de voir n'est pas assurée, je la modifie souvent. L'étudiant apprend moins par ce que je lui dis que par la mise en question de ce que je dis et de ce qu'il sait déjà. S'il en reste quelque chose, ce sera une faculté d'enthousiasme, une certaine avidité de l'esprit, cette curiosité intellectuelle que j'ai longtemps cru naturelle et qui fait si étrangement défaut chez les étudiants.

Face à la série de cours que l'on fait défiler devant lui, face à ces devoirs qu'on lui impose mais auxquels ils demeure étranger, l'étudiant n'éprouve souvent qu'indifférence et ennui . . . Pourtant, s'il ne connaît pas l'enthousiasme et l'exaltation, que lui restera-t-il de ces heures perdues? Que retrouvera-t-il en lui de ses années d'études s'il n'a pas connu la recherche fervente d'un mot, d'une pensée, ou de soi? Il fuira plus tard tout ce que ses cours auront touché, il croira que le travail n'est qu'une façon d'échapper à l'ennui, que la vraie vie est hors de soi. Pour qui a connu la ferveur de l'esprit, ne serait-ce que quelques heures, il se crée dans le souvenir une secrète possibilité qui transforme tout ce que l'on touche.

Pour ces étudiants dont j'ai oublié le nom, pour ceux que demain je retrouverai devant moi, que suis-je? Il m'arrive de me le demander. Les sociologues ont-ils cherché à savoir comment la société perçoit le professeur? Quelles sont les attitudes de l'étudiant à l'égard des professeurs? Cette perception est-elle trop individuelle, trop changeante pour la codifier? On connaît mal les étudiants. J'ai de moins en moins de rapports avec eux hors de la classe. Je crois peu aux activités dites para-scolaires, je ne suis pas animateur social, ni psychologue, ni conseiller en orientation. Ce sont pourtant des rôles qu'on voudrait m'imposer. Si mes heures au bureau se passent en conversations banales, et c'est à quoi se réduisent bien des rencontres avec les étudiants, l'essentiel de ma tâche ne s'accomplit pas. Le professeur doit d'abord travailler dans le silence et la solitude. Pourtant, que d'efforts il faut déployer aujourd'hui pour sauvegarder cette part de l'existence contre tout ce qui nous entoure.

Comment évaluer les succès et les échecs? Comment se fier au désespoir ou à l'exaltation que l'on ressent à la sortie d'un cours, quand on se retrouve détaché, seul et silencieux? Je n'ai d'autre mesure que le sentiment, si trompeur soit-il, de mon plaisir et de mon propre dépassement. Que vaut ce que je fais? Comment le savoir autrement que par l'ignorance où je suis de toute autre tâche qui me permettrait au même point d'être moi-même et de pratiquer mon plaisir? Enseigner, c'est se condamner, dans une société qui divise loisirs et travail, à n'avoir jamais de loisirs ou à n'avoir que le perpétuel loisir d'être soi-même et de vivre dans la ferveur de ce que l'on aime. C'est un jeu magnifique qui, permettant le pire, exige de soi le meilleur.

JEAN-LOUIS MAJOR

Né à Cornwall (Ontario) en 1937, Jean-Louis Major détient les titres universitaires suivants: B.A. (Hon.), B.Ph., L.Ph., M.A. et Ph.D. de l'Université d'Ottawa avec une thèse en philosophie et littérature, "Dialectique existentielle de Saint- Exupéry." En 1960 il enseigne la philosophie et le latin au Collège Bruyère, affilié à l'Université d'Ottawa, et l'année suivante il devient professeur au département de philosophie de l'Univer-

sité. Après l'obtention du doctorat en 1965, il est nommé au département de Lettres françaises. En 1968–69 il fait un stage d'études post-doctorales à l'Ecole pratique des hautes études à Paris, et en 1970–71 il est professeur invité à l'Université de Toronto.

Parmi ses publications on compte un livre, Saint-Exupéry, l'écriture et la pensée *(Editions de l'Université d'Ottawa, 1968) et des sections d'ouvrages collectifs: "André Langevin" dans* Le roman canadien-français; *"L'hexagone: une aventure en poésie québécoise" dans* La poésie canadienne-française *(Archives des Lettres canadiennes, tomes III et IV, Fides, 1964 et 1969); un chapitre sur le roman contemporain dans* L'histoire de la littérature française du Québec *(Beauchemin, 1969); et deux sections dans* Les critiques de notre temps et Saint-Exupéry *(Paris, Garnier, 1972). De plus, il a publié environ quatre-vingts articles et comptes rendus. De 1963 à 1965 il est critique littéraire au journal* Le Droit *et de 1969 à 1972 il tient la chronique annuelle de poésie québécoise dans* University of Toronto Quarterly. *Il est aussi l'un des directeurs des* Cahiers d'Inédits *aux Editions de l'Université d'Ottawa.*

Pendant presque toute la période à laquelle se rapportent les commentaires des diplômés, le principal domaine d'enseignement de Monsieur Major était la philosophie.

Selon ses anciens élèves, Monsieur Major possédait une connaissance très solide de sa matière, un enthousiasme contagieux, de la maturité dans ses rapports avec les étudiants et une "vaste culture dont il se servait avec modération sans jamais en faire un spectacle."

"Ses cours n'étaient pas des lectures de notes pures et simples, mais il rendait une matière, qu'il avait d'abord fort bien assimilée, d'une façon simple, sous forme de dialogue, où une discussion pouvait fort bien s'amorcer."

Il semblait aimer son travail et s'intéressait à l'étudiant; il possédait une voix chaude, plaisante à entendre. "Un grand homme—et quelle simplicité!" a conclu un diplômé.

Modest Miracles Do Happen

Brendan O'Grady

"How do you teach English literature?" you ask. What you really want to know is, "How do you promote a love for learning?" Regardless of the phrasing of the question, I am not sure that I can tell *how* the act is performed, only *what* I consciously do when I teach. A cautionary remark, therefore, may be in order at the outset: the fine arts have always eluded those who would profane them by looking only for tested recipes, easy formulas, or how-to instructions—even though these elements are fairly easy to identify and describe. The intangible, spiritual gifts of the artist, his inspired improvisations or disappointing lapses, various reflections of his distinctive personality: these cannot be readily captured; nor can they be easily evaluated, especially by the artist himself. As in any other art, then, to tell what one does when one is teaching is not to tell completely how one teaches. The best I can hope to do here is to state some of my beliefs and describe some of my practices. Perhaps it would be helpful to start with a few notes drawn from my own initiation into university teaching.

It is common knowledge that the educational philosophy, morale, and opportunities in a university can affect an instructor's attitudes and practices. It was my good fortune to have served my apprenticeship in a small college that had been in financial doldrums for over a century and, therefore, could provide only modest research facilities. Adversity, one could say, deprived the faculty of temptations enjoyed elsewhere. Partly for this reason there developed among staff members a genuine concern for the art of teaching. Especially encouraging was the response of students who were serious about learning. Sometimes staff members assisted one another by offering friendly advice or by exchanging general suggestions on teaching methods; but, thank heavens, these things were never done formally or officially. It is literally correct to say that each instructor had to learn his art by himself. It was a matter of survival, and of pride. The academic *esprit* at that time and place centred on classroom instruction. For the most part that meant lecturing by the instructor, and intensive rather than extensive reading by the students. Even under such favorable circumstances, however, each man had to be himself and had to teach in his own way. My own observations over the years support the view that what works well for one instructor, or in one class, or on one day may not work so well (or at all) for another instructor, or in another class, or on another day. Who can explain, much less control, such factors as personal charisma, group dynamics, or barometric pressure? To be more mundane: a recent survey revealed that students are noticeably less responsive the day after a dance or class party. Communication really breaks down if the professor, too, has been out late the night before.

Be that as it may. My particular experience has led me to some beliefs that many colleagues share, as well as some that are evidently singular. Here are several tenets that have been, and are, important to me.

First of all, I believe that a university teacher should display his love for his work. He should be deeply interested in what he teaches and he should openly share his enjoyment of his subject. Where there is no love, let him bring love. The rest is easy. For love is, by nature, productive. "And so it happens that the blind see, and the lame walk?" Well, not literally. And not always: for even the greatest teacher can do little or nothing for a person who obstinately refuses to learn; and even the most accommodating teacher sometimes fails to reach some persons who really want to learn. But, as a rule, in due time those who once had no taste for poetry learn to like it; those who have read little fiction resolve to read more; those who have written carelessly become conscious of style; those whose lives have been unremittingly drab now discover some signs of beauty. Modest miracles do happen.

Or, rather, they are caused. What I do as a teacher originates partly in the belief that if one treats a good poem, or short story, or drama with due respect, with reverence, it will reveal its aesthetic goodness. Once that goodness is seen the object will be attractive, desirable, valuable to the interested beholder. What the beholder comes to know intimately, particularly what he discovers for himself, he will tend to love.

Secondly, I believe that a university teacher must honestly know his work, his particular subject, and his special group of co-learners. Knowledge in this sense includes attitudes. Teaching in freedom is far from an authoritarian or despotic exercise: it is a highly personal and responsible task that makes great demands on both moral and intellectual virtues. A good teacher will study constantly, review, research his subject, perfect his knowledge; but he will not let his own growing expertness become an impediment to effective teaching. Excessive concern for the subject to the neglect of the student is sometimes a mark of scholarship, sometimes a sign of intellectual snobbery or pedantry. A teacher's standard of excellence should include a commitment both to learning and to learners.

Pedantry is one impediment to effective teaching; another is impersonalism. A certain "distance" is normal between an instructor and his students, but there is no need for barriers. Somehow we must think of our Freshman Composition or Sophomore Survey students not as anonymous groups assembled a few times weekly in a lecture room, but as individual learners, single human beings, each possessing a unique personality. Human dignity, the instructor's as well as the student's, is at stake. If he does not possess and demonstrate a genuine personal interest, the instructor might as well be replaced by the movie projector, tape recorder, or television tube. Look at the same problem more positively: useful as recorded lectures or filmed demonstrations may be, there is no substitute for the humane concern that a competent, dedicated person can and should bring to the learning process. For this very reason if, and when, live lecturers and conventional classrooms become obsolete, there will still be need, even greater need, for teachers.

Another belief of mine is that a university teacher should acknowledge both the limitations of his subject and its relationship to other studies. Literature, for example, has been called the mirror of mankind, the channel of culture, the fine art of verbal expression. It walks hand and hand with history and is related to such studies as psychology, sociology, life sciences, philosophy, theology. Inseparable from other studies, literature is nevertheless distinct from them, as they are distinct from one another. Literature is its own discipline, has its own objects, imparts its own power.

Granted: literature draws major themes and attitudes from sources which are the special concern of other branches of learning, and which are, strictly considered, within the *scientific* competence of those other disciplines. Literature does not stop there. The creative intellect transforms such themes to its own purposes, and in its own mode and by means of its own "communications system" offers to us new embodiments—representations refined in expression, style, form, arrangement, conception, and divination. A viable philosophy of literature will clearly acknowledge the various uses of literature, its philosophical content, and its indebtedness to other studies; but, especially, it will treat literature as a fine art, and thereby reveal its underlying reality, its distinctive discipline, the source of its integrity. If the proper object of the literary artist is beauty, then the proper criterion for judging value in this art is the beautiful. The central concern of literary studies, as such, is not logic or ethics or science, but aesthetics. "A poem," said Robert Frost, "begins in delight and ends in wisdom." Herein lies literature's distinguishing mark. No other subject, in this respect, can be its surrogate.

Finally I should like to mention a tenet that is particularly applicable to teaching practices: where there is no order, there is no beauty; where there is no beauty, there is no love. By thus asserting the need for design and structure I am not denying that there are many degrees of good order between the extremes of anarchy and autocracy. Nor am I denying the need for a reasonable flexibility. In fact, certain realities of recent history enforce the view that teachers should be prepared to adapt their practices to changing situations. Other contemporary events point just as clearly to the folly of precipitating change for its own sake. In my view pedagogical practices, provided that they maintain the principle of order, should suit the personality of the instructor, be appropriate for the subject, and be helpful to the learners. Personally I have always been a cautious innovator; but it is my general belief that, so long as the instructor is steadfast in his good purposes, and ethical in his practices, he should be flexible (but not flabby) in his methods of presentation. Even the Empire State Building is able to sway slightly in the wind because it is flexible, that is, firm without being rigid.

I shall now try to tell more concretely how I teach. Let me start with a few of the maxims I use in my classes:

(1) *"Give 'em the works."* This motto has been the keynote for all my courses. It means that my students and I emphasize primary works over critical or biographical commentaries. We want to read, to know personally, the original selections in preference to commentaries upon those selections; and to read, first-hand, as many of the primary author's works as possible. We do not ignore professional critics; we tend to postpone resorting to them until after we have exercised our own critical powers. Emphasis is what I am referring to here. *Prima primo.* Assuming that a choice must be made, I would rather have undergraduates read all the works of Nathaniel Hawthorne, for example, than all the critical commentaries on *The Scarlet Letter.* Surely, we do not denigrate Arvin, Matthiessen, Stewart, and Waggoner when we insist on giving primacy to Hawthorne. On the contrary, penetrating readers will give other critics their due by knowing, first, the very books the critics are talking about. Most of my class meetings therefore are spent in direct confrontation with the poems, plays, and stories themselves. We have no time for speculating on an author's "motivation," that is, for amateurish psychologizing about an author's private life. Genuine criticism certainly interests us, but in practice rarely do the professional critics upstage the principal performers, the primary works of art.

(2) *"Read out of the work, not into it."* Scores of times each year, I am sure, I repeat these words. This maxim, of course, is an application of a basic rule of literary criticism: "Judge a work for what it sets out to be." University students presumably want to be intelligent readers, that is, persons who deliberately exercise judgment and evaluate what they read. This particular critical process involves analysis and compari-

son. It demands close attention to the text. If judgment is to be fair, it must be based on a reasonable understanding of the work's inherent intention. Sometimes that intention is at variance with the reader's own desires or predilections, in which event the reader simply must adjust himself to the work; otherwise he may well distort the work to suit his purposes. It is so easy, it takes no training, to read into literary works all sorts of subjective meanings, personal wishes, introvertive significances. It takes detachment and discipline to read out of literary works what is there.

(3) "*What have you discovered*?" This question I ask, usually as an opener, more than any other. I believe that real learning is, after all, a matter of personal discovery. I do not mean that ideas must be strictly "original" to be considered as "discovered;" all ideas, no matter how ancient or how widely held, are "new" to the person who truly sees them for the first time. Effectively, I say, we have not learned until we have made truths our own, until we have seen the old anew and assimilated our discoveries in a systematic way. To clarify my meaning, imagine a college student with a copy of Wordsworth's "Tintern Abbey" before him. For that student, being asked what he has discoverd could mean, for instance: *What does the poem say*? *How does it say it*? *What is unique about it*? *What have you learned*? *Which lines are especially effective*? *What is the central theme*? *Where does the climax occur*? *How do you account for the appeal of the poem*? The practical virtue in asking the original question is that, regardless of the actual "discoveries," the very search develops personal discrimination, alertness, perceptiveness, attention to detail. Finally, "What have you discovered?" comes to mean, for some students, "What insights into reality have you gained?"

For my purposes as an instructor there are four means of promoting a mature understanding of literature: reading, composition, discussion, and listening.

(a) Reading is the *sine qua non.*

(b) Composition is also essential. Expressing views in writing for a discerning audience forces personal discoveries and convictions into the open where they can be assessed, puts to the test one's standards of taste, and thereby develops both critical perception and rhetorical precision. Such writing not only expresses convictions, it also helps to form and perfect them.

(c) Discussion, a natural outgrowth of shared interests, is also a very useful instrument. In this context, it is oral composition. This means that participants must have something significant to say, and they must say it clearly. The spontaneous interplay of vital ideas as they pass through the alembic of several informed minds tends to clarify thoughts, to test convictions, to introduce new possibilities, and to sharpen wit. Intellectual dynamics is never dull. This being so, discussion as a teaching technique will generally prove useful in proportion to the intellectual preparation that has gone into it. There's the rub. It is not sufficient that academic discussion be entertaining; it must also be enlightening. "Talking off the top of one's head," a normal practice in the coffee shop or barber shop, has no regular place in the university classroom.

(d) Listening (to readings, seminars, lectures, recorded materials) while it does less than discussion to make people articulate, presents another kind of opportunity for learning. I have in mind not passive absorption of spoken words, but listening that is active, even creative. Students should be resourceful listeners: people who think, take notes, sift and select, talk back, ask questions, evaluate, store ideas for future consideration and use. It has long been my opinion that many students who resent having to attend lectures do not know how to participate in them.

In any event, it seems, the old-style classroom lecturing is losing its place as the prime instrument of college teaching, and the oratorical method will probably be retained, if at all, only in a minor role. Informal lecturing—the illustrated, demonstrational, and "interrupted" types—has a longer life expectancy. Directors of seminars, tutorials, workshops, and independent studies are now superseding the formal lecturers as the workhorses of the academy. My own contention is that, whereas the magisterial monologue is an art that should be retained, the disciplined dialogue is an art that must be restored.

How to conduct and participate in seminars and tutorials so as to produce the maximum intellectual benefit is a continuing concern for all of us. Principles remain the same to me regardless of class size: enthusiasm (though it helps) is not mistaken for learning, rhetoric (though it may be a hopeful sign) is not necessarily reason, and pointless chatter is not an acceptable substitute for precise articulation. In the seminar the director must still instruct, and conduct students through a course, and lead by precept and example. Even though his methods will be different from those he employs in a lecture room, he must still be the master of his art. I am aware of so-called "non-teaching" approaches, but my own experience leads me to think that the nondirective road to learning is generally unreliable for undergraduates and the unstructured course is self-contradictory.

Over the years I have conducted a score of seminars and workshops, each attended by from four to twelve undergraduates. Normally it has been easier for me to promote worthwhile discussion in such small groups than in my more typical assemblies of from forty to seventy-five students. I do not mean that one is inherently superior to the other, but that each requires different techniques and achieves a different result: the seminar discussion is usually more intensive, the classroom discussion more discursive. I should like to explain some of my seminar techniques first.

Usually I begin a seminar series by outlining goals: primary and supplementary books to be read, methodology to be employed, papers to be prepared, topics to be discussed. Either I distribute a selected bibliography or, more often, I ask the students to work up their own bibliographies; and I provide a relevant introduction to the works under consideration. Discussions usually focus on assigned topics: for example, one two-hour period might be devoted to Emerson's essay on Nature, the next to selected poems by Emerson, a third to Emerson's influence on Thoreau, and so forth. Each member reads appropriate selections in preparation for each weekly meeting and speaks to the topic of that day. Ideas are freely exchanged, arguments ensue, and issues collide, giving off at least faint sparks of truth. Meanwhile, privately, each seminarist has several weeks to prepare a research paper on an approved topic. These papers are usually duplicated, distributed and presented—sometimes actually read aloud, usually synopsized, and always defended orally—by the writers, whose peers must comment upon the essays. Finally, the essays are submitted to me, and I evaluate each one personally and privately. For each student, then, the seminar is designed to provide training in research, discussion, formal reporting, and criticism. It is intended for students majoring in English literature and is used in courses whose scope is comparatively restricted, even specialized.

To return to our main theme, teaching in the general classroom:

When you interpret a poem, for instance, you exemplify what you expect of your fellow-readers. You enter into the poem, believe it, elucidate it, reveal its meaning and spirit. Exactly how you do this differs from poem to poem, but always the poem—not the instructor-reader—is the main thing. As far as possible you submerge yourself, in the interest of the work at hand. First and last, it is the poem which must capture the imagination of the audience, the poem which must radiate its singular order, its distinctive beauty. By concentrating on the poem, not on the author, certainly not on yourself, you impart it to an audience. The poem speaks through you; you are its vocal chords.

There is more to it than that. You are not merely an impersonal medium in the communications system; by the very act of reading aloud you are an actor. Precisely, you are an interpreter. Moreover, when you comment directly upon the poem you are explicitly a critic. In any event the poem should speak through you: it has a being of its own apart from the way *you* see it and what it may mean to *you*. So you suppress your egoism and interests in favour of the *other*-ness, the special *that*-ness of the poem. The cultivation of such detachment makes more meaningful the experience of empathy, because both you and your audience then may hope to know the work for what *it is* rather than for what *you are*. Without this objective element, reading could easily degenerate into an exercise in egocentricity. Without the subjective response, on the other hand, reading would lose its aesthetic pleasure or rapport. We need both. Unfortunately the inordinate romanticism of recent times has inflated and distorted the value of empathy, leading many to judge significance and beauty almost solely in terms of personal interests and individual reactions. Empathy for such misguided people is akin to narcissism.

One task of the instructor, then, is to combat such heresies. His aesthetic theories, part of his total philosophy, provide the principles which his day-to-day practices must exemplify, concretize, and validate. The instructor personifies the theory. How to communicate the theory most effectively is always a challenge.

Usually I invite (indeed, implore) my audience to read, say, W. B. Yeats's "Lake Isle of Innisfree" as though they had never read or heard it before, as though they did not know who wrote it and had never heard anything at all about the author or this poem. First we read the poem, slowly and thoughtfully, but without affectation. "What do we discover here?" I ask "Who is the speaker?" "What is he talking about?" By question and answer we call attention to form, theme, structure, figures of speech, diction, mood, and so on. We uncover problems of both style and content, which we attempt to resolve by citing the lines and words of the poem itself. Sometimes we may allude to other commentaries to spur our own explorations, or to assist us in drawing conclusions, or to enrich our own experience. Gradually, by observations and insights we come to recognize the poem in its parts, features, and facets. Having thus identified each of the several components we are prepared to appreciate their special fusion into an orderly artifact. By this time we have read the selection, or parts of it, several times. As the ear and voice assist the eye, we always read aloud. Our minds and our senses have been concentrated on the object, alerted to its various nuances by such analysing and linking together, hearing, seeing, feeling. Having done our part, we are prepared for the poem's total revelation. This comes, one hopes, in the final oral reading, which can now be affectionate and meaningful.

Perhaps several times each year all systems work perfectly, and a lyric by Frost or Hopkins, Keats or Eliot, comes alive, transmits itself through your instrumentality, and proclaims itself in a kind of epiphany. This experience, as unmistakable as it is undefinable, is known in part by the inaudible tribute produced by the shock of discovery: "*Silent, upon a peak in Darien.*" Some call this empathy. At its best, it surpasses ordinary communication and becomes communion.

I favour classes devoted to exploration and explication of texts, but sometimes I find I must deliver specialized lectures on individual writers or works, or background lectures on such topics as "The Romantic Movement" or "Naturalism and Realism." Though students may interrupt to ask questions or to offer comments, ordinarily these lectures are monologues. I may give lectures on several consecutive days or I may intersperse them through the term, depending upon the needs and capacities of each new group. When lecturing I use a "notes-and-quotes" outline (which assures coherence and permits spontaneity of expression) or a complete script (which assures reasonable thoroughness and precision of expression). I deviate from these carefully prepared materials only if I feel that I am reciting rather than delivering ideas. Whether my lectures are quite formal or apparently casual, they are never, from my point of view, routine. When enrolment exceeds, say, thirty students, anonymity sets in. After that point, the larger the class the more reluctant are the students to participate in discussions, and the more the professor is inclined (or required, in self-defence) to lecture. Over the past two decades my classes have tended to exceed fifty students. Hence I have had to do a great deal of talking. Fortunately, so far, my Hibernian heritage has held me in reasonably good stead.

Even in these larger classes I do employ a variety of discussion techniques that are potentially more beneficial than a steady stream of lectures. I should like to describe three such techniques now.

(1) *The questionnaire.* At least three weeks in advance of specified discussion dates I distribute a mimeographed list of twenty-five questions on, say, *The Adventures of Huckleberry Finn.* Most questions require the reader to focus close attention on the story. In class we select a question such as, "What are the functions of the Mississippi River in this novel?" and solicit tentative, brief replies. As members have read the book and are already acquainted with the question, they normally offer answers without very much urging. These answers I jot on the blackboard. A reasonable consensus having been established, the next step is to classify, bring order to the information received. Support for each major point is then sought, argument being based on direct references to the story. Sometimes lively debate ensues, the only restriction being that speakers must confine themselves to the specific topic. From the evidence supplied by the class and abbreviated on the blackboard we are usually able to compose a reasonable answer to the question. I point out the merits or defects in the consensus, suggest supplementary readings, and invite further comments. The process takes anywhere from fifteen minutes to one hour, depending upon the complexity of the question and the perceptiveness of the readers. I normally use the questionnaire method only two or three times each year in each course, and then only for major or full-length works.

(2) *The smaller groups.* This method assures total participation in discussions and permits wide coverage of material. Moreover, it is easy to administer: I simply divide the class into several discussion units of five or six students, who form circles and choose a spokesman who will report their findings to the class. Each group may be assigned a different task, or all may work on the same one. Suppose our topic is Wordsworth's Sonnets. I assign six or seven sonnets for study, a different one to each group. Usually I suggest a basic study format so that the same approach or order will be followed in each study group. Normally about one-half hour can be allowed for discussion, before each group reports to the entire class. Special points of interest made by the spokesmen are jotted on the blackboard; so are any conflicts. Depending upon this feedback, I then summarize the evidence, take issue with statements made, supplement the findings, or recommend further study. The smaller

groups method I use several times each year in each course, especially when I wish to open up the multiple possibilities inherent in a topic.

(3) *The panel discussion.* This technique offers opportunities to capitalize on the interests of several students at a time. This is how it works. First we ascertain the books the students have recently read, or intend to read for the course. Then we ask five or six students to study a particular theme or book or collection, with a view to presenting their discoveries several weeks later. The panelists choose their chairman, pursue their own private research, and in due time meet with me to rehearse a few questions or plan procedures. Having agreed upon a basic format for the presentation, on the date assigned the panelists are allowed at least half an hour to express and exchange views, and to question and challenge one another; and then the discussion is thrown open to the entire class. (I take a place near the rear of the room so that I may observe and take notes on the proceedings. Occasionally I participate directly by asking questions or making statements, but normally I wait until the exercise has run its course before I offer any comments.) The panel discussion I have described is merely an "open" seminar conducted in the presence of many other students who are invited to participate in the discussion. Obviously it can be employed often, with variations, and in any sort of course. In the Modern American Literature course, for example, we stage a series of panels on the Nobel laureates, with each student serving on at least one panel of his choice and competence. On balance, this is the technique that I have found to be most effective for engendering intelligent group participation.

What do I do about essays, term papers, and other assignments?

At one time I required each student to write several short essays each term. I used to annotate most of these essays and return them to the writers. As I have never employed a reader or assistant, I was annually overwhelmed by the sheer volume of this paper work. Moreover, my students generally regarded these compositions as dutiful assignments and not as meaningful statements.

Several years ago I adopted an approach that, everything considered, has proved much more effective. In my lecture courses, I now require (besides examinations) one major paper per term. Each student selects a manageable topic, usually discusses its possibilities with me, and several weeks later submits an essay of approximately twenty pages. This paper is expected to be unified, coherent, and adequately developed, and to adhere to a standard methodology. The topic must be significant, the treatment appropriate, the composition correct.

After I have read and annotated the paper, I arrange a private interview with the writer and offer a "personalized" critical evaluation of the work. To accommodate all my students I must schedule appointments at half-hour intervals over a period of three weeks or so each semester. In this way I am certain to meet with each of my 120 students at least twice each year. Of course, I see many of them privately, especially English majors, on other occasions as well. We do not always confine these tutorial meetings to consideration of the term paper. Sometimes we discuss such matters as other assignments, readings, class participation, or preparation for further studies.

Conducting tutorials in this manner cuts heavily into the time an instructor would normally devote to other interests, such as his own research and writing. It also takes its toll in physical and nervous energy. But it has its compensations. Many students have expressed appreciation for the personal attention given to their efforts, and some of my colleagues have told me that they regard these tutorial practices as my particular forte.

I have recounted some of my tenets and practices as an instructor, not because I believe that these factors alone account for success or failure, but because, it seems, there may be some usefulness to others in these revelations. I have asserted no claim to originality: in philosophy I am a traditionist, and in pedagogy a moderate. I do, however, accept title to uniqueness: my own personality, for better or worse, necessarily invests and individuates my work. This element, however, I am in no position to assess. During the two years I served as dean of arts and science, several students and a few faculty members urged me to give up front offce work and return to the classroom. I have done so. But to this day I have not found out–frankly, I have been afraid to ask–whether my friendly advisers meant that I was a good teacher or that I was a poor administrator.

BRENDAN O'GRADY

Born in New York City, Brendan O'Grady studied for his first degree at the University of Notre Dame, a master's degree at Columbia University, and a Ph.D. at the University of Ottawa. He joined the staff of St. Dunstan's University as an instructor in English in 1948 and rose to be professor and head of the Department of English, then dean of arts and science and vice-president. He served as vice-chairman of the University's Board of Governors for two years and finally for three months as chairman.

He was a member of the University Planning Committee which brought about the merger of St. Dunstan's University and Prince of Wales College to form the University of Prince Edward Island in 1969. He then became a professor of English in the new University.

Earlier public service included the role of conciliation officer for the P.E.I. Department of Labour, directorships in the Catholic Social Welfare Bureau, the Cooperative Union of P.E.I., and the Charlottetown Credit Union, and he served as a member of the P.E.I. Civil Service Commission.

Over a period of twenty-five years he has engaged in occasional free-lance journalism, given more than three hundred public lectures and written a dozen essays and booklets ("some anonymous, some pseudonymous; none I wish to claim"). He is currently engaged in research (when his teaching leaves him time, which is seldom) on the major characters in Hawthorne's romances and ("a labour of love") a study of modern Irish fiction.

According to his former St. Dunstan's students, Professor O'Grady loved his subject and thus inspired others to love it. He personalized English literature for each student, demonstrating that it was a living part of the society from which it evolved. The variety of methods he used called forth comment: lectures, term papers, tutorials, seminars, panel discussions, and group discussions.

He had a sense of humour, personal integrity, and self-discipline. He showed a personal interest in each student, and a respect for the intelligence and opinions of students. "He never forced his views on us," said one of his former students, "but he never accepted ours unless they were valid. He was always ready to change his mind—for a good reason. You felt you were learning with *him as well as* from *him."*

Breaking the Sound Barrier: A Dramatic Presentation

R. W. Packer

Probably the most violent and aggressive act that any person can do to other persons is to invade their minds with ideas and twists of meaning which disturb the comforting security of things known and faith kept. Yet this is what I, as a teacher, am required to do. Recognition of this fact has three facets. There is first of all the difficulty of finding the opening words to begin the intercommunication process. Each teaching situation is different. Each has its own tensions and constraints, for each situation new phrases, sentences, actions have to be found. Repetition of what worked yesterday may not work today. A colleague who had recently joined the academic world after years spent in research once said to me, "I envy your ability to go in and meet a new class without any nervousness." I quickly assured him that all I had learned to do was to disguise the tension and to channel its energy into breaking the mental barriers which everyone establishes in an even slightly unsure situation.

Secondly, the mental attitude of the taught to the teacher is established very rapidly. I find that I can easily influence those who take a positive attitude towards me, I can teach those who do not like me but I can do almost nothing with those who take a blotting paper, "I'm here, teach me!" attitude. So, because I'm paid to teach, extra effort is needed to stimulate the amorphous middle group.

Thirdly, the success or nonsuccess of a lecture is often determined by the initial impact. In the same way that an orchestra conductor sets the tempo of a piece of music by the speed of his upbeat, the whole character of response to a lecture is determined by the energy of the beginning. This is a matter not simply of speed but of the intensity of meaning of the words.

Effective teaching must include a deliberate attempt by the teacher to warp the minds of the taught. After a teaching session neither the taught nor the teacher should be quite the same. Both should have gained incrementally in knowledge and/or understanding. I wish that I could always find the right combination of words to convey meanings and ideas. I am sure that every teacher wishes that he could remember the exact phrases he has used which were not in his notes but which appeared, apparently extemporaneously, and seemed to be just right. Perhaps it is the learning/teaching situation that is just right and not the words themselves.

I never, willingly, put myself into a teaching situation for which I have not prepared both substantively and mentally. Those last five minutes before lectures or seminars or field work during which the mind can review the material are to me as important as the many hours of reading and writing which preceded them. This is the time when my mind rotates at speed and checks off the various items and the emphasis to be placed on those items, and this frees me from the tyranny of notes. I abandoned the completely written lecture about twenty years ago, after a lecture during which I was trying to point out the similarity between the annual migration of Canadians to the summer cottage and the widely reported "transhumance" of Swiss farm families together with herds of cattle from the lower part of the valley to the alpine meadows above the tree line. I said, reading from my notes, "from the cows they obtain milk for butter and cheese," the students wrote it down and yet no one in the room was learning anything that they had not known for years. On the other hand, notes for both instructor and instructed are valuable. But the only ways to ensure that notes are kept is to mimeograph them, to write on the blackboard, or to include a numerical statistic. Mimeographed notes in my opinion are a waste of time. They go directly into the students' notebooks where they remain in pristine condition, untouched by mind or thought until eventually they are thrown out or regurgitated to some other group of students. Ideas, not facts, usefully deserve the time and effort of transcription from notes to board to notes. Most people have difficulty remembering numbers, so that if a number is included in the thought or concept it is usually recorded for later use.

I have found it most ineffective to display beautifully drawn finished graphical material. It is much more effective to show, even inaccurately, how the graph, diagram or map is developed step by step than to have a neat finished product. The finished result is suitable for books not for the classroom.

We have a student population which is, from infancy, faced with imaginative presentation of coloured pictures, slides, photographs, films, and television. They have been conditioned to see them either as a transitory phenomenon in advertising, which they can accept or reject, or as part of an entertainment. They have to be taught how to look at these as a means of education. In reply to the much quoted "A picture is worth a thousand words," often ascribed to Dewey, but probably coming from Comenius, I would like to submit "A picture without words is without educational value." This has a corollary that a bad picture is an educational detriment. Learning with visual aids is more demanding than without them. It is difficult enough to listen, comprehend, and take notes, but when seeing is added it becomes an even more strenuous process.

Because the teaching/learning process requires work in the full sense of the word, the question of the attention span of the individual has also to be considered. I think my attention span is about twelve minutes so that I consciously put a break in my lectures at somewhere between 10 to 14 minute intervals. These breaks, in general, are attempts to obtain some release of mental tension. I may change my position, perhaps by sitting on a table or removing a jacket, or displaying a map, or I may tell a story or make a joke. Jokes have to be an integral part of the subject matter and not mere attention-getters. It is unfair to attempt to compete with the Ed Sullivan show before a relatively captive audience, so the jokes and stories must have immediate mnemonic relevance.

I have tried teaching by correspondence with notable lack of success. I found it possible to make up quite interesting and effective assignments. Then I would be faced with a mass of written submissions. Those students who understood the instructions caused little difficulty, their assignments could be rapidly shipped back to them. The problem for me was that the correspondence students who could not or did not understand the written or printed word in the first place were most unlikely to be able to take advantage of written comments and yet it was these papers that took the most time. I found myself unable to overcome this dilemma.

Some of the most time-consuming but worthwhile teaching I do by talking to students. I do not subscribe to the notion that the best thing to do is to refer the student to books, articles and other references, since most of the students' problems arise not from an inability to read but an inability to comprehend what they have read. To say "read it over" has never impressed me as a good teaching device, I much prefer to say, "read what someone else has written about the same subject and then we can discuss the similarities and differences."

I have been annoyed in recent years by the usurpation of the term "Programmed Learning" for a specific type of progressive system of questions, answers, and reinforcements. It is not the type of learning device that I object to, but the fact that progressive sequential learning and instruction is the only method that has been used by teachers for millennia. I am committed to the concept that understanding is not a matter of intuitive, random quantum jumps, but a series of building blocks which gradually lead to the understanding of a total structure. This does not necessarily mean that it is at all times possible to go step by step. Sometimes it is necessary to use the "carrot technique;" that is the way you get a donkey to move, you dangle a carrot in front of his nose and he really doesn't get the carrot until he reaches home. At times it is necessary to say to students look, learn this and when you have it you will see what it is all about.

I have great sympathy and understanding for those students who are not too bright. I am happy to try endless variations of explanations to try to reach some degree of understanding. The students who annoy me most are the bright, intelligent ones who are too lazy to do the work to their best ability. My oft-used phrase, "the stupid I like, the indolent I will not tolerate" is probably too extreme, but it has had some positive results in shocking some of the bright into productivity. Perhaps they respond to the notion of not disappointing me.

It is quite obvious that the attempt to squeeze all students into a uniform educational mould is not realistic. Choice of methods must be available, but it is possible to envisage some kind of minimum subjection of one mind to another; unless this occurs or if a mental block is set up the time of everyone is wasted.

The urge to pontificate is irresistible. A university consists of an organized mass of books and students. Some students, through accidents of age, are in a position of instruction. No professor should be really satisfied until one of his students knows more at the end of a course than the professor did at the beginning. By the end of the course, the "student instructor" will have learned too and so continue the process of incremental learning. So many acts and attitudes of the students with whom any professor comes in contact show that most students do not understand what the faculty members of the university are trying to do.

Teaching probably is the most frustrating of all occupations. When a plumber repairs a leaky pipe, a business man sells a new product, or a financier floats a bond issue there is an end to the process. The pipe is fixed, the bank account is increased, the bonds are sold. Personal satisfaction in terms of a finished product is a rare reward for the teacher. Years of honest and best effort can only be evaluated by the later results. Perhaps the good student would have done as well without instruction, perhaps he or she succeeds in spite of professorial activities. This is not an appeal for sympathy nor a request for gratitude but a demand for understanding.

Professors, believe it or not, are human, they do not teach solely for their own gratification. They do not give assignments, select essay subjects, or insist on tests for their own self-aggrandisement. They do it because after years of experience, consultation with colleagues, and careful consideration they have found that these are the best ways they know to develop the knowledge, techniques, and ability of the persons under instruction.

A student will often question the mechanics of courses, the unreal values, the evaluation procedures which are often improper because they are based upon a lack of understanding of what teachers are trying to do.

"When do you want this handed in?" No professor really wants it for himself, he wants it only so that he can use it, after marking, as a foundation for future learning by the student.

"What are we responsible for on the exam?" There is no finite limit to learning, the student who places an artificial achievement level on his efforts denies the opportunity available to him.

"Where have you got to in the text, you don't seem to be following it?" The assumption that one of the university entrance requirements is the ability to read seems to be a reasonable one. When an instructor is reduced to following slavishly the outline of a "text" book his function as an interpreter, a stimulator, or a mentor has ended.

"What good will studying geography be to me?" If the next half-century could be foreseen, each person could be easily trained to fit into an allotted slot, just as each machine is designed for a specific function. Every teacher hopes that the mind that he is attempting to warp, twist, brainwash, and otherwise coerce into operation will be able to develop greater flexibility than a machine. All knowledge is additive, none of it is subtractive, and the denial of the opportunities for knowledge on the ground that an immediate use cannot be seen is a process from which the young person must be dissuaded for his own protection in the future. In spite of the fact that very few people in our society are doing now what they thought they were going to do when they were in school or university and that change will probably be accelerated, the demand for immediate relevance continues to be presented as a substitute for the more difficult and rigorous process of accumulation of basic knowledge.

"How much of this should we memorize?" My objective as a university teacher is not to fill the mind but to sharpen it. The procedures of analysis, correlation, sorting, computation, synthesis, and regurgitation are the aims of education. However, none of these goals can be reached by working in a vacuum. Of course, all the material is in the books, and a system of filing and cross-indexing will be able to produce it, and the human mind is more than a storage unit. Nevertheless, all the energy of the world applied to nothing produces nothing.

"You failed me in Geography 20." This is just not true. No instructor ever failed anyone. The function of the instructor is like that of a rock in the face of an oncoming wave, if the wave breaks over the rock, so much to the good, if the waves does not reach the rock, it will remain there waiting for the next wave which, with a little more energy, may succeed.

"Do you mark on a curve?" Undergraduates may find some relief in the knowledge that this is not necessary, there is a sufficient number of good students that the standard is set by one's classmates. Most professors are so unsure of the efficiency of the examination system and their own ability to apply it, that whatever marking scheme is planned the lower fifteen percent are usually helped. It is equally possible to have a class with all first-class grades and also all failures, but such occurrences are extremely rare. No pressure to allow any percentage to pass or fail has ever been placed on me, perhaps because I would reject it so vehemently.

Since I like to use the didactic, expository approach in lecturing and to a certain extent am involved in an emotional and, if I may be presumptuous, dramatic presentation, the timing and flow of the presentation is important to me. For this reason I try to give students enough time to arrive before I start to lecture, and of course this backfires in two ways. First, I am accused of being late for lectures, which is nonsense for it is extremely difficult for the lecture to begin without me being there, and secondly, since I do not start when the Pavlovian bells sound, some students arrange their timing to arrive even later. I must admit to having made sarcastic and scurrilous remarks to such individuals, which can be unfortunate since they may not be late of their own volition.

A further result of this approach is that questions from the students are not always easy to cope with. If my lecturing has been good, then the "right" questions are asked at the appropriate moment and the flow of concepts and information is neither interrupted nor changed. I still do not know what to do about the questions asked about the topic covered twenty minutes previously. It is often obvious from the groans and grimaces of the other class members that they too recognize the inopportune question. The only thing to do is to offer to discuss the matter individually later. This is usually ineffective teaching, for frequently the whole matter has become self-evident after consideration.

I have never yet taken attendance at lectures although I do insist upon total participation in laboratory and field work. Since attendance is therefore voluntary I try to maintain the involvement of everyone in the room. Since I use only the minimum of notes I can watch the responses and activities of the students. At the same time I retain the right to exclude people who go to sleep, talk, hold hands, write history essays, study for tests, do crossword puzzles, or otherwise not participate. I do not know whether I have this right. I don't care very much, for I intend to continue to use it, when needed—perhaps once or twice a year. When it is necessary to exclude peremptorily a young gentleman or lady from the lecture hall, I soften it by offering my office, which is always empty when I am lecturing, or a dime for a cup of coffee, or a suggestion that the beautiful tree-dotted grassy campus is a better place for giving vent to those inevitable bisexual impulses which occur in the spring. Even so the interruption is a double one, the flow of the lecture is broken as also is the mental coupling which I have been working hard to attain. To put it mildly, to have to do it annoys me.

One of the many things that makes teaching a pleasure for me is the fortunate fact that I teach a subject which in itself is intrinsically interesting. Everyone has had and is currently having geographic experiences: weather changes, rivers flood, cities expand, industries pollute, so that it is relatively easy to develop abstract principles which fit within the experiential background of the student. There is also an element of the "outside" in the sort of physical geography that I am involved with, and this gives the subject matter an aspect of virility. This, in a society in which both sexes are conditioned from childhood to make the value judgment that virility is both important and good, makes the material of geography both in series with and parallel to previous concepts. It seems necessary to be enthusiastic about the subject matter yet obviously no one can be equally enthused about all things. I have solved this problem by choosing to talk about only those things with which I have some kind of emotional/intellectual involvement. The result is that the "course description," the "course of studies," or the "course outline" which satisfies my academic colleagues bears little resemblance to what I actually choose to talk about from year to year.

The cliché, "what do you know for sure?", is to me not a mere verbal patting but a real question. Naturally, further study of everything reveals gaps in knowledge but more important is the fact that perhaps we only "know" those things which we can relate to a sensual experience. I accept as an intellectual abstraction the scientific truth, in other words a very high probability, that the planet earth is roughly spherical. I am prepared to lecture on the various approximations of spherical excess in relation to the shape of the geoid, but my experiences and sense observations all point to the surface of the earth being flat. It is the transference from what is "known" to what is "known for sure" that represents the real challenge. It is a corollary of this point of view that field observation by the learner, tactile learning through models, samples, and practical work, and use of analogies all have become an integral part of my teaching/learning process.

Since this essay is to a certain extent a public confessional or a psychiatrist's couch I am forced to say that for me teaching requires not only patience but a willingness to indulge in hypocrisy. It is necessary to regard the student as an adult, otherwise he or she will not think in an adult or nonbinary manner. This means that the teacher has to pretend that the student's response to a situation is both mature and new, even though it may be neither, lest the idealism, interest, and confidence of the developing mind be destroyed. This means that I have to listen many times to poorly stated opinions and questions from freshmen, which I have heard over and over again, as if this were the first time. Only after the bait has been firmly taken can the line be pulled, the direction to the relevant literature be given, and genuine criticism be attempted. This technique does not work with senior or graduate students since they are firmly hooked anyway and are prepared to make critical evaluations between opinions. They do not or should not expect to arrive at earth-shattering conclusions or entirely new concepts. To illustrate this point

I like to tell the story of my "great discovery." I was working with rainfall periodicities, particularly the daily rainfalls of Canada, to see if certain days were rainier than others. There tended to be a repetition, both in frequency and in amount, of rain on certain dates. In looking around for some kind of causal factor, I examined the phases of the moon. I was excited to find that every 27 years the new moon occurred on the same date. This was new to me, perhaps I had located a repetitive cause not previously noted. Unfortunately, it was known to the Egyptians in 2000 BC and is the basis of the Jewish Calendar. My new idea was 4000 years old! Such a rebuff might well cause a neophyte to lose confidence! I find I must let the student find out his or her evidence to refute ideas and not contradict them as if from the seat of judgment.

The problems faced by the new instructor include that of when and how to stop. One rule is to stop when you have finished all you have to say on a particular topic. I learned years ago that no students are fooled by waffling or padding to fill a time period. Secondly, do not start on a new topic which you have not completely prepared. You will spoil your next lecture. On the other hand, reiteration, is never a waste of time in the inexact process of communication. The clock is meant as a guide not a tyrant. I have adopted the position that the lecture ends when I do, not when the noisiest student with another lecture to go to or a pressing lunch engagement decides to close his notebook and put his coat on. Yet after years of the fifty-minute lecture period I am conditioned to that time-length. I found it most obvious when I taught a summer session at another university where the periods were fifty-five minutes long. At my conditioned time I dried up. When this happens all one can do is to hope that some part of the teaching/learning process has taken place and just stop.

R. W. PACKER

Robert W. Packer was born in Shropshire and educated at the Ludlow Grammar School. Both before and after war service in the Royal Air Force, he studied geography at the University of Cambridge (M.A. 1949).

After brief periods of employment as assistant planner for the Hamilton Planning Board, in the Geographical Bureau of the Canada Department of Mines, and as a member of the Nauja expedition making a coastal survey of James Bay, Hudson's Bay, and West Baffin Island, he joined the Department of Geography of the University of Western Ontario as an instructor. There he rose to the rank of professor.

Professor Packer has devoted his research especially to the physical geography of the region of Southwestern Ontario, contributing articles to such journals as the Canadian Historical Review, Western Ontario History, *and the* Canadian Geographer, *and papers to the Canadian*

Association of Geographers of which he served as president in 1972–73. He is joint author of a Workbook in Introductory Physical Geography *(McGraw-Hill, 1966). "I like to think of myself as a field man," he says, "both as an observer and a teacher of field technique."*

Some notion of his almost flamboyant approach to teaching may be gained from the following extracts from the outline of his course, "Introduction to Geography."

1. *Where in the world are you?*
   (Where the hell do you think you are?)
2. *Longitude and time*
   (Everything good comes from the east)
5. *Modern meteorology*
   (It's all wet)
6. *The general circulation*
   (The semi-permanent permanent wave)
18. *Physiological and psychological limits of habitability*
   (It's not the heat, it's the humanity)

Professor Packer was a "very human, highly opinionated, witty lecturer, with an excellent command of the Socratic method," said one of his former students. Another described him as "an actor" who "mixed a great deal of humour with each topic, starting each lecture with what would seem to be a humorous title, then going through the lecture with jibes and, in retrospect, horrible puns. Little did we realize at the time that by remembering the humour we inadvertently remembered the lecture."

He had a sound grasp of and a keen interest in his subject, his former students testified. He organized his courses well, made meaningful local references, used slides effectively, and employed a variety of teaching techniques.

Evidently he showed real interest in his students, was easily accessible, and often mixed socially with them but was never too familiar. He made his students earn their grades, one graduate reported, and was respected for this. One student who had taken both undergraduate and graduate courses from Mr. Packer marvelled "at his ability to completely change his style of presentation, even his apparent personality, as he moved from level to level amongst his students." He created a more personal atmosphere in the smaller, more advanced classes.

Commitment Is Catching

Frederick A. Aldrich

The invitation to prepare this essay made me reflect very seriously and try to analyse what, for the want of a better name, may be called my "teaching method." In the first instance, I don't believe I have a teaching "method" as such. I do not claim to be a pedagogue. If anything, I am a scientist trying desperately to get some research done in my chosen field of marine invertebrate zoology while administering the Marine Sciences Research Laboratory of Memorial University of Newfoundland. But, at the same time, and of no less importance, I attempt to impart knowledge of my field, that is, the broad field of biology, to the students to whom and for whom I am responsible. But there is more to it than imparting knowledge. Unashamedly, I admit that it is an attempt to inspire them and to instill in them enthusiasm for biology—an enthusiasm which is akin to my own. At this point I feel I have come to my first rubric, or criterion, and that is enthusiasm. At best, teaching is communication, and communication is most easily accomplished when the communicator is enthusiastic about the product which he is hawking. Anyone can convey his subject, at least in part, if it is important to him, for commitment is catching. Students know when a person believes what he is saying, and they respond to personal commitment and a personal involvement. This enthusiasm, or involvement, in my opinion, can go a long way to compensate for other failings in a lecturer's methods.

To put it in the modern vernacular, it is my mission to "turn them on." To turn them on, however, does not really say it adequately. No one can turn them all on. But I am committed to the belief that even for those for whom you must turn in a failing grade (and there are always some, for only if you are capable of reporting failures does a grade of distinction mean anything) you should be able to make a difference. Now, how do you do this? Rather, I must ask, how do I do it? I don't think that one method does it, and indeed my "teaching method" encompasses a kaleidoscope of many roles. In my teaching I must not only wear, like Joseph, a coat of many colours, but a coat that changes colour to fit a number of roles. I maintain that not the least of these roles is that of a dedicated scientist true to the integrity of his science, but not over-impressed with himself as a scientist. In this role I do not stress the fact that I am a scientist, but that I am a practitioner of a science. And this brings me to my second rubric. We all know about watered-down texts and general guides, but in my opinion they are a hindrance rather than a help. Students don't want to be taught by watered-down scientists and they don't want to be taught watered-down science. And I submit that in the dilution of the science, as some sort of an aid to instruction, you are defeating your purpose. The rubric to which I refer then is that the students want to know it the way it is, and not the way that you think they can understand it. The commitment to the integrity of the science, along with your involvement and your enthusiasm, work hand in hand, or at least I have assumed that they do so for me.

How fortunate I am that I teach biology, for I definitely feel that biology is the ultimate science. Like other salesmen, my job is therefore made easier because I have a product to sell which is not only saleable, but is one with which I am proud to be associated. To teach, I believe the scientist must be part actor, evangelist, and even charlatan. Like the old snake oil salesmen, I must entertain, astound, amaze, but above all, sell the snake oil.

But what is the snake oil? The snake oil is no less than a confrontation with life. Living processes, living forms, living destinies, evolutionary histories, evolutionary projects, and the very stuff (some call it protoplasm) of life itself. The subject is so vast and it lends itself to a myriad number of ways through which it may be taught. I cannot teach it dully, drily, or even quietly. For life is not dull, or dry, or even quiet. We here in Newfoundland are extremely fortunate for our very lives are touched by the sea and its contained biomass. As a squid biologist working in Newfoundland, symbolized by some as the traditional "squid jigging grounds," I am continually amazed that many of my students have never seen a squid and equate most fish with cod.

And so I have the opportunity, through the teaching of biology, to introduce these students to something of which they are themselves a living part, and by so doing place them in that totality. I have had an opportunity granted to few people, not only to teach such things as marine ecology and the consequences of environmental deterioration, but also to do it as a medium helping students to become aware not only of much of what we know as biology, but also of themselves as part of the biological world. The scientist's ultimate concern in his science. The teacher's ultimate concern is human beings. How fortunate I have been to see that really these are one and the same thing.

Specifically, I try not to teach facts. That's what books and libraries and laboratories are for. I try to teach a feeling, an appreciation, an awareness, to arouse an interest. The books and the facts will follow. Facts are for learning, and learning, like prayer, is an individual, private process. It is my responsibility to get them to want to learn and to make the investment of themselves, for themselves, for they must invest themselves in the learning process.

I am sure that many teachers would disagree with this, but I really do not put too much reliance on laboratory sections alone. Beginning students either drop the scalpels on their feet, or faint at the sight of blood, and most important, I have found more often than not that laboratory experiments just do not work. Now, I do not want to go on record as saying that laboratories are not valuable, but I really would equate labs with libraries as far as the professor is concerned. If, through teaching, one can "turn the students on," to invest themselves in learning, then that learning process will carry on into the lab and into the library.

Nor do I subscribe to the necessity of small classes. To paraphrase a great educator, mediocrity in small packages is not a virtue. There is a place for small classes, i.e., discussion groups, but evangelism and theatrics are best expended on large groups.

In conclusion, I repeatedly find that the most important items in my teaching bag of tricks are the students. On any number of occasions I have had to try to adapt my methods to closed-circuit television, or public television, or radio, knowing that somewhere out there were breathing people who were hearing and/or seeing me and whom I was instructing. But for me, something was missing, and that something was the living students. They just were not there to be taught, and it is they that make one a teacher. It is their needs that I must meet and it is the students who show one what succeeds, and what fails to meet their needs. So many times I have had to alter course, adopt new means, anything to get ideas across, when they, most often silently, but not always so, communicate to me that the ideas are not going across.

The following is a passage from Shakespeare's *King Lear:*

FOOL: Canst tell how an oyster makes his shell?

LEAR: No.

FOOL: Nor I neither. . . .

Nor can I. To me, the key word in this passage is "how." Like Lear and the Fool, I could say that I don't know either, but I do know something about oysters and other similar pelecypods, and I know something about their shells and their pearls. In teaching biology, the important thing is to tell them about oysters and to tell them about shells and pearls in such a way that the students want to learn how the oyster makes them. Not knowing how an oyster does so, I can only hope that some of the interest that is generated among the students will someday result in one of them filling in the missing information.

A teacher needs students. May I always have mine.

FREDERICK A. ALDRICH

Frederick A. Aldrich was born and grew up in New Jersey. Zoology was his major subject for the A.B. degree at Drew University, and the field in which he took his M.S. and Ph.D. at Rutgers, The State University, New Jersey. Later he studied at the Marine Biological Laboratory, Woods Hole, Massachusetts, and at the Graduate School of Hahnemann Medical College of Philadelphia.

In 1954 he became assistant curator (later associate curator) of limnology, Division of Estuarine Science, Academy of Natural Sciences of Philadelphia. Seven years later he joined the staff of Memorial University as associate professor of biology. By 1970 he was professor of biology, director of the Marine Sciences Research Laboratory, and dean of graduate studies.

Dr. Aldrich was invertebrate zoologist with the Catherwood Foundation Peruvian Amazon Expedition in 1955. He has served as president of the Atlantic Estuarine Research Society and of the Canadian Society of Wildlife and Fishery Biologists (Area I). He is a fellow of the Zoological Society of London and of the American Association for the Advancement of Science, a director of the Canadian Society of Zoologists, and vice-chairman of the International Committee for the Scientific Exploration of the Atlantic Shelf.

His many articles and reports in scientific journals and collections reflect his research interest in the invertebrate fauna of the northern North Atlantic, with primary emphasis on the functional morphology of decapod cephalopods (squid).

The picture of Professor Aldrich sketched by his former students is that of a friendly extrovert, enthusiastic about his field, and anxious to share his enthusiasm with his students.

According to those reporting, he knew his material, organized it carefully, spoke well and with humour, illustrated his presentations with visual aids, including diagrams "drawn with a flair," topical examples and references to his research, and engaged his students in questions and discussion. He was at his best, it was said, in undergraduate courses. His use of frequent short tests was noted, and also that he was a "strict marker."

He was "friendly and personal with each student—knew each by his first name," said one graduate. Another added that he "made each student feel important."

Elements of Creativity in Teaching

George Setterfield

A particularly critical, nonteaching research scientist I know claims that my teaching activities are little different from selling shoes. While I am prepared to admit that teaching involves a degree of such over-the-counter salesmanship, I also believe emphatically that there is creativity in teaching and that it is precisely this element which separates teaching from more routine occupations. Furthermore, I would suggest that the degree of creativity in a given teaching operation largely determines its quality and therefore it is this aspect of teaching with which this book is, or should be, primarily concerned.

I have personally experienced a striking example of creative teaching. My interest in academic things in general, and science and biology in particular, stems directly from the influence of a single teacher, the late Mr. R. Hammond of Victoria High School. In the space of a few months, in a crowded classroom, this man aroused in me a respect for learning, an interest in and curiosity about science, and a desire to contribute to both knowledge and teaching. At the same time he taught me most of the basic descriptive biology that I know. No doubt I was at a particularly receptive age for such stimulation and had the necessary abilities to respond, but the influence of this man was so decisive and in such contrast to that of other teachers I have experienced that for me Mr. Hammond was clearly an exceptional teacher.

Since that time I have often attempted to analyse the factors which were responsible for Mr. Hammond's influence. It is relatively simple to list some obvious qualities which contributed to his success: he was well-informed and interested in his subject, organized, a clear communicator, and a warm and sensitive person. Yet many teachers who made little impact had the same qualities while several others I have encountered lacked some of these qualities but were very effective. Clearly, these obvious positive characteristics were important in Mr. Hammond's performance but were not sufficient, or perhaps even completely essential, in themselves. I believe his success depended additionally on a complex interplay of subtle aspects of his attitudes and personality which defies analysis, i.e., an indescribable creative element. The components of this element, of course, vary greatly with different teachers but I am sure that all effective teaching has such an element and it is only when it is lacking that the teaching exercise is reduced to "shoe selling."

I emphasize the indefinable character of creativity in teaching because I have been unsuccessful in analysing it myself and I have not heard it adequately described by others. In fact I have ceased attempting to rationalize the subtleties of teaching and in my own operation I essentially function intuitively. This is not to say that the creative element in teaching cannot, or should not, be analysed, but I am content to leave this work to others. For myself, I can only describe some attitudes and approaches I have to teaching and hope that when taken together with other such statements, as in this book, it will aid in the understanding of creativity in teaching.

For purposes of description I will break the teaching process down into three elements: underlying attitudes of the teacher, practical teaching methods, and student responses. Of the three I personally consider the first of major importance, the second of lesser significance, and the third an element in the system upon which I can only make limited comment. The three components are, of course, not clearly distinguishable during teaching but rather are closely interdependent and the separation is an arbitrary device to aid description.

Attitudes and Characteristics of the Teacher

I place great emphasis upon the teacher's attitudes because I feel that probably the key to the creative part of teaching lies there. If the integrity, motivation, and attitudes of the teacher are "together" the other components of the process will fall out more or less naturally and some success will be achieved; if they are not, no amount of sophisticated technique or curricular juggling can substitute. The main attitudes which I consider to be essential to creative teaching may be grouped under three headings: honesty, involvement with subject, and sensitivity.

Honesty. Most intellectual pursuits are concerned with revealing or experiencing truth and as a result are closely bound up with honesty. Science, for example, only proceeds by continual unrelenting honest appraisal of results and hypotheses. Similarly, I believe that teaching can only flourish in an atmosphere of maximum honest interaction between teacher and students. As I have suggested, one essential element of teaching depends on a subtle projection of the teacher's personal characteristics and nothing is more injurious to this subjective process than insincerity or falseness. Students in reacting to the teacher can sense such negative qualities almost immediately and although they may not be able to analyse precisely what is wrong they know that something is, and as a consequence rapport is lost. With rapport gone, with distrust or even hostility aroused, the teaching operation is reduced to a struggle to sell shoes to a wary buyer.

Dishonesty in the teaching operation may appear at different levels. It almost goes without saying that the teacher must not attempt to bluff his way through material he is unfamiliar with or does not understand. Rather, he must master the material insofar as he is able and then openly admit to his ignorance beyond this point. The important result of such a process is that the student is able to build up a realistic picture of the teacher's strengths and limitations and the teacher then emerges as a real person to whom the student can genuinely relate.

Of course, if the teacher is simply incompetent and the limitations on his abilities are too severe no amount of admission of the fact can save him. But this is not the usual problem; the hiring processes insure that most professors are reasonably competent in their subject. Most professors are not, however, as I know from association with numerous colleagues, master scholars in their fields. Yet many professors would attempt to project this image. By stick handling through subject material they attempt to give the impression of vast knowledge coupled with incisive intelligence. This approach creates an initial awe in students which usually dwindles into anything from qualified respect to disgust as the real abilities of the professor emerge in spite of his performance. The sad thing is, such teachers never give students a chance to form a relationship with them; they play a game and force students to uncover the rules as the game proceeds. Most of these professors might be very successful teachers if they could find in their true abilities a satisfactory image for projection.

Apart from the act of teaching, honesty must also be present in the motivations of the teacher. Basically he must teach because he really wants to teach. If a person merely teaches to earn time in the research lab or because it offers material advantages I find it unlikely that he will be more than a technically competent communicator. Again, the underlying insincerity would prevent any strong interaction between teacher and students. Fortunately, in my experience this form of dishonesty does not seem to be widespread in universities, or at least among the scientists there; most of my colleagues seem to be at the university primarily because they want to teach. For the minority of people involved in teaching for the wrong motives I can only suggest that they admit this openly and at least establish an honest relationship with the students on this limited basis. It should be better than nothing.

At this point some people may take issue and say that an element of acting and sham is essential to teaching technique. Certainly I occasionally calculatedly mislead students for the sake of emphasis or clear exposition and I have seen other teachers engage in questionable histrionics with marked positive effect. Doubtless one can take students in, but I suggest that one can only do this successfully after a firm, honestly based relationship has been established and students realize what is happening. In other words, although it may sound paradoxical, one may con students only when they know they are being conned. Also, let me emphasize, this is a "special effects" technique which must be used discreetly.

Involvement with Subject Matter. Given an honest person with a strong interest in teaching, the really important prerequisite for success seems to be that he have something to teach. This apparent statement of the obvious points directly, I believe, at the source of most of the weak teaching in universities today. In my opinion many professors, although sincerely involved in education in general, are not intimately enough involved in any particular subject to really have something to teach. As a result really exciting teaching becomes impossible.

What I am trying to say here is that the teacher is not a communications device. You don't simply supply him information and have him digest it and deliver it up in palatable form. If this were so the university faculty would be largely irrelevant and the library and a few visual-aid centres would be the important elements on a campus. Although a few might argue that this is a correct picture, I think most people who have experienced higher education would agree that the quality of the faculty is central to the success of a university. I would argue that this is because it is the faculty which must provide the main creative element in the institution. I would then further suggest that creativity in teaching begins with a teacher who is creatively involved with the subject matter he teaches and only by being so involved does he have anything to teach.

As a scientist I can restate this in more concrete terms: good teachers of science are usually active in scientific research! I realize that this statement is by no means universally accepted and certainly the converse is a widely extant myth: i.e., that research scientists are poor lecturers and are usually not interested in teaching. The largely phoney controversy about "publish or perish versus good teaching" grows out of this misconception. My experience in several universities, large and small, both as student and professor, simply does not support a conflict between teaching and research. Almost all of the good teachers I have experienced were active or interested in research while as far as I can recall all of the bad ones made little or no original contribution in their fields. Admittedly there are a few exceptional individuals who teach well and are not active as scientists but they are so rare as to be exceptions which prove the rule. The main point is that creative teachers must be involved in the creation of new knowledge as well as in its dissemination.

If one accepts the proposition that teaching involves creativity then this situation does not seem exceptional. In fact it would seem most surprising if a nonscientist could simply read about a subject in books, assemble a body of second or third-hand knowledge and then present a personal, exciting, and critical synthesis. Rather, it seems obvious that only an active scientist can make such a synthesis. In his own narrow field, of course, he speaks with immediate involvement, authority, and originality. Beyond this, however, in areas outside his immediate research interests he is able to approach the work of others as an original contributor in his own right. He can readily appreciate the difficulties, limitations, and significance of hard-won knowledge and separate fact from fiction, data from speculation. Apart from established knowledge he can introduce students to areas of ignorance, i.e., to current challenges in the field. Since he is entitled to demand the same standard of performance from others that he asks of himself his critical appraisals carry authority. Furthermore, since the researcher necessarily reads widely in original literature and attends major scientific meetings, he should be well informed on current knowledge in his field. I grant that it is possible for the nonresearcher to keep up with recent advances but in my experience this is rarely done unless people are actively doing science. Finally, the active scientist is a member of the international scientific community in his field and knows either personally or indirectly many of the experimenters who contribute to the body of knowledge he teaches. He is therefore in a position to describe the immediate, human side of scientific progress, an activity too often presented as a sterile mechanical process.

These factors taken together explain, I think, why it is the active researcher who is in a position to develop a genuinely original and personal synthesis of a subject. His courses then become unique intellectual events and students may sense that they are experiencing not just a commentary on the field by an observer but the field itself as interpreted by one engaged in making it. There is, in my estimation, no substitute for this situation in university teaching.

When I state these ideas verbally, I inevitably receive a rejoinder at this stage to the effect that this may be true for graduate and advanced undergraduate teaching but does not apply to the introductory level where a "grand synthesis" is required. While I am willing to concede there is something in this argument my experience still dictates that it is largely myth. Most of the really good first-year teachers I have known were actively concerned with research. I think the reasons for this are still those raised in the previous paragraphs. Basically, only those active in science have the right combination of personal experience and perspective, up-to-date knowledge, and critical ability to give the unique and stimulating overview of the field required in introductory courses.

There is one important corollary to the concept of researcher as teacher. Clearly, the values of having an involved scientist teaching are lost if he is asked to present a great deal of specialized subject matter with which he is not involved. Avoidance of this situation requires relatively low teaching loads and, often, restricted curricula. As a rule of thumb I would suggest that most competent scientists have no more than a total of two good specialized courses in them. If they teach these at alternate times and contribute to a general elementary course they are probably giving optimum performance. If much more is asked, or allowed, most will deteriorate both as researchers and teachers. This situation requires, then, that a department with limited staff carefully curtail the scope of its course offerings. I would argue strenuously that this is a good thing; better to present a limited group of excellent courses than offer a complete catalogue of mediocre ones. If a department cannot accept this approach I suggest that it not bother to attract people involved in research but rather just hire good technical lecturers or buy a bank of television tapes.

Finally, at this point some readers may question my discussion on the basis that it perhaps applies to science but lacks relevance for teaching in fields where research is impossible. One may ask, in fact, how I could explain Mr. Hammond, the exceptional high school teacher, who lacked both opportunity and facilities for research. I reply emphatically that any university or advanced upper school teacher active in a subject area where formal academic research is impossible must develop an equivalent substitute involvement in his subject. Although Mr. Hammond did not make original scientific contributions he was an excellent amateur naturalist and was able to take students far beyond the prescribed book content of the course with his first-hand knowledge of field biology. This amateur involvement in his subject was sufficient at the senior high school level. I suspect that, unfortunately, a great deal of weak high school teaching stems from the failure of overtaxed teachers to develop any such form of personal involvement in their subjects outside the classroom. As one goes to lower levels of teaching subject matter becomes less important and the need for such involvement gives way to other factors. At the university level, however, where subject matter is of central importance in all fields, I believe teachers must have serious personal involvement in their field beyond that simply essential for teaching.

Sensitivity. Even with the best of motivation and strong subject involvement on the teacher's part the operation may founder. In such a case the element quite possible lacking is sensitivity on the part of the teacher. If, as I have suggested, successful teaching depends on a complex, indefinable interaction between teacher and students the good teacher must be intuitively aware of the subtle needs, feelings, and reactions of the students. This awareness must be operative both in the planning and execution of the course and must lead to constant re-evaluation.

I must emphasize that what I am speaking of here is *subtle*. It is not sufficient just to ask students what they want or how they feel; often they don't really know or cannot articulate their true feelings. Yet they have real needs and feelings which the teacher must try to appreciate. Somehow the teacher must look behind the overt comments and actions of students and try to understand the reasons underlying them. He must discover the minority of more sensitive students, develop rapport with them and through them gauge reactions of the less responsive mass. Basically, I suppose, he must learn to think like a student himself. At the same time the teacher must not unduly compromise his own ideals and attitudes. He must in some way harmonize student needs and responses with standards that as scholar and teacher he feels are essential to maintain.

One might suggest that what I have called sensitivity may be largely replaced by experience. I think not. Teaching situations are not static but rather vary with level of teaching and with different groups of students in the same course. The subject matter of a given course also changes with advances in knowledge and the teacher himself evolves in attitudes and outlook. Experience tends to be in effect conservative, to influence one to think he has solved problems and to apply previous solutions to new situations. Experience thus tends to deaden sensitivity, a situation which must be actively resisted by the teacher. I very much discount the value of experience in teaching; certainly I feel I was at least as good a teacher when I began as I am now.

I am unable to rationalize further the characteristics of sensitivity; it is without doubt the most elusive term in the teaching equation. It is also possibly the basis of the aphorism "teachers are born not made."

Teaching Methods

Most discussions of university teaching centre around methods. Certainly this is the component of teaching which students are best able to appreciate and the area most amenable to rational analysis. However, as I have intimated, I feel that methods are of secondary importance in the teaching process. This is not to say that one can ignore methodology but I believe that given a teacher who possesses the general characteristics outlined in the previous section almost any method will get good results. Furthermore, the sensitive teacher will continually adjust the methods to suit his and the students' needs. Methods will thus vary with teacher, students, and subject. I have personally experienced most of the main teaching methods and they all work reasonably well in the hands of good teachers. On the other hand, none is perfect or sufficient in itself and one must experiment, compromise, and adjust to varying needs in selecting different approaches.

Choice of particular teaching methods depends primarily on what they will achieve. In structuring, or unstructuring, a course one must first look at the aims of the course and then meld together the approaches which it is hoped will achieve these aims. My own teaching aims may be briefly summarized thus: to impart knowledge in an understandable fashion, to arouse interest in this knowledge, to stimulate curiosity about associated areas of knowledge, and to generate independent, critical thought on the part of students. To approach these aims I have used a variety of major methods: the professorial lecture, student lectures, long and short student seminars, discussion sessions, the set-piece laboratory exercise, and the open-ended laboratory. I have mixed feelings about all of these approaches and no set formula for how or when they should be applied.

The professorial lecture is presently the mainstay of university teaching and I believe that despite criticism it will continue so. In my experience the lecture is unquestionably the best single method of imparting information and arousing interest. The written word, which is often held as a substitute, lacks the flexibility necessary for really clear exposition and fails to generate excitement and emotion the way a good lecture can. Certainly I have had the best responses from students through lecturing and I continue to rely heavily on it. This may be in part because I believe that in undergraduate science teaching there is a great body of established knowledge and theory to which students must be exposed before they can react in a meaningful independent way. I thus place prime emphasis in undergraduate teaching on communication of information, which is best done through lecturing. In addition, since I always strive to make my own synthesis of a subject in lectures it is primarily through this approach that I am able to develop an original, personal view of the subject.

Professorial lecturing is not without problems as a teaching method, however. Its prime weakness lies in the fact that the students remain essentially passive. Even if they enjoy the lectures and are aroused they still largely react to the teacher and subject rather than actively contributing. A steady diet of such passivity is, I am sure, destructive to students.

To counteract this situation, over the years I have used a variety of classroom methods which centre on direct student participation. With large second-year classes I instituted short seminars based on original papers, selected by the students from research journals. The aim was to introduce young students directly to real data and experimentation and to induce them to make critical appraisal of results and theory before their peers. Although there were some disastrous individual efforts these were in a minority and most feedback indicates that students considered these short seminars a valuable experience. I expanded this approach with smaller, fourth-year Honours classes where students presented major seminars on special aspects of the subject complementary to my lectures. These were in the main very successful and well received by students.

Despite the reasonable success of these seminar approaches I still felt that student participation was too limited. I obtained much more student involvement in a very small graduate class where the students and I lectured and led discussions alternately on an equal footing. As a result, last year in a fourth-year class composed of thirty students I turned the entire lecturing of the second half of the course over to the students. I functioned in the role of "resource man" and critic and gave occasional summary lectures in an attempt to develop an overall synthesis of the field. Unfortunately, I am afraid I must report that this experiment was not a success. The level of information in the course dropped seriously, consistent overall viewpoints failed to appear, and student excitement dwindled. Reactions from perceptive students were generally negative although some felt the basic approach, with modification, might have merit. The only truly positive note was that performance on the final exam, an essay type, was noticeably better than I had previously experienced. I cannot analyse this situation further here but I raise it to point out the problems involved in combining different methods so as to achieve a balance of the aims involved in teaching.

Apart from the purely discursive approaches of lectures, seminars, discussions, and so forth, science teachers have available another approach to student involvement, the laboratory. The laboratory component of a course primarily serves two purposes, it exposes the student first-hand to material discussed in lectures and it teaches experimental techniques. Unfortunately, with large classes the types of exercises possible in laboratories often become trivial or routine and serve to alienate students. I believe it is a central responsibility of university scientists to prevent this destructive situation. They must plan challenging, modern laboratory exercises and strive to obtain the facilities and assistance necessary to mount them. The laboratory is potentially an invaluable opportunity for a student to experience his subjects directly and to learn by doing and it should be fully exploited. I admit that this is easier said than done.

Finally, I should comment on various ancillary techniques in teaching which can be termed audio-visual aids. There is, currently, considerable pressure to use televised lectures, taped laboratory exercises, film loops, programmed texts, and other communications devices. The proponents of these techniques often resemble religious missionaries who are quick to attack those who resist their blandishments as reactionary or even immoral. From my limited experience I am convinced that most audio-visual devices are really not compatible with my teaching style and I hope the reasons for this are obvious from the preceding discussion. While occasional films or lantern slides might dramatically reinforce lecture and laboratory material I feel that extensive use of technical aids merely erects a "hardware" barrier between teacher and students. Achievement of teacher-student rapport is a tricky enough job without this.

Student Response

Taken in its broadest sense student response is the sole purpose of teaching. The actual creative result of teaching is the change it brings about in the student. If the student's intellectual development is enhanced significantly during a course he becomes a different person and the teacher has aided in the creation of something new. Student response thus becomes a central element in planning, executing, and evaluating a teaching operation.

It would take another essay to analyse the complex facets of student response and I raise it here only because of its basic importance. Student reactions are as variable as students themselves. Just as there are good and bad teachers for many reasons, there is a similar variety of good and bad students. Furthermore, while the teacher must be continually introspective about his own role in teaching, I believe that students also must analyse their position in teaching and education. Some students are careful and sensitive in their analysis of courses but there are far too many superficial blanket assessments offered by others. Many of these assertions remind me of simplistic analyses by teachers of what is important in teaching. I suggest that we should ask of students that they review their attitudes, motives, and approaches in learning so that we might better integrate their role with that of the teacher. Perhaps a book complementary to this one, written by selected students, would be a valuable beginning to this process.

Most people, I think, believe secretly or otherwise that they could teach successfully if given the opportunity. Certainly most people hold strong opinions about teaching. In recent years as universities have, appropriately I believe, received the main thrust of overt social unrest, a deluge of criticisms, analyses, and suggestions about teaching has poured in from all sides. Most of this comment is ill-informed and poorly thought out. If this essay has any single message it is that teaching is a complex and subtle endeavour and there is no simple or single route to success. As a result, sincere professional teachers must resist or at least discount much of the superficial clamor from outsiders. However, the clamor is a symptom; there is much wrong with university teaching and teachers must criticize and reexamine their own functions and strive for improvement. I hope that this short essay, and this book, will aid the process.

GEORGE SETTERFIELD

George Setterfield was born and started school in Halifax but his early education took place mainly in British Columbia. He was an undergraduate at the University of British Columbia where he took first-class honours in biology (genetics). From there he went to the University of

Wisconsin for a Ph.D. in botany (cell biology) with a minor in biochemistry. Then back to U.B.C. for two years as an instructor in the Department of Biology. There followed six years at the laboratories of the National Research Council of Canada, Biophysics Section.

Dr. Setterfield was appointed to the Department of Biology of Carleton University in 1962. He was chairman of the department from 1963 to 1968, and then went on leave for a year as an NRC Senior Research Fellow in the Department of Biology of Laval University. He is a member of the Advisory Committee for Academic Planning of the Ontario Council on Graduate Studies and of the Plant Science Grant Selection Committee of the National Research Council.

Dr. Setterfield's general field of research is cell and molecular biology with particular emphasis on the relation of cell structure to the mechanisms of cell growth and differentiation. In the past he has concentrated largely on plant cells but he is currently investigating animal systems as well. His publications in periodicals, usually in collaboration with colleagues, number more than thirty. With F. Wightman he edited Biochemistry and Physiology of Plant Growth Substances *(Runge Press, Ottawa, 1968).*

During the period under review he taught undergraduate courses in introductory general biology, genetics and cytology, and advanced cell and molecular biology for graduate students.

The image of Professor Setterfield which emerges from the comments of his former students is of an unusually intelligent, competent, well-organized and hard-working man with a keen interest in his subject, who inspired awe in his students. Some said he was dominant, demanding, impatient; others (and sometimes the same ones) that he was sensitive to students' capabilities, was willing to clarify points of difficulty and to take time outside class to help students.

He organized his lectures well, prepared them thoroughly and delivered them in a way which was forceful and called for special comment on his speaking voice and diction. His laboratory exercises were interesting and relevant, he used visual aids well and made frequent reference to recent research findings. One graduate reported that "he lectured on material which in one case was only one week old." "He had each student give a seminar on a current paper or series of papers which gave students an insight into problems involved in presenting seminars." His ability to control a large class, even to the point of making possible meaningful discussion, was noted by several graduates.

To See a Chemist Thinking

Zdenek Valenta

Just what should a university professor do to perform his teaching duties most effectively? How can he best transmit available knowledge to his students and, at the same time, get them to participate in at least a part of the discipline's thinking process and spirit of discovery? I honestly do not have the slightest idea. Having naively tried to answer these questions, I can only come up with the conclusion that the answers cannot be usefully generalized or at least that I am incapable of generalizing them. And I am very pleased about that. For, were there an ideal way, the *only way* to do it well, there would be just no hope for widespread first-class teaching at the university. Individual specimens of *Homo sapiens* are just too different for that kind of programming. And even if it were possible, using some idealized professors, it would then be hard to protect the students from extensive boredom caused by uniformity. And whatever else happens to them during the learning process, the students must not be bored. They might occasionally get frustrated because the professor is "talking over their heads" or "preaching down to them," they might have misgivings that he is too theoretical or not theoretical enough and they might get upset when they disagree with his ideas, deductions, or interpretations, but they should not get bored. Come to think of it, perhaps that is one reasonable generalization.

This then leaves me with a simpler question. What should *I* do to teach effectively? Well, I know of only one way in which I personally can attempt to reach this desirable goal. My only chance is to enjoy my own lectures and I believe that the only way I can achieve that is not to know precisely and ahead of time what will happen in any one of them. Thus, I can possess at least a part of the anticipation which the students hopefully have before and during the lecture. In addition, there is always the hope that by fresh thinking about the particular topic during the lecture I can induce the students to do the same. A discovery of an interesting explanation or application during the lecture period (even if it has been already encountered in the course literature) can be an exciting experience for everybody.

One might well ask whether this is not a rather elaborate way to talk oneself out of lecture preparation. But the point is, there are many textbooks available in the discipline which I teach, organic chemistry, both on the introductory and advanced levels. Should one find that none of these textbooks is even partly suitable, then of course one would have to make the necessary and very extensive effort to create one's own full course or textbook. Since several of the available textbooks are in fact very modern and of first-class quality, it makes more sense, at least to me, to take advantage of them. The question then arises: What are the lectures for?

To me, in my discipline, the answer is quite simple. They provide the opportunity for the students to participate, personally and fully, in the thinking process of the discipline. There are of course other important purposes. Teaching of new knowledge accumulated since the textbook and reference books have been written, discussion of topics of particular new relevance, and extensive elaboration on subjects not sufficiently covered in the textbook are some examples. But clearly, all of these could be served—possibly equally well—by simply guiding the students to the proper reference material without a recourse to lectures. Even beyond that, it can be argued that a student—particularly an exceptionally imaginative one—can use the available literature as the sole source for the development of curiosity and creativity. This is no doubt true, but in science this transmission method is by no means perfect.

First of all, there is the problem of selectivity. The available literature in my field and in related fields is now truly vast. It contains a staggering number of accomplished experiments, important results, and subsequent conclusions. These results and conclusions must be made known to the new generation, but it should not happen in a "telephone book" fashion. After such an initiation, it would just not be reasonable to expect that many—or any—of the students would get excited by the prospect of adding, during their lifetime, a few more pages of new words and numbers to the body of knowledge. It must therefore surely be one of the purposes of the lectures—and of the textbooks—to present a logical development of thought within the discipline and a summary of the available knowledge which is as simple as possible. By that I do not mean that "complicated" facts and problems should be omitted. But it seems to me that—at least in my discipline—most of the truly important generalizations, conclusions, and ideas are really quite simple and that most of the complications one introduces into them are artificial. As a consequence, as far as the known body of facts is concerned, I make an attempt to show to the students that they can acquire a workable understanding and knowledge of the discipline during the course and do not try to impress upon them just how complicated and perverse is the behaviour of organic molecules and just how long it will take them to understand what is going on.

There is another problem involved in learning only from scientific literature. The articles, reviews, and books contain the accumulated body of *answers*, small ones, partial ones, and big ones. The *questions* are, however, often hard to find, particularly for the novice. For one thing, a scientist who would attempt to publish an extensive treatise containing mainly topical questions is likely to get a polite letter from the editor pointing out the increasing publishing cost of the particular journal and suggesting that the article might be accepted after the author has provided some of the answers. Furthermore, this situation is not likely to arise too often, because when a scientist thinks up a truly good question, he is likely to keep it and attempt to answer it. Now, it is quite obvious that the formulation of the right question at the right time is often as important, or even more important, for the advancement of science than is the provision of the answer. In many instances, there is in fact no chance to get a useful answer if the right question is not asked. To use an example, after young van't Hoff—as a student—asked himself towards the end of the 19th century whether the optical activity of some organic compounds and related properties could not be explained by a certain fixed geometry of the molecules, the postulate of the tetrahedral nature of the carbon atom in organic compounds logically followed. Both the question and the answer are staggeringly simple and now, *post facto*, explicable to a ten-year-old child. It is probably not relevant to this discussion that van't Hoff had a hard time to get his solution accepted for publication and that—after this was finally accomplished—he was advised, to put it mildly, to get back into the laboratory to do some useful experimental work instead of indulging in useless theorizing. Surely, we are much more tolerant of new ideas nowadays. Aren't we?

It seems to me, then, that one of the truly important functions of lectures at the university level is to show students that there are many important questions left, to provide an atmosphere for formulating them, and to provide some guidance for spotting them. Certainly, the acquisition of quite a bit of knowledge should come first, but I do not see how one can wait until they get degrees before one takes the students right into the unsolved regions. They can certainly take it and they seem to enjoy it. I therefore do not hesitate—starting with the first lecture of the introductory course—to extrapolate the first simple principles to complicated systems and to their possible application in organic chemistry and in other fields, theoretical and practical. The textbooks, reference books, and other reading material provide a well-ordered, carefully thought-out compilation of knowledge; I feel that I can add to them during lectures the somewhat unsettling, but at the same time invigorating, influence of unsolved problems and imperfectly understood phenomena.

Without a doubt, however, I believe that my most important task as a teacher is to think and solve problems—prepared and unprepared—right in front of the class. I do not claim that this is the best way, or even a reasonable way, but it happens to be the only way in which I feel that I am accomplishing anything. Obviously, under such circumstances the lectures may be far from polished; in fact, they can become quite disorganized. But it is not my purpose to show the students how a perfect lecture can be achieved when one works hard enough at it. All I want to show them is how the only live organic chemist available to them for that particular year does his thinking in his discipline. It is this, the "live exhibit," which it is impossible for the students to obtain from printed sources. Obviously, there are many masters of the discipline, past and present, who are superior to the lecturer in intellect and accomplishment and, one hopes, there are many students who will surpass their teacher in these respects. But in the meantime, the students need to see, at leisure and in detail, how questions can be formulated. They need to realize that the first "elegant" answer obtained while solving a problem is not necessarily the only one, or the right one. They need to have it demonstrated to them that the human mind is capable of unbelievable "mental blocks," of faulty thinking and of wishful thinking. In short, they need to see a real person—no matter how imperfect—involved in the scientific thinking process. If the students can at the same time actively participate in this process, then a rather important step in their education has been taken. There is then a chance that they will realize how science actually works: by the formulation of a problem, by the careful and reliable execution of experiments, by subsequent deductions which usually predict the outcome of further required experiments and, finally, if nothing goes wrong, by the formulation of conclusions. They might also become aware of the extreme care which is required in performing experiments and in interpreting them and of the imagination necessary for major scientific advances. All of this is, of course, contained in the scientific literature, but seldom in that order, with that emphasis. By the time a scientific article is written, and particularly after a whole field is reviewed, all is often quite polished, clear, logical. The trouble is, that is not the way the problems look when one is in the middle of them. The established principles, the discovered laws, the accomplished tasks are often beautiful in their simplicity; but the way to them is purely human—uncertain, hesitant, complicated.

These, then, are the elements which I consider important in giving my lectures. All the remaining problems are just technicalities. One interesting question in this category is the following: Since meaningful and important scientific problems often require months or years to solve, can one really hope to present them honestly and realistically during a lecture or during an academic year? It is obviously difficult on the undergraduate level. But there are ways by which one can come close to reality. A very interested graduate student was recently put in charge of the elementary organic laboratory in our department and he introduced a program during which the students extracted an organic natural product from a plant, performed a complete structure elucidation using all modern techniques and, finally, constructed this compound by total synthesis using store-room chemicals as starting materials. This method which had previously been described in chemical education literature and is now, no doubt, used in many universities, represents a very successful attempt to show the students how science actually works. It has, of course, a small flaw. The results are known beforehand, the element of uncertainty is not fully present. I occasionally use one or more of the unfinished research problems which are currently being studied by graduate students under my supervision. Most of these problems are perfectly suitable for this undergraduate teaching purpose. At the beginning of the year, I describe the problem, the purpose and the state which has been reached. Together with the class, the problem is then completely analysed, whatever can be explained is explained, and predictions are made. Quite regularly, many of these prove to be wrong as the year progresses so that new explanations and predictions have to be made. No acting or pretense is required in this process; it is almost the real thing.

A related question concerns final examinations. What, if any, is the correlation between solving relatively easy problems in three hours and difficult problems (the *real* problems) in several months or years? Well, there is probably little correlation, but if one does not take too ambitious an attitude towards examinations, this should not matter. I feel that an undergraduate examination is a very imperfect tool for the assessment of a student's promise as an imaginative and productive scientist, but it is a quite adequate method to test approximately his present state of knowledge. And let us be realistic: it continues to be a good incentive for the student's continued effort. I should perhaps add that the undergraduate science students, at least in our department, have shown no preference for a system without testing and examinations.

Finally, there is the question of the atmosphere in the classroom. As a logical consequence of the concept of the lecture which I happen to prefer, the atmosphere is and must be completely informal. First of all, the students may or may not attend individual lectures depending on their assessment of the lecture contribution to their study of the subject. Secondly, they are expected to participate—and do participate—during the lecture by asking questions, presenting problems, and making comments. This does not, in fact, convert the lecture into a seminar. But it often converts the planned lecture into an entirely different one. If in the process a topic is reached in which there are serious gaps even in the lecturer's knowledge, a future lecture can be planned based on a prerequisite search of the available literature. I find that the number of students in the class makes less of a difference than one might expect. There is possibly a slight hesitancy on the part of some students to make a comment when the student number reaches forty or fifty, but I do not think that I am fooling myself completely in believing that even a group of hundred or more students can participate quite effectively in an open lecture. Certainly, one sometimes gets too many questions and comments, but then again there is a better chance of getting some really good ones.

In conclusion, it does not seem particularly wise to try to devise a blueprint for effective science teaching at the university. Having just attempted to analyse myself, I am not even certain that it is possible or useful to formulate in detail one's own chances and possibilities. Perhaps one can hope, however, that the students will always be eager to learn from teachers who are truly interested to teach.

ZDENEK VALENTA

Zdenek Valenta is one of the four natives of Czechoslovakia contributing essays to this collection. He qualified as a chemical engineer (Dipl. Ing. Chem.) at the Eidgenössische Technische Hochschule in Zürich, Switzerland, and later as M.Sc. and Ph.D. in chemistry at the University of New Brunswick.

Except for the year 1956–57, when he was a research associate at Harvard University, Dr. Valenta has been at the University of New Brunswick from the time of his arrival from Europe in 1950. He became assistant professor in 1957, associate professor a year later, and professor in 1963. He served as departmental chairman 1963–72. In 1967 he was winner of the Merck, Sharp and Dohme Award for research in organic chemistry, which is his field of study, and in 1972 he was elected a fellow of the Royal Society of Canada.

Between 1952 and 1973 he was author, or joint author with his former teacher and present colleague, Professor K. Wiesner, of more than 60 articles in chemical journals.

"Dr. Valenta possessed great knowledge of his subject, but more important was his enthusiasm for the subject and his ability to communicate this to his students. His lectures were well organized, but he could always take time to clarify any point, or, should the occasion require, he could lecture equally well on questions presented by the students during the class period." This comment is representative of many made by Professor Valenta's former students.

They found him a dynamic person and an interesting talker. ("His accent helped a bit.") When a discovery was made in his field he was eager to tell others, especially his students, about it.

In class, his presentations were clear and usually simple. The principle was the thing. Complex explanations were repeated and illustrations were given. His style was informal, relaxed, and he spoke without notes —conversing with the group, of which he was a part.

He treated students as persons, with respect. He was kind, approachable, fair, and had a sense of humour. He was interested in and took an active part in campus activities. "He was always so keen, so interested and so happy," reported one graduate. "He was not doing a job but living a life."

Teaching Teachers

Earl W. Buxton

After I emerged from the Camrose Normal School in 1929, I wrote sixty-seven applications for a position, and interviewed school boards all over Northern Alberta, before I found a sanctuary from the rigours of the Depression in a rural school north of Edmonton. It had one room, twenty-six double desks, about thirty books in the library, forty-eight students in all grades from one to eight, and a salary of $800 per year, providing I acted as janitor.

During my first week in Cloverdale School, I made the disconcerting discovery that if one has eight grades, then each grade is going to get only one-eighth of his teaching time. That is, I had about 35 minutes per day to teach each grade all the subjects outlined in a rigid curriculum guide: reading, writing, arithmetic, spelling, literature, history, geography, art, science, and health. For six weeks I struggled with a task that seemed to be about as frustrating and unproductive as the labour of Sisyphus. Then I found an answer to my problem: instead of trying to teach everybody everything, I encouraged them to teach themselves and each other. In one cloakroom, a grade 2 girl used flashcards to help grade 1 with word recognition. In the other cloakroom, a grade 3 pupil listened to grade 2 read. A grade 4 pupil dictated spelling to grade 3 and a grade 5 to grade 4, and so on. At the back of the room, the grade 6 students created a coloured map of North America on the blackboard and took turns testing each other on the names of rivers, lakes, gulfs, bays, peninsulas, cities, and mountains, as well as the locations of natural resources and industries. I discovered that many of my pupils were very competent artists; and the blackboards bloomed with maps, diagrams, drawings, and time charts in coloured chalk. In short, my function seemed to be acting as manager for an educational enterprise.

I need not dwell at length on the conclusions that resulted from my initiation to teaching in Cloverdale School. I suppose the most important ones were that learning is most effective when the teacher reveals his faith in his students' interest and ability; that pupils like to share their learning with others; that many students have creative talents that will emerge when the environment is favorable; and that the most valuable "teaching aides" that any teacher can have in the classroom are the students themselves. In recent years, studies have revealed the implications of the "self-fulfilling prophecy"—the principle that if a teacher is led to believe that some of his students are more intelligent than others, then his attitude toward students in the "selected" group "can lead to their improved intellectual performance."[1]

These are some of the principles I have attempted to apply—not always as successfully as I may have hoped—to my work in elementary and secondary schools and in the University of Alberta where I teach Curriculum and Instruction courses at the undergraduate and graduate levels to prospective teachers of English.

In each class I want to know my students and I attempt to establish the kind of personal relationship that will engender a cooperative classroom climate—an attitude that we are working together to develop the knowledge and skills that will lead to effective teaching.

To begin this process of getting acquainted, I memorize a seating plan during the first week of lectures so that in subsequent classes I can call each individual by name. As the term progresses, students' oral and written reports and their contributions to class and small group discussions enable me to gain information about each individual's background, his ability, his interests, his control of language, and his commitment to learning and to teaching. Occasionally individuals and small groups come to my office to discuss their reading, their reaction to educational issues, their projects, or their response to the comments I have made in evaluating their written assignments.

Abraham Maslow, William Glasser, and others point out that most students are concerned about "the impersonality" of the large high schools and universities. Discussing his experience as chairman of a student panel, Glasser states:

> . . . complaining that in junior or senior high they didn't get to know the teachers very well, the students said that they therefore had trouble figuring out what was expected of them. . . . Again and again they asked, "Is there some way we can get to know our teachers better and some way our teachers can get to know us better?"[2]

Many critics of modern education decry the rigidity of high school and university programs and the lack of what Carl Rogers has called "freedom to learn."[3] The most radical of these critics suggest that the student be given freedom to set his own curriculum, follow his own interests, and in general "do his own thing." My experience suggests that though high school and university students appreciate opportunities to make their own choices, they are more satisfied with their achievement when this freedom is complemented by some knowledge of the structure of the program, the areas that might be explored, and the instructors' objectives and expectations. I therefore begin each semester by using handouts which indicate the topics we may find worth discussing, the assignments, and the bases we might use for evaluating each individual's progress. To provide a degree of flexibility, I supplement this syllabus with a comprehensive bibliography of books and articles on research in English, curriculum, literary criticism, linguistics, and methods that may be used in the teaching of reading, composition, language, and literature. During a class discussion of these materials, I suggest that each individual read books and investigate problems which he finds interesting and which he believes may be most valuable to him. Because the curriculum and instruction course and practice teaching are taken in the same semesters, students usually find that their reading lists can help them to find answers to problems which they encounter in the schools.

In addition to assigning research papers, I encourage students to record suggestions they may find useful in the classroom, and to present to the class ideas gathered from books and articles, and from their teaching experience, when these ideas are relevant to a topic we are discussing. For example, in a recent session on the writing of poetry in the junior high school, one student had gathered information on the haiku from *Let Them Write Poetry*;[4] a second student discussed her experience in working with "diamond poetry;" a third was interested in parodies; and a fourth brought in a handout of "Impressions" created by members of her grade eight class after their reading and discussion of several short poems, including Carl Sandburg's "Fog," Carlos Williams's "Red Wheelbarrow," Tennyson's "The Eagle," and Humbert Wolfe's "The Gray Squirrel."

During the five weeks before my students begin practice teaching, I emphasize certain approaches which I think may be of value in their classrooms. One of these approaches, which I think vital to the study of literature, is effective oral reading. I begin by reading or reciting a variety of selections ranging from "The Enchanted Shirt," "The Ballad of William Sycamore," and "The Deacon's Masterpiece" to "Prufrock," "August Bank Holiday," Keats's "Ode to a Nightingale," and Ferlinghetti's "Constantly risking absurdity." I attempt to vary tone, pitch, stress, and tempo to interpret the ideas and feeling which I think each writer has endeavored to express. I have found that if an instructor attempts to use his voice to interpret literature, his students may overcome their reticence and try to follow his example; therefore, I encourage my students to acquire a degree of competence which may help them to make literature an exciting experience for their pupils.

So we practise reading selections in class—sometimes in parts, using a deep voice for the walrus, a lighter voice for the carpenter, and a shrill voice for the oysters. We assume the role of Shylock considering Bassanio's request for the loan of three thousand ducats, or Jacques pointing out that "All the world's a stage," or the witches concocting their brew, or the tribunes during their encounter with the commoners in the opening scene of *Julius Caesar.* We try to produce the cacophony of sounds in Sandburg's "Chicago," and to express the tranquility of London as Wordsworth saw it from Westminster Bridge. We read excerpts from "Buck Hanshaw's Funeral" and "Haircut" to illustrate varieties of English usage; from Leacock's "Good and Bad Language" and Ross's *The Education of Hyman Kaplan* for fun; from poetry and novels and short stories to support our interpretations and opinions.

During these practice periods we discover that when a student is preparing to read a selection to his peers, he must first interpret the selection to himself. He must make his own decisions about meanings, purpose, and tone. He must sense the changing moods of Shylock, the bombast of Falstaff, the vigour of Shelley's west wind, or the "drowsy numbness" of Keats as he listened to the nightingale. When oral reading is followed by class discussion, pupils can develop some appreciation of the care with which the first-rate writer shapes linguistic and rhetorical resources into a pattern that may create the effect he hopes to communicate to his readers.

As I have indicated, a considerable proportion of class time is devoted to class and small-group dialogue. Some of our discussions focus upon educational issues, objectives in the teaching of English, research studies, and materials and methods described in books, articles, and curriculum guides. During these sessions, I encourage students to support their statements or opinions by referring to their reading or to their experiences in the classroom. Sometimes our discussion involves the exploration of literary selections which may be appropriate for study in the junior or senior high school. We may let our conversation flow from topic to topic, sharing ideas and arguing about the validity of different interpretations. An extended example follows.

After the students had read several short stories that appear in recent anthologies, we began a class discussion by trying to determine why Shirley Jackson's "The Lottery" elicits a powerful emotional response from most readers. Some students suggested that the impact of this selection resulted from the sharp contrast between the relaxed behaviour of the villagers in the first part of the story, and their brutality, so unexpected and so horrifying, in the concluding paragraphs. A few members of the class objected to this analysis, pointing out words and phrases that dramatize the villagers' tension and create suspense: "The men began to gather, *surveying their children.* . . . They stood *away from the pile of stones in the corner*, and their jokes were quiet, and *they smiled rather than laughed.* . . ."

Some students called attention to the irony that runs like a thread through the fabric of the story. For example, Mrs. Hutchinson, who joined her friends with the laughing comment that she "almost forgot what day it was," died under their volley of stones two hours later. Other students observed that though the sacrificial ritual seems so fantastic when placed in a contemporary setting, society still has its lotteries which select victims for a variety of destructive treatments. When asked for examples, they mentioned the "numbers game" used to select young Americans for military service, as well as the lotteries in which such "scapegoats" as Negroes, Canadian Indians, and children of "disadvantaged" families are selected at birth. We concluded that Jackson is implying that all kinds of traditional beliefs, primitive practices, and archetypal rituals may persist long after the situations that initiated them have been forgotten.

This interpretation led us to consider the various kinds of fetters—tradition, superstitution, and prejudice—that restrict human freedom. We discussed the dilemma confronting the individual who has to decide whether to respond to a critical situation in the light of his own convictions or to submit as did the villagers to the pressure imposed by the rules, conventions, expectations, or traditional practices of the society in which he lives. We then turned to other selections in the high school program and discussed the ways the problem was resolved by the young police officer in "Shooting an Elephant," Dr. Stockmann in *An Enemy of the People*, Huckleberry Finn, Thoreau in "Civil Disobedience," and the members of the lynching party in *The Ox-Bow Incident*.

After this introductory session, the class divided into groups of three, and each group prepared to lead a discussion of one of the other selections that the class had read. The list included James Joyce's "Counterparts," Morley Callaghan's "Two Fishermen," Sinclair Ross's "The Lamp at Noon," Graham Greene's "The Destructors," Willa Cather's "Paul's Case," Eudora Welty's "A Visit of Charity," Nathaniel Hawthorne's "Young Goodman Brown," Wallace Stegner's "Butcher Bird," and William Faulkner's "That Evening Sun."

During these discussions I sometimes interjected comments or questions to suggest topics that might merit attention. For example, after the class had discussed the ways that Farrington had tried to satisfy his need for recognition and approval after his humiliating experiences during the afternoon, I asked why Joyce had chosen "Counterparts" for his title. Students looked up Webster's definition of the term, and some of them suggested that Farrington and his cronies fitted the definition: *a thing or person very like another*. When I wondered whether Farrington and Mr. Alleyne could be considered counterparts, a few students were doubtful. However, after examining the second part of the story, the class gradually assembled items that might be relevant. They suggested that during the evening, Farrington's boasting, his "showing off," his ogling of the plump-armed young lady from the Tivoli, his temper tantrum in the bar, and his brutality in the concluding scene all paralleled the behaviour of Mr. Alleyne during the afternoon. After I suggested that they had been talking about Alleyne and Farrington as if they were real people, we read and analysed several passages to determine how Joyce had achieved his realism.

In these discussions, we are attempting to combine the "free response" technique advocated by a number of British educators with an application of the formalistic, psychological, sociological, and archetypal approaches described by Wilbur Scott, Cleanth Brooks, Welleck and Warren, I. A. Richards, Northrop Frye, and other critics.

During one analysis of our discussion sessions, students suggested that these activities may help secondary school students to examine literature, to express their ideas, to avoid unproductive digressions, to support their judgments, to revise opinions in the light of new evidence, and to abandon the belief that all answers must be considered either right or wrong.

I suggested that some educators, psychologists, and philosophers believe that through verbal interaction an individual gains not only an understanding of others, but also insights into his own thoughts and feelings, his opinions and prejudices, his view of the world.[5]

When we turned to a discussion of teaching techniques that may help to achieve these objectives, the students decided that the following approaches may be worth testing in their own classrooms: a) asking "open-ended" questions that encourage a variety of answers which pupils can attempt to support by referring to the text; b) encouraging pupils to question each other—to interact in a dialogue that can become student-centred rather than teacher-centred; c) providing *time* for pupils to weigh and consider, to organize their ideas, and to phrase their responses. During our discussion, I mentioned some research which indicates that we teachers, like disc jockeys, seem to be afraid of periods of silence during our "program"; we are usually in a hurry to cover the course, to offer our interpretations, and to disgorge information that we consider important.[6]

To gain experience in selecting and organizing materials for study and supplementary reading, groups of three or four students in each class cooperate in developing teaching units that may be used in either the junior or the senior high school. The titles of units produced in one recent term include "Myths and Legends," "Man Versus Nature," "The Generation Gap," "Canadian Humorists," "All About War," and "Satire." The topical or thematic unit permits the inclusion of poems, stories, essays, novels, a play, and articles from periodicals. Because all members of a group can contribute, the units usually include a wide range of materials. Occasionally the students ask whether I have any suggestions. For example, a group recently visited my office to discuss a project entitled, "Our Future?". They were planning to include George Orwell's *1984*, Aldous Huxley's *Brave New World*, Nevil Shute's *On the Beach*,

B. F. Skinner's *Walden Two*, Garret De Bell's *The Environmental Handbook*, Paul Ehrlich's *The Population Bomb*, Alvin Toffler's *Future Shock*, Van Tilburg Clark's "The Portable Phonograph," and relevant articles from periodicals. They were searching for materials like Margaret Mead's "Three Votes for the Age of Anxiety" that might present a more optimistic outlook. I suggested that they might be interested in looking at Buckminster Fuller's *Operating Manual for Spaceship Earth.*

The plan was that the authors of each unit should list their materials in a handout and discuss teaching approaches and student activities in our seminars during the first week of student teaching so that other students might try out some of their suggestions in the schools.

To supplement students' reading, I use a variety of mimeographed materials. Some of these are designed to outline the program, or to initiate individual or group projects. Many handouts are used to summarize information that I might have presented in lectures on such topics as research in the teaching of grammar and usage, teachers' experiences in motivating student writing, or suggestions concerning the evaluation of students' themes. Other mimeographed handouts are used to introduce a discussion of materials and methods that might be used to encourage pupils to examine their language in terms of its history, its structure, and its variety. For example, an exploration of the origins of such words as *disaster*, *dialogue*, *trivial*, *biography*, *mansion*, and *calico* can initiate an investigation of how the English language has been created and enriched by words from the languages of the peoples who invaded England, from Britain's continental neighbors, and from distant lands reached by British ships during more than three centuries of exploration and trade.[7]

To discuss rhetorical principles including the ways that language can be used to inform, amuse, convince, persuade, or manipulate readers and listeners, we may examine essays on controversial topics, news reports, editorials, "Letters to the Editor," television and radio programs, commercials, and even such columns as "Your Horoscope," "Ann Landers," and "Dear Abby." Articles like Robert Fulford's "Who's Crazy?"[8] that analyse human idiosyncracies, can provide a basis for stimulating discussion and student writing, particularly in the junior high school.

My discussion of oral reading, classroom dialogue, group work, and mimeographed materials does not mean that I avoid lecturing. However, because a lecture on education can become rather abstract, especially for beginning teachers, I try to illuminate theory by using illustrations and suggesting practical applications drawn from my experiences or from those of other teachers in secondary school classrooms. I also endeavor to provide opportunities for student participation by asking an occasional question or by welcoming the response of a student who indicates that he has a contribution to make. Usually, in a session following a lecture I set up situations in which students can apply the principles we have discussed.

I encourage students to use the excellent resources of our media centre to illustrate their reports to the class. For example, a group interested in film study presented films based on Poe's "The Masque of the Red Death," Jackson's "The Lottery," and Earle Birney's "Espolio" in order to compare the film versions with the original selections. Another group used a series of slides developed from photographs of sod houses, threshing machines, and prairie towns to introduce their unit on "Canadian Prairie Fiction."

During the year my students do a substantial amount of writing: short pieces on a variety of topics; book reviews; two or three lesson plans for teaching a poem, short story, or novel; a group project; and documented research papers on teaching practices or issues in which they are particularly interested.

In evaluating written assignments, I view each student's paper as part of a dialogue between him and me. If our dialogue is to be authentic, I think I am justified in expecting that he will make every effort to express his ideas clearly, accurately, and honestly. He has the right to expect that I will contribute to the dialogue by making an honest response to what he has to say. Therefore, at the end of each paper I usually write a paragraph or two in which I comment on his ideas and his success in communicating them to me. Sometimes I suggest that the dialogue be continued in my office or in the classroom. I find that two of the most encouraging comments I can make are, "I'd like a copy of this for my files" or "I'd appreciate your presenting these ideas to the class during the next period."

I tell my students that these principles may apply to their teaching of writing in the schools. For example, an English teacher may be able to reduce what Lois Arnold has called "writer's cramp and eyestrain"[9] by ensuring that her pupils edit their papers carefully before handing them in. Some teachers have found that pupils can help in editing by working in small groups, reading their papers to each other, and discussing revisions.

Basic to the approaches I have described is the principle that reading, thinking, speaking, writing, and listening can be closely integrated parts of an English program. Research has indicated that practice which results in increased competence in one area will lead to increasing proficiency in others. For this reason, I believe that one of the important tasks of the English teacher is to create a classroom climate and a variety of challenging situations in which these activities can occur.

I realize that the methods I use may not be appropriate for all courses, particularly at the university level. When I taught first-year courses in literature with the Department of English, I believe that I lectured more than I do in teacher education. My objective in Curriculum and Instruction is to illustrate a variety of methods and to discuss materials ranging from books that may engage the interest of "reluctant" readers to selections that may provide an intellectual challenge to advanced classes. It may appear that in emphasizing student contributions in the form of reports, discussion, and projects, I am just as lazy as I was in Cloverdale School when I let my students do most of the work. If this conclusion appears justified, I hope that no one will communicate it to the Dean of Education in this University. He has enough problems.

EARL W. BUXTON

Born in Toronto, Earl Buxton grew up in Alberta in the prairie town of Lougheed (population 250). He attended the Camrose Normal School and, while teaching, qualified by extramural and summer courses for the B.A. and B.Ed. degrees of the University of Alberta. This took him twelve years. In another ten he had qualified for a master's degree at the University of Washington and a doctorate at Stanford University. From 1929 to 1936 he taught in rural schools, then served for five years as a high school principal, and for seven as a demonstration teacher in city secondary schools—all in Alberta. He joined the Faculty of Education of the Calgary Branch of the University of Alberta in 1948 and moved to the main University campus at Edmonton in 1955.

In his youth ("now long gone," he says) Professor Buxton held the Alberta middleweight and welterweight boxing championships. He was cartoonist for the Alberta Teachers Association Magazine *from 1945 to 1949. On three occasions he was elected to the Edmonton Public School Board and served one term as chairman. He was a member of the Alberta Department of Education Curriculum Committee on High School English from 1956 to 1966.*

His articles have appeared in publications of the National Council of Teachers of English, The Alberta Journal of Educational Research, *and* The English Teacher *(Alberta). He has compiled three anthologies of literature for use in Alberta secondary schools:* Creative Living *(Book Five),* Points of View, *and* Prose for Discussion, *all published by W. J. Gage and Company. He is the author of* Teachers' Guide to Literature *(Gage, 1956), and prepared* Guide to Modern English, *a Canadian revision of a language textbook by Richard Corbin and Porter Perrin (Scott, Foresman, 1960). He wrote the introduction to* Looking at Language *by Penner and Scargill (Gage, 1966; Scott, Foresman, 1969).*

His field during the period covered by graduates' comments was methods in the teaching of English in secondary schools.

Teacher trainees he taught said he was exuberant, friendly, humorous, genial, approachable, and genuinely interested in every one of his students. He obviously loved literature and teaching. "He often got carried away quoting a passage, tapping out a rhythm, or otherwise responding to something in a poem or story. His knowledge of English literature was amazing—he could quote from any work that any of us in the class ever mentioned."

Notes were distributed in mimeographed form so classes could be devoted to discussion. "He not only encouraged rousing discussions, he created them." From his experience Professor Buxton offered many examples and anecdotes, and he used his sketching ability to demonstrate word meanings. His tests were searching, and his assignments fair. As for the latter, he obviously read them carefully and made helpful written comments on them.

NOTES

1. Rosenthal and Jacobson, *Pygmalion in the Classroom* (Toronto: Holt, Rinehart and Winston, 1968). Other investigators have shown the importance of the roles assigned to students. For example, pupils who were placed in the role of tutors for other children used a more mature, more elaborative form of language than they used when confined to the role of pupils. Frances Conn, "The Effect of Change from Pupil Role to Teacher Role on Language Production of Sixth Grade Children;" Charles Herbert, "Social Role and Linguistic Variation" (Ph.D. dissertations, The Claremont Graduate School, Claremont, California, 1970).

2. William Glasser, *Schools Without Failure* (New York: Harper and Row, 1969), p. 218.

3. Carl Rogers, *Freedom to Learn* (Columbus, Ohio: Charles E. Merrill, 1969).

4. Nina Willis Walter, *Let Them Write Poetry* (Toronto: Holt, Rinehart and Winston, 1962).

5. See, for example: Postman and Weingartner, *Teaching as a Subversive Activity* (New York: Delacorte Press, 1969); Carl Rogers, *Freedom to Learn* (Columbus, Ohio: Charles E. Merrill, 1969); Abraham Maslow, *Toward a Psychology of Being* (Toronto: Van Nostrand, 1969); William Glasser, *Schools Without Failure* (New York: Harper and Row, 1969); Martin Buber, *The Knowledge of Man* (Harper and Row, 1965).

6. After analysing tape recordings of a large number of "discovery" lessons in elementary and secondary schools, investigators reached these general conclusions: a) teachers talked far more than pupils in response; b) most teachers' questions were close-ended, so that pupils were seldom invited to think aloud, to generate new sequences of thought, or to explore implications; c) children learn to give back to the teacher what they think the teacher wants, and teachers "snow" their pupils with masses of information, or complicated proofs, or "authoritative references." See: Douglas Barnes, *Language, the Learner and the School* (Harmondsworth: Penguin Books, 1969); also: Adams and Biddle, *Realities of Teaching: Explorations with Video Tape* (Toronto: Holt, Rinehart and Winston, 1970).

7. A bibliography listing twenty-four references includes Albert Baugh, *A History of the English Language* (New York: Appleton-Century, 1935); Wilfred Funk, *Word Origins and Their Romantic Stories* (New York: Grossett and Dunlap, 1950); Robertson and Cassidy, *The Development of Modern English* (Englewood Cliffs, N.J.: Prentice-Hall, 1954).

8. Robert Fulford, "Who's Crazy? Our Don or the Whole Country?", *Saturday Night*, 87, no. 9 (September 1972). (Don is a lonely fellow because he cannot share in the nation-wide hockey fanaticism.)

9. Lois Arnold, "Writer's Cramp and Eyestrain—Are they Paying Off?", *The English Journal*, LIII, 1 (January 1964), 10–15.

Faire aimer

Paul L'Archevêque

Ce que je fais en classe! . . . C'est un passé total, à la fois personnel et professionnel, qui, en partie mais inévitablement, le détermine; c'est un passé ineffaçable qui s'insinue encore sous tous les changements que, sans cesse, lui impose une expérience cumulative projetée dans le crépuscule d'un futur, à travers un passé plus long, de mieux en mieux entrevu.

Ce que je fais en classe s'explique donc aussi par les objectifs que je poursuis: les uns, immédiats, se font divers et changeants; les autres, éloignés, restent dans leurs profondeurs à peu près immuables comme la nature humaine elle-même qui, d'ailleurs, aux autres et à moi-même, les impose.

Antécédents

Mon passé personnel, on le devinera assez bien, dans ses grandes lignes synthétisé, à travers la personnalité que, même malgré moi, manifestera cette description de ce que je fais en classe.

Quant à mon passé professionnel, il a commencé par une pratique de dix années d'enseignement au service de la Commission des Ecoles catholiques de Montréal, au niveau primaire surtout.

J'ai l'impression—presque aussi forte qu'une certitude—que ces dix années m'ont été d'un grand secours même dans mon enseignement universitaire. Ne serait-il pas vrai que, de la maternelle à l'Université—et en première année surtout—les difficultés fondamentales de l'apprentissage et de l'enseignement ne changent pas beaucoup? Ces difficultés, normales, se posant à l'état brut plus chez les enfants que chez les adolescents ou chez les adultes, ne s'y feraient-elles pas aussi plus facilement saisissables et maîtrisables?

J'en suis maintenant à ma vingt-deuxième année d'une carrière universitaire qui a débuté peu de temps après la fondation de l'Ecole de Pédagogie et d'Orientation, maintenant devenue la Faculté des sciences de l'éducation de l'Université Laval.

Les problèmes que pose la naissance d'une telle institution ont fait que j'ai dû accepter la responsabilité d'une assez grande variété de cours durant les dix premières de ces années: statistique, méthodes de recherche, docimologie, mesure de l'intelligence, mesure des intérêts professionnels, et questionnaires de personnalité.

A partir de 1952 et durant sept ans, j'ai eu la possibilité de me soumettre à toutes les exigences théoriques et pratiques d'une licence en psychothérapie.

Ce fut là le point de départ d'une seconde phase de ma profession d'enseignant qui me faisait passer d'une certaine psychologie "quantitative" ou objective à une autre psychologie plus "qualitative" ou subjective.

Peu à peu, les cours qu'on me confia depuis lors furent les suivants: psychopathologie descriptive et M.M.P.I. psychologie de la personnalité, sexologie, théories de la personnalité, psychogénèse, et psychologie de l'affectivité. Ces trois derniers cours demeurent actuellement l'objet principal de mes intérêts et de mes responsabilités d'enseignement.

A cela se sont ajoutés quelques séminaires portant sur les sujets suivants: "counseling," nouvelle approche psycho-philosophique de la relation éducateur-étudiant, l'observation du comportement du maître, et psychologie rogérienne.

Cette grande variété de tâches m'a imposé un travail considérable dont je suis maintenant heureux croyant avoir ainsi élargi une certaine compétence telle au moins que semblent la percevoir les étudiants qui en seraient satisfaits!

Ceci eut également pour effet un enrichissement progressif de chacun de mes cours par suite d'emprunts divers et variés provenant de la matière des autres cours antérieurement faits.

Les objectifs

Ce passé professionnel, à mesure qu'il s'édifiait, donnait une force croissante à ma conviction déjà ancienne, mais de plus en plus claire et ferme, que l'être humain, quels que soient son âge et ses autres conditions, ne se met en mouvement que par une seule puissance fondamentale et dont la force a un coefficient d'universalité: l'énergie affective; cette affectivité qui pousse ses racines jusque dans le dynamisme de la primitivité indestructible des instincts, pour toujours, à divers degrés, déterminants de toute activité ultérieure, la plus évoluée qu'elle puisse devenir.

Il est intéressant de noter qu'au niveau des mots déjà, il n'y a qu'une seule lettre de différence entre "mouvoir" (faire agir) et "émouvoir" (faire sentir). On pourrait dire que, même pour comprendre (prendre avec soi et non passivement recevoir), il faut vouloir, c'est-à-dire, s'émouvoir d'abord d'une certaine façon pour se "mouvoir" ensuite, intellectuellement, vers l'objet de connaissance à saisir.

C'est l'amour en ses manifestations innombrables qui déclenche et féconde l'activité humaine et la rend heureuse tant dans son exercice que dans son produit. Est-il nécessaire de noter qu'au niveau universitaire cette activité, qui doit être mentale avant tout, se fera d'autant plus auto-créatrice et créatrice qu'elle sera plus intensément réfléchie, à l'inverse de ce qui se produit dans les jardinières d'enfants, mouvementées et bruyantes.

En leur profondeur, tous mes objectifs s'inspirent donc d'un seul et s'y réduisent: faire aimer.

Il faudrait avoir la conviction inébranlable que la communication des connaissances ou l'information stricte ne remplit qu'un rôle instrumental par rapport à la formation vraie—affaire affective—et qui devrait constituer toujours l'objectif principal de toute action pleinement éducative. Les puissances productrices de l'affectivité peuvent devenir incommensurables au service de l'intelligence dont elles disposent pour le mieux comme pour le pire, dans tous les domaines de la vie humaine, personnelle ou collective.

Il faudrait accuser l'humanité enseignante tout entière de n'avoir de tout temps songé qu'à la communication des connaissances et à la formation exclusive de l'intelligence. Or, un homme instruit, fût-il génial, s'il se réduit à ça, réprime en lui-même un monstre terrifiant et toujours menaçant. De tels génies sont rares, heureusement. Mais les monstres à demi instruits foisonnent et, par leur nombre augmentant, ils se font effarants.

Ainsi, l'état présent des sociétés, résultat de cette erreur millénaire et actuelle, ne manifeste-t-il pas en grande partie, les effets accumulés d'une affectivité malade, depuis toujours par les éducateurs abandonnée à elle-même et qui, de nos jours dans une contestation aveuglée et généralisée fait éclater—même avec des bombes—la haine et l'"amour", dans leurs destructions plutôt que dans leurs créations.

La haine de soi-même d'abord telle que, dans ses profondeurs et sous ses apparences contraires, on la devine; cette haine qui en partie atteint les autres et, inassouvie, semble chercher l'infini en se dressant contre la divinité. Notre siècle, de plus en plus, s'enivre de drogue et de sexe dans un rougissement de fureur folle. Il écume toujours de guerres et de crimes qui vont parfois du masochisme au suicide, du sadisme au meurtre comme de l'irréligion au déicide.

Faire aimer! Voilà donc mon objectif principal, à la fois immédiat et éloigné et sans cesse sous-jacent à tous les autres. Faire en sorte que les étudiants en viennent, à travers une meilleure connaissance, à aimer vraiment l'objet qui, déjà, les avait attirés en leur première année d'université, même avant de bien connaître cet objet pour eux d'abord plus ou moins fascinant. Il s'agit, au fond, d'exciter indirectement les besoins fondamentaux et les plus puissants de tout vivant, ceux de l'autoconservation et de la reproduction, pour en faire jaillir une sublimation partielle en des désirs affamés de ces connaissances qu'exige l'affective activité créatrice, pour soi-même et pour les autres, de toutes les professions.

Quant à mes objectifs plus purement d'ordre intellectuel, ils ne peuvent être autres que ceux de la taxonomie officielle qui n'a rien, en définitive, que de très traditionnel.

Préparation

Pour ce qui est de ma préparation éloignée à l'enseignement, il suffit, je crois de s'en reporter à mon passé professionnel.

En ce qui concerne ma préparation immédiate, je tiens, chaque fois que j'entre en classe, à y avoir consacré au moins une heure. Quand ce m'est possible, je préfère encore y mettre deux heures, surtout si je dois remplir trois périodes consécutives de cinquante minutes de cours.

Je tiens très fortement à cette préparation immédiate, même s'il s'agit d'un cours que je répète depuis un certain temps. Il me serait très désagréable et même pénible de redonner un cours sans rien y changer. Je risquerais ainsi de m'ennuyer beaucoup, donc d'ennuyer mes auditeurs qui, par leur propre ennui, augmenteraient encore le mien. Evidemment, le contenu fondamental d'un cours répété doit rester substantiellement le même; mais une foule de détails, plus ou moins accessoires, peuvent y changer: présentations, illustrations visuelles, graphiques ou autres, exemples concrets, etc.

Cette préparation me permet aussi d'introduire toutes les nouveautés dont j'ai pris connaissance depuis la dernière fois que j'ai fait tel ou tel cours: observations ou expériences nouvelles, résultats de lectures, actualités diverses et changeantes, etc. J'y prévois les synthèses à édifier, des illustrations variées et, surtout, des tableaux synoptiques auxquels je crois beaucoup par suite de leur caractère à la fois synthétique et analytique qui est aussi celui de la connaissance.

Ces tableaux synoptiques représentent des unités conceptuelles détaillées en leurs éléments constitutifs, le tout y étant aperçu d'un seul coup d'oeil dans lequel l'ordre logique diminue de plus l'effort de mémorisation.

En classe: Enseignement magistral

La plus grande partie de mon enseignement se fait sous la forme du cours magistral que je crois, suivant certaines conditions, plus adéquat au niveau de la première année universitaire.

La résistance que ce mode d'enseignement, traditionnel par excellence, oppose à toutes les critiques séculaires et actuellement si virulentes ne ferait-elle pas déjà penser que "les portes de l'enfer ne prévaudront pas contre lui"!

Il s'agit là, semble-t-il, d'une permanence "envers et contre tous" qui, pour être telle, doit s'enraciner dans l'immuabilité fondamentale de la nature humaine, elle-même en ses profondeurs génératrice des traditions par lesquelles elle se manifeste et qu'elle ne pourrait, par suite, anéantir qu'au prix de son propre anéantissement.

Désignant le lien qui continue le passé dans le présent où germe le futur, le mot tradition, comme la chose qu'il désigne, implique déjà l'idée d'une nécessité inéluctable ainsi qu'il en est au plan même de l'évolution physique où le temps se fait inséparable de la vie; corrélativement, la tradition implique donc aussi quelque chose de "magistral" et qui s'impose quand on définit cette tradition par la transmission orale d'abord et millénaire, puis écrite et visuelle de doctrines et de faits.

On pourrait peut-être distinguer trois grandes phases dans l'évolution de la tradition et de ses civilisations en ce qui concerne la communication et l'apprentissage.

Ces trois phases, préhistorique, protohistorique, et historique se trouveraient justement, avec leurs chevauchements, comme densément vécues dans le raccourci de l'ontogénèse, elle-même "traditionnelle," c'est-à-dire pour tous et en ses grandes lignes toujours semblable depuis la naissance—et même un peu avant—jusqu'à l'âge adulte.

La période de l'ouie d'abord, pour l'humanité primitive comme pour le bébé et l'enfant où la communication de l'information ne pouvait être que "révélation" orale, donc magistrale dans le sens le plus large de ce mot. Et ceci, sans cesse, tout en diminuant à mesure que l'humanité—comme le bébé—montait vers une maturité, pour l'une comme pour l'autre, vague et imprécise.

Viendrait ensuite, dans une émergence graduelle mais aussi depuis longtemps commencée, la phase de la vue, s'ajoutant à la précédente sans l'annuler, à partir, approximativement, de l'écorce des arbres devenue le papier jusqu'en notre siècle de l'image par excellence, celui des journaux, des livres, du cinéma, de la télévision, et des satellites artificiels.

Une troisième phase enfin, synchronique aux deux premières, mais sous nos yeux accélérée et s'affermissant, celle de l'action personnelle dans l'apprentissage en particulier et sous toutes ses formes. Depuis l'école "active" des maternelles jusque dans ses prolongements actuels et adolescents de la participation, de l'auto-éducation, et de la cogestion, le besoin d'action, si longtemps frustré, devait fatalement éclater d'abord dans la violence des contestations diverses et dans celle de l'inévitable enseignement magistral en particulier.

En somme, il y a eu d'abord les mots pour l'oreille et, pour les yeux s'ouvrant de plus en plus, le spectacle de l'univers proche ou éloigné offert à la curiosité visuelle, puis intellectuelle et enfin à l'action qui en vient à exiger la lune et maintenant s'en empare.

Donc, rien de vraiment nouveau sous le soleil, mais rien de moins non plus: le tout de la communication en général n'ayant été qu'amélioré par la technique, sous la poussée du développement des sciences, lui-même lancé par les enseignements magistraux des époques antérieures et depuis les commencements.

Dans l'ordre chronologique, en ce qui concerne la communication et l'enseignement, l'humanité est donc passée de la nécessité primordiale de la parole pour l'oreille "passive," à l'importance de la vue moins passive avec les dessins, les manuscrits, les imprimés et les photos et, enfin, à la combinaison audio-visuelle qui entraîne plus fortement vers l'action.

Ce qui était au commencement primordial, l'enseignement "magistral," doit demeurer jusqu'à la fin essentiel.

En effet, si, comme nous venons de le constater, il est naturel à l'être humain d'entendre d'abord pour ensuite mieux voir—au sens propre comme au sens figuré—avant d'agir, tout système d'éducation qui briserait absolument cette continuité, en ses commencements surtout, serait voué à l'échec.

N'est-ce pas un peu là ce que semble inversement démontrer, à nous en crever les yeux, la négation de plus en plus forte et généralisée de toute autorité, sans doute auditivement perçue comme "magistrale" et dans le sens abusif et détestable de ce mot. De nos jours, il faut vraiment, pour être sage, se faire pardonner d'avoir quelque chose à enseigner. L'autorité vraie ne sera toujours à l'avenir que celle qui sait se faire accepter pleinement, sans la moindre violence de sa part.

De plus, si, pour atteindre les objectifs fondamentaux de l'oeuvre éducatrice pleine, il faut passer par l'affectivité, c'est encore par l'oreille—que traversent aussi les mots de l'amour—qu'on y arrivera le plus surement.

Il y a peut-être des incompétences diverses, plus ou moins bien senties et justement dissimulées sous la résignation facile de certains de ces éducateurs qui acceptent de se taire de plus en plus en classe pour laisser la parole aux étudiants. Il y aurait peut-être aussi chez certains de ces enseignants cette illusion simpliste que l'abolition des distances de toutes sortes favorisent le rapprochement sur le plan affectif—ce qui n'est pas toujours vrai même dans l'intimité sexuelle. L'affectivité est beaucoup plus clairvoyante qu'on ne le croit par sa puissance intuitive. En fait, d'ailleurs, beaucoup d'étudiants restent profondément déçus de ce rapprochement "spatial." De plus, leur besoin humain fondamental d'entendre, frustré, attend encore plus et se révolte au fond contre cette attente même.

Ajoutons que naître à la science, en première année d'université, c'est un peu comme naître à la vie autant pour la personne que pour l'humanité: il faut en respecter les phases essentielles. L'activité intelligente se situe au terme d'un processus qui présuppose une certaine passivité réceptive des commencements où germe l'action future un peu comme l'immobilité précéde le mouvement. Celui qui ne sait pas encore et qui veut savoir a besoin d'entendre d'abord et de voir ensuite pour s'élever même jusqu'à la visualisation intellectuelle de l'invisible et ainsi éclairer l'action de toute la lumière possible. De toutes façons, l'oreille est antérieure à l'oeil, pédagogiquement comme génétiquement: le nouveau-né entend avant de voir. L'ouïe se développerait même durant la vie intra-utérine obscure alors que la vue ne fonctionnera que dans la clarté extra-utérine. De la même manière, quand, spirituellement, on naît à la science faut-il entendre d'abord dans le clair-obscur d'une ignorance relative avant de voir par soi-même. La lumière artificielle vient d'une électricité invisible. Si la polarité audio-visuelle était verticale, on pourrait dire que, face à la réalité inépuisable, la hauteur où s'est élevée la vue se mesurerait à la profondeur où l'oreille serait d'abord descendue. L'oeil est plus près de l'esprit, dit-on, et l'oreille plus près de la matière, mais de cette matière sensible—et même sensuelle—à travers les sens perçue et qui se fait indispensable à l'affectivité comme à l'intelligence elle-même.

Je reconnaîtrais assez facilement comme bien fondées la plupart des critiques que l'on formule contre l'enseignement magistral, mais j'admettrai difficilement qu'il soit devenu inutile. Aujourd'hui, comme depuis toujours, les mots de l'enseignement magistral restent nécessaires pour ce qui est de l'acquisition des connaissances premières surtout et dans tous les domaines.

En classe: Le cours

Ce que, concrètement, je fais en classe! C'est difficile à décrire parce que c'est trop simple.

Je crois pouvoir affirmer qu'il ne m'est arrivé que très rarement d'entrer en retard en classe où je veux être ordinairement cinq minutes avant l'heure indiquée à l'horaire.

Avant cette entrée en classe, j'ai toujours un peu peur, une peur légère et dissimulée le mieux possible, mais que je crois maintenant, pour moi, inévitable. J'en reste malgré tout assez heureux, si cette peur peut être celle dont on dit qu'elle est le commencement de la sagesse!

Je salue amicalement l'ensemble des étudiants déjà arrivés et quelques-uns plus en particulier qui se trouvent plus près de la tribune. Avec ces derniers, s'approchant parfois, j'échange quelques mots, le plus souvent, gais.

J'attends les retardataires quelques minutes, puis, je prends le micro dont je vérifie le fonctionnement par certains bruits qui font naître le silence.

Je reste debout et en mouvement, le plus possible, durant chaque période de cinquante minutes.

M'inspirant de circonstances diverses, j'essaie que mes premiers mots fassent rire. Ce qui se produit assez souvent!

Je procède ensuite au résumé du dernier cours pour enchaîner graduellement avec la matière dont je me propose de parler.

Je réduis la lecture de mes propres notes au minimum possible: tout au plus quelques citations importantes et très choisies ou quelques références précises.

Pour la plupart de mes cours, les étudiants peuvent se procurer des notes polycopiées et reliées qui comportent de cinquante à cent cinquante pages, selon la matière.

Ces notes de cours, je les fais toutes de la même façon. On y trouve, en somme, le plan détaillé du cours entier sous la forme d'une grande synthèse réunissant des synthèses de moins en moins vastes. Ces notes, je les rédige de façon qu'elles soient en elles-mêmes facilement intelligibles, mais en même temps incomplètes. Je fais ces notes de cours incomplètes aussi pour me garder une certaine liberté de détails dans le développement des idées générales qui restent évidemment invariables sous un même titre.

Ces cours magistraux, donc auditifs, je m'applique de toutes les façons possibles à les rendre "visuels" au maximum et en autant que le permet cette méthode d'enseignement prise en elle-même.

Pour y arriver, j'ai recours à toutes sortes de petits moyens: stimuler par des mots l'imagination au point de l'amener à "voir"; j'ajoute à cela des illustrations diverses et nombreuses surtout d'ordre graphique comme des tracés de figures géométriques régulières.

Je m'applique à devenir moi-même "visuel" (il n'est pas ici question d'esthétique ni d'art dramatique), par tous les mouvements que je fais spontanément: la marche qui accentue peut-être parfois ce que je dis, les gestes, les mimiques. Quand c'est possible, j'ai recours à certains films ou projections visuelles diverses.

A tout cela s'ajoutent, me dit-on, certains "tics" ou certaines distractions qui amusent les étudiants et . . . les reposent.

A partir des réactions que j'observe chez mes auditeurs, j'essaie, sur le plan verbal, de soutenir l'attention par tous les petits moyens que m'offre la parole. J'ai recours à beacoup d'exemples très circonstancés et concrétisés au maximum. Je simule parfois l'éloquence grandiloquente; je fais de l'humour; j'affirme certaines choses avec beaucoup d'exagération que j'atténue aussitôt; je fais suivre le comique par un grand sérieux et inversement; j'exploite aussi l'étonnement et la contemplation chaque fois que c'est possible.

Je varie les tons que je fais, suivant les circonstances, solennels, majestueux, poétiques, naïfs, ou péremptoires et surtout provocateurs tout en invitant les réactions verbales qui souvent se produisent.

A plusieurs reprises, après certaines affirmations importantes, j'invite encore les étudiants à poser des questions, à formuler des commentaires et même des objections. Il m'arrive ainsi, à l'occasion, de consacrer à cela jusqu'à trente minutes sur cinquante durant lesquelles les discussions se font aussi parfois entre étudiants.

Je pose aussi à mes auditeurs des questions auxquelles je sais qu'ils ne pourront pas répondre parce qu'il n'y a pas encore de réponse connue à fournir. Je me sers même parfois du silence qui durant quelque secondes permet une réflexion ou une prise de conscience.

En général, je vise à atteindre le plus possible l'affectivité de ces auditeurs avec la mienne, car je crois en ce que j'enseigne, surtout, j'aime beaucoup en parler; j'aime donc aussi ceux qui veulent bien m'écouter.

Je termine chaque cours à l'heure indiquée en annonçant la matière du cours suivant et de façon à piquer la curiosité, à en faire naître le besoin.

Enfin, cette description de ce que je fais en classe n'a probablement porté que sur quelques éléments constitutifs d'une certaine atmosphère que, pour bien connaître, il faut peut-être avoir respirée.

Dans une prudence dernière, je ne résiste donc pas à dire que les cours que je fais sont probablement beaucoup mieux que ceux que je décris!

PAUL L'ARCHEVÊQUE

Paul L'Archevêque est Maître ès Arts (littérature française) et Docteur en Pédagogie de l'Université de Montréal.

Avant sa nomination comme professeur à l'Ecole de Pédagogie et d'Orientation de l'Université Laval en 1947, M. L'Archevêque avait été professeur durant douze ans à la Commission des Ecoles catholiques de Montréal. De 1950 à 1960 il a été directeur des recherches à l'Ecole de Pédagogie et d'Orientation, puis directeur adjoint de l'Ecole jusqu'en 1964. De 1965 à 1967 il était vice-doyen de la Faculté des sciences de l'éducation.

Il est "Psychological Officer" pour la Mensa-Canada.

Il a fait des recherches sur le rendement scolaire à tous les niveaux, y compris la construction des tests. Ainsi, il a publié des tests collectifs d'intelligence générale pour des sujets dont l'âge varie entre huit ans et l'âge adulte. Ses articles ont paru dans diverses revues et ouvrages de collaboration dont L'Ecole pour tous *(Beauchemin, 1968),* L'Education dans un Québec en évolution *(Les Presses de l'Université Laval, 1966),* Les Valeurs chrétiennes en éducation *(Les Presses de l'Univesité Laval, 1967), et* Index analytique des Oeuvres de Teilhard de Chardin *(Les Presses de l'Université Laval, 1967 et 1972).*

Pendant la période à laquelle se rapportent les commentaires des diplômés le domaine principal d'enseignement de Monsieur L'Archevêque était la docimologie.

Selon ses anciens élèves, Monsieur L'Archevêque était un homme brillant, maître de son sujet, avec beaucoup d'expérience comme chercheur.

Il avait l'esprit profond, très modeste, simple. "Sous des dehors timides il savait communiquer son enthousiasme pour la méthode expérimentale," a dit un diplômé. C'était un homme sympathique, disponible, "qui savait voir ses élèves, les aimer, se soucier de leur compréhension et être très près d'eux."

Rien de révolutionnaire dans sa façon d'enseigner; il donnait son enseignement avec ordre et méthode, illustré d'exemples ou de cas tirés de sa vie professionnelle. Ses notes de cours étaient toujours à la disposition des étudiants.

"Ce qu'il livrait était tellement senti et vécu qu'il nous permettait de participer à sa découverte et nous donnait soif de découvrir à notre tour," a dit un diplômé. "Il m'a marqué," a témoigné un autre. "Par la suite j'ai obtenu mon Ph.D. en psychologie générale et expérimentale."

All the History of Man

A. W. Jolliffe

The reason for my inclusion in this distinguished coterie should be made clear at the outset. Over the past twenty years more than five thousand students have entered engineering at Queen's University and only a handful escaped having to sit through my Geology 010 lectures. None of my colleagues has been granted anything like equal exposure or contact.

The course in which all engineering freshmen, about a dozen laboratory assistants, and myself are involved is labelled "Elementary Geology." Neither the title nor the brief elaboration in the University Calendar is truly informative. In general, a *multidisciplinary* approach is attempted, organized and taught by the one individual (with all the severe limitations this entails), as contrasted with an *interdisciplinary* course where these responsibilities are shared by several teachers, each from a different field.

Few engineering schools require all first-year students to take a course labelled "geology." Its inclusion at Queen's came about prior to my joining the teaching staff in 1950. The course had to serve both as a foundation for subsequent geological studies taken by students opting for mining, metallurgical, civil, and geological engineering (about half the class), as well as a non-professional or "cultural" subject for the other half. Geology 010 can thus be said to have three objectives: "introductory" for the first group, "terminal" for the second, and "cultural" for both.

The whole class (about 350 students) meets for a 50-minute lecture twice weekly throughout the academic year. In the first term the topics relate mainly to physical geology and follow a well-worn path around the rock cycle. All the laboratory and field work is taken in this term, in sections of 40 to 90 students. Two-hour laboratory sessions on each of "Minerals" and "Rocks" are succeeded by two 3-hour field trips, and by a final laboratory period on rock structures and the geology of Canada. Three 3-hour tutorials are offered during the first term with the instructor and several teaching assistants present; attendance is optional.

Departures from the customary "Elementary Geology" approach become more drastic in the second term. Economic geology is especially stressed, and conventional historical geology is used primarily as a launching pad for discussions on the rise of man over the last 2,600,000 years and on his technological accomplishments. If I pace them properly, the lectures conclude with brief treatments of the roles of technology and science in history, and of those scientific revolutions that most altered man's views on nature and his place in it.

At the end of the first term the students take a one-hour test on mineral and rock identification. This, plus a one-hour "short-answer" test, counts 30 per cent towards the final course mark, the balance being based on a three-hour examination in April, most of which calls for essay-type answers. Usually about 15 per cent of the class achieve "A" standing and about the same proportion fails (if one includes the January drop-outs).

A teacher faced with the responsibilities of such a course may be forgiven conflicting emotions. It has been said that a professor's enthusiasm for an introductory science course varies inversely with the square of the likelihood of his having to teach it. The difficulties and disadvantages are many: twice a week he will be confronted by an intimidating horde of critical and demanding students; he must make a stab at maintaining touch with advances in all science from astrophysics to zoology; those cherished research projects that yield publications and academic kudos have to be curtailed or abandoned; and there is always the prospect of wading through stacks of final examination papers. Not the least of his concerns is that some colleagues may regard his efforts as a shallow survey, of dubious inclusion in a university curriculum. But, on the other hand, this sort of course does present a challenge and may carry hidden or potential benefits. Large numbers in a class can provide an exciting stimulant; the necessity of exploring writings remote from one's own discipline can open new doors; broad syntheses can be regarded as research as well as specialized investigations; and examination papers can supply invaluable feedback.

But how can such a course which attempts to cover the interconnected permutations of physical, chemical, and biological principles, processes and events across the 4,600,000,000 years of earth history, and then attempts to weld all these into one continuum with the story of man—how can such a course be other than superficial? And how can it be made meaningful to freshman engineers, many of whom may resent its inclusion within a crowded and demanding first-year curriculum?

These questions raise formidable problems and I have tried to keep them constantly in mind over the twenty years Geology 010 has evolved. They can best be countered, I believe, by building the course around a laboratory-supported basic science core, by pursuing some few selected topics to reasonable depth, and by linking all together under one unifying theme.

The total of four hours allotted to laboratory studies of minerals and rocks is far less than is customary in equivalent courses. Yet those members of the class who subsequently take advanced courses in mineralogy and petrography do not seem penalized thereby. The reasons for this may lie in limiting the selection of minerals (20) and rocks (12) to the most common and important types; in emphasizing economic aspects of mineral and rock identification; in being able to examine most of these in their natural settings on field trips; and not least, in having dedicated laboratory instructors who have done their homework.

A prospector's approach seems to lessen the drudgery of learning the diagnostic properties and chemical compositions of minerals, particularly for that half of the class which will take no further geological training. Engineers of any stripe are likely to find themselves in parts of Canada where weekend prospecting might profitably be linked with the pleasures of a fishing trip, and specific examples can be cited to bolster this proposition. Instead of beginning with the physics and chemistry of minerals (a legitimate approach if time were available), the very first exercise in the initial laboratory period requires each student to draw the point of a magnetized knife blade across the surfaces of three yellowish metallic minerals (pyrite, pyrrhotite, and chalcopyrite—any of which might be termed "fool's gold"), and to note how this one simple test serves both to identify each of the three and to differentiate all of them from native gold. The economic connections can be fortified further by noting that chalcopyrite mined in Canada last year yielded about half a billion dollars worth of copper, and that pyrrhotite is by far the commonest and most easily recognized associate of nickel ores in Canada, the world's largest producer. Similarly, the laboratory study of rocks can be lightened by stressing economic aspects. Conglomerate becomes a far more intriguing rock if samples can be passed around that come from Witwatersrand and Blind River, the world's largest known sources for gold and uranium. Such approaches smooth the way for the subsequent nitty-gritty of isomorphous substitution, Bowen's Reaction Series, and so forth.

Geological studies at Queen's University are favoured by proximity to a remarkable variety of mineral occurrences, rock types, geological structures, and landforms of glacial origin. The two field trips taken by the first year engineers also include visits to a meteoritic impact crater (Holleford), to a limestone quarry containing abundant Ordovician fossils representing seven phyla, and to a road-cut which exposes a subeconomic sulphide occurence containing chalcopyrite and molybdenite.

Unfortunately, the field trips have to be scheduled early in the first term, long before some phenomena seen on them can be dealt with in the lectures, and this is only partly remedied by liberal handouts covering the various field stops. Next year's class will be able to refresh their memories near the end of the second term by viewing a colour film on these.

To lift the stigma of superficiality from Geology 010, some matters are examined in detail, far beyond their treatment in elementary texts and even at the expense of topics long and firmly entombed in such texts. Continental Glaciation is stressed at the expense of other agents of gradation, not just because it has been so important in shaping both the landscape and history of Canada, but also because it was contemporaneous with the rise and spread of man. Uniformitarianism, Time and its Measurement, and Darwinism are some of the topics selected for special emphasis. Current interest may dictate some choices, like Moon-rocks, in 1969–70, and Environmental Geology in 1970–71. A decade ago Continental Drift was a barely respectable hypothesis warranting only passing mention, but its modern counterpart in the new global tectonics now has such compelling support that it demands extended treatment. Here, as in so many cases, much of the significant and exciting evidence is not to be found even in the latest textbooks but only in current scientific periodicals. Such papers can hardly be assigned as "required reading" to a class of 350 overworked freshmen, so the task of searching scientific journals and summarizing appropriate papers for inclusion in the lectures devolves on the one overworked instructor. Because of these annual shifts in course emphasis and content, the students are allowed some latitude in their choice of textbook, and are warned that examination questions will be based on lecture material.

One apparently frivolous topic receives intensive coverage. Some years ago I acquired an "advanced model" dowsing-rod from a disillusioned prospector. This is introduced in the form of a demonstration in connection with subsurface water. But the prime purpose of devoting a whole lecture to this, including lengthy readings from the polemics of Kenneth Roberts and other pro-dowsers, is to contrast science with pseudo-science, and to enquire into what constitutes scientific "evidence" and scientific "proof." In this Age of Aquarius, scientism, UFO's, Immanuel Velikovsky, and Edgar Cayce, it may be my most important lecture.

A class of 350 students has difficulty in establishing effective communication with the instructor. I have tried various experiments designed to foster feedback but with indifferent success. Students are encouraged to interrupt a lecture at any time to ask for clarification but not many risk it, nor is the allocation of a few minutes for questioning at the close of a lecture any more popular. Informal tutorial periods were instituted in 1969 and student attendance (optional) has been heartening, but instead of the lively bull-sessions that were anticipated, most students have spent the time studying minerals and rocks.

Although these attempts have fallen short, messages from the class do reach me loud and clear and in great volume via two routes: comments collected during the last week of lectures, and final examination papers. From a student's standpoint these come too late; any benefits resulting from his submissions will accrue to subsequent classes but not to his. From my standpoint, the information I get from close annual scrutiny of examination papers and comments is invaluable. It pinpoints just where I must take immediate remedial action, and the cumulative effects over the twenty years the course has been offered have been profound.

By convention, the main purpose of an examination is to supply reliable student grades. If this be taken as the sole objective, marking the papers can become a dreadful and tedious chore. However, if one adopts the unorthodox view that the chief function of examinations is to yield feedback (including lecture-evaluation), reading the papers becomes more rewarding.

Examinations are preferred targets for attack these days but on this matter I am a dedicated reactionary. Across twenty-five years I have been responsible for university courses under a dozen different titles, and have lectured to classes that ranged from two or three graduate students to about 400 freshmen. In the evolution of all these courses, but particularly those with larger numbers of students, examinations have proven so indispensable that I would set down almost as an axiom: The larger the class the greater is the need for holding formal examinations, for including some questions requiring essay-type answers, and for requiring the lecturer to read the papers.

Some 350 papers were written in a recent year's three-hour final examination in Geology 010. Reading the essay-type answers took me about three weeks. From the conventional standpoint the examination could be regarded as satisfactory—any students I talked with agreed that the questions were fair and representative, and the (unadjusted) grades plotted along a reasonable curve with mean and median values between B and B-plus. All this information is now filed in the Faculty archives, readily accessible for any sort of computer analysis that might be dreamed up in the future. But the most significant set of grades remain safely hidden from everyone except myself, recorded only in the copious notes that I accumulated during the marking—the grades I gave myself.

During the previous winter, for example, I would have awarded at least an A-minus for my lectures on Bowen's Reaction Series or on Darwinism; later, after reading hundreds of student answers to questions on these, I would have regarded a B-minus as over-generous. My unwitting slips were revealed in embarrassing clarity. Many answers to a question on sea-floor spreading, for example, used a puzzling term variously spelled "bedding-off" or "bending-off." Next year I would remember to write "Benioff Zone" on the blackboard. How can a teacher possibly gauge his performance except through careful personal scrutiny of examination papers? Perhaps it can best be likened to his annual medical check-up, where hidden disabilities are brought to light and remedial measures indicated.

Solicited comments from the students afford a useful supplement to information obtained from the examination papers. During the final week of lectures each student is asked to hand in a statement of what he found most interesting, what he found least interesting, and suggestions for improvement. Up to half the class may contribute comments; these need not be signed but many are. The longer submissions usually come from those students who believe that my casual dismissal of 4004 B.C. and "separate creation" places me in some jeopardy.

"Man is explicable by nothing less than all his history," wrote Emerson in the 1840s. In a broad sense this supplies the unifying theme for Geology 010. But what is *all* the history of man and where does it start? If it be limited to written records, it began a bare five or six thousand years ago. If "man" signifies *Homo sapiens*, he has been around a hundred thousand years or so. But tool-making near-man antedates him by more than two million years, and to find a likely ancestor for both man and ape one must go back some tens of millions of years further. So if the road to man can be regarded as part of man's history (in the same fashion as a century or two of prior events would be included in a historical study of the French Revolution of 1789), and if organic evolution proceeds by imperceptible steps through natural selection, should not one reach back successively through the earliest primates, mammals, and vertebrates to the very origin of life some three or four billion years ago?

Even this is hardly enough. The history of life on earth cannot be divorced from the earth's physical history. For it was the constantly changing environments across the sweep of geologic time that brought about the infinite variations in life, past and present. So the full story of man is necessarily involved with land and sea in restless interchange, with mountains gradually uplifted and sculptured and reduced and uplifted again, with ice sheets that grew and stagnated and shrank, with continents that wandered and joined and divided, and with all the other multitudinous events of geological history.

This, then, is the unifying theme for Geology 010: Time is a continuum and any subdivisions are arbitrary; the history of man is to be treated not as separate from nor as an adjunct to the history of nature, but as an integral part of it— man in time, man in life, man in the cosmos and on earth; the study of man in nature is essential for understanding the nature of man.

What specific relevance does all this have for first-year engineers? It rests mainly, I believe, in the intimate interconnections between minerals, rocks, archeology, and technology. Except for the very last 1/500th part of his existence, almost everything we know about man (and near-man) has to do with his use of mineral and rock materials. And we know more (and with greater surety) about his proto-engineering activities than we do about almost anything else that concerns him. An artifact from any age—whether it be a flint scraper or a bronze urn, the remains of a dwelling place or an irrigation system—speaks the engineer's language. Built into each artifact is unequivocal information on materials and processes, and on a host of hidden skills best appreciated by the engineer.

In this way—by regarding artifacts as "technological fossils"—the freshman engineer can become excitingly involved in archeology. And he is relieved to find that the basic methods and principles are the same as those he had studied in Geology 010 a month or so previously or had encountered earlier on field trips: superposition supplies the relative ages, radiometric dating supplies the time "fixes." His natural bent already links him with the earliest tool-makers, with fire-using *pekinensis*, and with a whole host of history-shapers who invented pottery, smelting, the loom, the wheel, and so on. He can appreciate the irrigation and construction methods employed ten thousand years ago at Jericho, and can trace a connection therefrom through the plumbing system at Mohenjo-daro, the aqueducts and *cloaca maxima* of classical Rome, right down to sewage disposal problems of his own city.

Lead beads recently found in a 6400 B.C. level in the Anatolian settlement of Çatal Hüyük supply a case in point. They antedate the earliest known mention of lead and its minerals by some five millenia. Their use is conjectural, but no such uncertainty pertains to the technologies implicit in these lead beads, many of which can be interpreted with confidence by the engineering freshman. He already knows (or knows where to find) the "vocabulary" and the "grammar" by which their messages can be read. From chemical data he can infer that lead is most unlikely to occur in nature as a metal, and he can confirm this by consulting any mineralogy text, *ergo* some smelting process must have been carried out. From additional information available to him he can calculate that certain minimum temperatures had to be reached and appropriate reducing conditions maintained during these operations, all of which imply a good deal concerning furnace construction, fuel selection, and so on. Many other equally sophisticated technologies are clearly implied by the beads—all those skills connected with the recognition, discovery, and mining of the highly restricted sources from which lead metal can be smelted. The engineering freshman will end such an exercise with new appreciation of the dignity and antiquity of his craft.

Nor does the usefulness of artifacts for reconstructing the science and engineering of the past end with the beginning of writing. The history of chemistry as recorded in almost all writings up to the seventeenth century tells quite a different story from that revealed in the artisan's products over the same period. Until the last few decades the history of science and technology was a largely neglected field. The last few lectures in Geology 010 attempt to bridge some of these gaps.

So much for Geology 010 course—its structure, content, and what I have thought to be its unique features. What remains are some miscellaneous reflections on teaching, mostly having to do with the "generalist" approach. All this is presented with many misgivings. What I report is fashioned only by twenty-five years of hard experience because, like so many university instructors, I received no formal training in the art of teaching.

Any success a teacher may have surely stems in large part from the attitude he brings to his subject. All else—the teaching methods and gimmicks, the well-structured pedagogical approach and sequence, the little dramatic devices designed to lure the student on—is secondary. If the teacher is not possessed by an enthusiasm and evangelical zeal that literally drive him to demand that his students find truth and beauty where he himself has glimpsed them, and fascination and excitement where he has experienced them, he had best find another subject or profession. He must never reveal it to the class, nor is it wise to divulge it to the friendliest of colleagues, but he has to believe, almost as a prime article of faith, that his is the most significant course his current crop of students will ever encounter.

But such fervour can be condoned only if it is tempered by a deep respect for all other disciplines, wide reading therein (even to the neglect of one's own specialty), and a constant search for all possible interdisciplinary linkages. And this sort of approach need not be limited to broad elementary courses. Queen's engineers of a few decades ago testify that "Sandy" MacPhail lecturing on sewage systems contributed more to their cultural development than almost anyone else on or off the campus.

Teachers in every discipline and at all levels have a pressing obligation to foster this multi-culture symbiosis, and those in the life and earth sciences bear special responsibility since they deal with matters more immediately relevant to human experience than do physics and chemistry. Accordingly, every chance must be seized, however tenuous the connection or remote the analogy, to link science and technology with literature, the fine arts, history, sociology, and all the rest. This is an area where the scientist must toss his customary caution out the window and where, to paraphrase Thurber, it is better to fall flat on one's face than to lean too far over backwards. Many illustrations and analogies used in my lectures are farfetched, and many inferences range from the naive to the ridiculous. Can Bohr's complementarity principle be cited with propriety to suggest that the diametrically opposed viewpoints of the emotionally involved poet and the objective scientist need not mean that the one is right and the other wrong? Is it proper to mention in class that two different propositions of Einstein may have equal validity —"$e = mc^2$" and "God who creates and is nature, is very difficult to understand, but he is not arbitrary nor malicious"—and from this to weave a connection with geological uniformitarianism, a corollary of which is that the laws of nature seem to be independent of time? Perhaps inept, unwarranted, or even false analogies are pedagogically pardonable so long as they carry shock benefit. Various writers from Coleridge to Koestler have advocated the juxtaposition of quite unrelated topics or frames of reference as vital in the learning process. The student must furnish his own "hooks and eyes of memory," but the instructor has to catalyze these linkages in the student's mind.

Herein may lie the main justification for the lecture system. The "transmission of knowledge" has always been a traditional function of the university, and lectures were the obvious vehicle for this a few centuries back when books and journals were rare and expensive. Today the system is not so readily defended. Yet the lecturer must hope for his efforts as Francis Bacon did for his essays: that they should serve "as grains of salt, that will rather give you an appetite than offend you with satiety." Surely this must be the teacher's prime function: to strike sparks, to build fires, so that the student's own enthusiasm will carry him through those dreary stretches that exist in all learning. Nor do I believe that "taped" lectures by world authorities can supply more than a useful supplement to the "live" lecturer. Only he can respond intuitively to the unasked question, or to the increasing boredom or enthusiasm of the class.

Many illustrations can spark response. Geological phenomena are everywhere, and geological events are frequent. Almost any issue of the local newspaper or the weekly newsmagazines may carry an article on some earthquake or volcanic eruption, or on moon-rocks, drifting continents, a uranium discovery, pollution problems in the Arctic, and such like. A surprising proportion of the class is apt to read this, so a few minutes on it at the next lecture encounter already seeded ground. Scrutiny of innumerable examination papers has proven to me that the few casual remarks thrown out under such circumstances remain firmly in a student's memory, whereas some meticulously honed exposition of a concept that lacks such associations is more likely to have gone down the drain.

Literature supplies another fertile source. Some quotations are directly applicable, others may be quite out of context, all seem fruitful. Many passages from *In Memoriam* are valid statements straight from Lyell, others are anticipatory of Darwin. Shakespeare on earthquakes exemplifies the tenacity of the Aristotelian hypothesis, whereas John Wesley views them as "divine visitations" no other of which "is likely to have so general an influence upon sinners." These can serve as the starting links in a loose chain through Poseidon, Thornton Wilder, and *Candide*, to the sloppy engineering job at Siloam recorded by St. Luke, and the whole can serve as a background for the present theory of earthquake origin and the evidence upon which it rests. Myths and legends known to all may appear in a new light to engineers if an empiric core can be demonstrated. Thus Jason's golden fleece can be linked with certain modern methods of mineral separation, and the same physico-chemical principles hold for the technique of dragging feathers through sands to recover gold, as described by Herodotus (although his further stipulation that the procedure must be conducted by virgins lacks any obvious scientific base). Coleridge's poem on "the two and seventy stenches" he counted in Cologne fortifies the engineering student with evidence that pollution has been a problem for a long time and that today's technology is not the sole culprit.

Common ground is abundantly available in the other arts. Materials engineering, usually regarded as a modern development, has its roots deep in the paleolithic. The sculptures of ancient Egypt may be contrasted with those of classical Greece or of the modern Eskimo from the standpoint of rock types available to the artists. Minerals used as pigments can serve as a connecting link from Lascaux to the Sistine Chapel, the Group of Seven, and the prevailing colour of rural Ontario's older barns. And the "peculiar virtues of minerals" play a lengthy role in the history of the healing arts.

Emerson, who supplied the theme for my freshman engineering course: "Man is explicable by nothing less than all his history," may again be enlisted (in paraphrase) in conclusion: "Every *student* I meet is in some way my superior; and in that I can learn from him." A textbook dedication I once came across said "To my teachers—those who taught me and those whom I have taught." To both of these I subscribe.

A. W. JOLLIFFE

Alfred Walton Jolliffe was born in Winnipeg, went to school there and in Kingston, attended Queen's University for his first two degrees—one in chemistry, the other in mineralogy—and then on to Princeton University for a Ph.D. in geology. During his years as a senior undergraduate and as gradate student he spent his summers as a field assistant on parties of the Geological Survey of Canada, mainly in the Northwest Territories. He spent the first ten years of his career as a working geologist in the same setting. (There is an island near Yellowknife which now bears his name.) There followed five years as associate professor in the Department of Geological Sciences at McGill University. Then, in 1950, he accepted the Queen's professorship from which he retired in 1972. Throughout his professorial career he has acted as a geological consultant to various Canadian mining companies.

He is a fellow of the Royal Society of Canada, the Geological Society of America, the Mineralogy Society of America, the Geological Associa-

tion of Canada, and the American Association for the Advancement of Science.

Dr. Jolliffe's main fields of research are the geochemistry of ore deposits (particularly iron and uranium), evolution of the Precambrian atmosphere, and the origins and evolution of chemistry. His publications include more than a score of reports and papers, mainly scientific and technological. In collaboration with his brother, H. R. Jolliffe, formerly of the School of Journalism, Michigan State University, he is preparing the first English translation of Georgius Agricola's Bermannus sive de re metallica *(1530), "a work which," Professor Jolliffe explains, "marks the birth of the sciences of mineralogy and mining geology." In 1973 he was one of fifteen Ontario university teachers chosen to receive OCUFA Teaching Awards.*

Most of the graduates who commented on Professor Jolliffe and his teaching had come to know him in the introductory course in geology which was required of all first-year engineering students. Evidently he overcame the handicap that implies. Indeed it is said that as a result of their experience in that course many students chose careers in the field of geological sciences.

Former students testified to his "depth of understanding and concern for both his subject and his students . . . in all his classes, whether on the introductory level or graduate, whether a class of 200 or 10." His experience as a long-time hard-rock geologist and the breadth of his interests ("from biology to statistics") enabled him to illustrate every principle he stated–by practical examples, experiences, or anecdotes. And all this with humour, joy, vitality, enthusiasm, even missionary zeal, and with humanity and sincerity. Basically, said the graduates, he was an interesting person.

Only brief references were made to his teaching methods. Mention was made, however, of his use of visual aids and his helpful habit of writing on the board a skeleton outline of the topics to be presented in the day's lecture.

To Interest and Inspire

G. G. Meyerhof

During my years in high school I enjoyed those courses most which were given by good teachers. These classes included both humanities and sciences and were given by men who knew their subject well, as shown by the contents of their instruction and by their answers to our questions. Their lectures, illustrations, and any experimental demonstrations were well prepared, arranged in a logical manner, and clearly and simply presented. They made the subject sufficiently interesting and stimulating for the students to delve further into it and to do their homework with some pleasure. The good teachers combined capability with enthusiasm. They had a sense of humour, a pleasant personality, and treated the students with respect.

At the time of my university studies in engineering my friends and I occasionally discussed the common qualities of our best professors, who were good educators in the broadest sense. They had not only the attributes mentioned for good high school teachers, but they had also made some original contributions to engineering research and had a good deal of practical experience. These qualities gave us confidence in and respect for their teaching. For instance, one of our best professors had developed a new type of aeroplane and illustrated his lectures with some practical problems which he had solved. Another professor had contributed a new principle in engineering analysis which he compared with previous methods, while a third professor brought various design problems from his extensive consulting practice into the classroom.

These professors not only knew their subject thoroughly, but also had themselves done something in the creation of the subject which they presented. The best professors lectured in a simple manner and made frequent reference to new problems arising from their engineering activities. Their lectures were interspersed with problem and design sessions and with laboratory periods for experimental verification of engineering principles and illustrations of the applications and limitations of different theoretical methods. Thus, the students also learned how to obtain practical data and present the results in engineering reports, while seminars allowed the presentation of experimental results and the discussion of new developments of original research. In this way the students received not only a good training in the fundamental sciences and basic engineering subjects but also learned how specialized engineering analyses and designs are used in the solution of current engineering problems in their chosen branch of engineering.

These professors inspired me to supplement my university studies with practical experience in the design and construction of engineering works by working with consulting engineers and contractors. Later on I joined a government research establishment to specialize in foundation research, which formed the basis of my extramural postgraduate studies and brought me into renewed contact with university professors. Meetings of various engineering societies gave me an opportunity to lecture and present papers on some of my work and take part in discussions. At first I had to prepare each lecture carefully and write it out in full. Sometimes a lecture had to be redrafted several times before I was satisfied. However, the full text was never read but remained in my pocket, while the salient points of the work were described and usually illustrated by slides. Gradually these public lectures required less preparation until a few notes sufficed, especially because oral presentation of a subject for discussion differs from papers written for publication. Thus, it is usually better to explain any difficult points simply during the lectures and to treat them more fully in written papers. Occasionally I was invited to give lectures at universities, conduct seminars, and participate in short courses in the field of my specialization.

As a result of this experience I have joined a small engineering college where I could combine teaching with research and occasionally do some consulting with government or industry in order to keep abreast with modern practice. Since I give courses on subjects in which I have had experience for many years and also continue to make personal contributions to research and practice, I no longer need any notes for my undergraduate lectures. I prefer to speak freely and attempt to present the material in a simple and clear manner. I always try to bring something new and interesting to the students' attention. The lectures and discussions are illustrated by practical examples from my consulting experience, the results of my research and other work with which I am thoroughly familiar. Starting with simple and specific cases which a beginner can easily understand, I try to discuss the subject without extraneous details. After the student has familiarized himself with the fundamentals and can appreciate a more sophisticated approach, I embark upon a more general discussion and more rigorous form of presentation. However, the lectures include only the highlights and the more important latest developments of the subject, while the textbooks and reference works are available for details.

During the first phase of teaching the subject, I integrate the lectures with problem periods, laboratory work, and some field experience. In this way the students see the practical application and interpretation of the fundamentals and experimental data to solving simple engineering problems and they become familiar with the behaviour of engineering materials and components. During the second phase of teaching I give the students an elementary knowledge of the theories required for carrying out engineering designs. Therefore, this stage of teaching is closely integrated with projects to illustrate the application of theories in engineering works. I also include some laboratory testing of models of engineering constructions to familiarize the students with actual behaviour of simple engineering structures and comparison with theoretical estimates. I try to be present during the problem periods and the laboratory and design sessions to assist students on a more individual basis and answer their questions. By special projects and thesis work I allow students to study a particlar subject of their choice more thoroughly and give them an opportunity for some creative expression. This also enables each student to pursue some independent study to a greater depth and then work together as a team. Students enjoy such team effort in which each one contributes his solution in a particular area to a complete design project which may include a report to indicate how the work would be constructed. For example, in the case of a suggested bridge design, one student deals with the geology of the site, another one covers the soil exploration, the results of which are applied by those students in designing the foundations, while the structural design is distributed among various other students and then coordinated by all of them. Whenever possible, this program also includes some field visits and guest lectures by visiting professors and professional engineers.

By attempting to conduct these courses in a way similar to those of my own best former professors I hope to arouse the interest of the students in the subject, inspire them to do creative work in that field, and indicate to them the areas which still require further study or development. Special emphasis is placed on the gaps in our knowledge, the approximations and simplifying assumptions made in various theories and the uncertainties and limitations of different methods of analysis and design. Students are always interested and surprised to hear that the semi-empirical methods used in engineering design can only provide rought estimates at best. I try to indicate to them that engineering is both an art and a science and that engineering decisions require a great deal of personal judgment. My lectures, therefore, include case records of successful designs and investigations of failures of engineering works.

Such accounts support the need for more field observations and a better understanding of engineering behaviour.

In general, I encourage students to take a broad view of engineering, including its social and economic implications and its place in human environment and civilization as a whole, in the hope that engineering knowledge may be advanced through the joint effort of the students and myself for the benefit of our profession.

G. G. MEYERHOF

After studying at Heidelberg Gymnasium in his native Germany, Geoffrey Meyerhof graduated from the University of London in 1938. He worked for several years with consulting structural engineers in England and subsequently qualified for the Ph.D. in engineering. In 1946 he joined the staff of the British Government Building Research Station near London where he carried out extensive research on soil mechanics and foundation problems. For his distinguished contributions in this field the University of London conferred on him the degree of Doctor of Science.

In the mid-fifties Dr. Meyerhof moved to Canada where he became supervising engineer in the Montreal office of the Foundation of Canada Engineering Corporation, designing buildings, bridges, and other structures.

Dr. Meyerhof is the author of numerous papers on structural and soil mechanics subjects, published by scientific and engineering societies in various countries. He is a registered professional engineer, a fellow of the Royal Society of Canada, and a member of many scientific and engineering societies in Canada, the United States and England. He is a council member of the Engineering Institute of Canada, and first president of the Canadian Geotechnical Society.

He joined the staff of Nova Scotia Technical College in 1955 as professor and head of the department of Civil Engineering. He was director of the School of Graduate Studies for three years and then dean of engineering from 1964 to 1970. His teaching field during the period with which we are concerned was soil mechanics. In 1973 the Technical University of Aachen, West Germany, awarded him an honorary degree of Doctor of Engineering for his contributions to geotechnical engineering.

Professor Meyerhof's mastery of both the theoretical and practical aspects of his subject impressed his students, and they bore testimony to his ability to present both in ways which were uncomplicated and interesting. His vast experience as an engineer provided practical examples which he used with authority. In addition, he kept the class abreast of new developments.

He gave teaching high priority, lectured simply, without notes, and made effective use of the blackboard. He treated students with respect and dignity, worked hard himself and expected his students to do the same. He was friendly and approachable.

"The subject was new to me," reported one graduate. "My interest was so aroused that I specialized in it at graduate school. Looking back, I feel this was largely due to the teacher."

The Profit and Pleasure of the Protestant Ethic

Muriel Armstrong

There are, I think, two cardinal rules of good teaching. First, a teacher must like his students. He must enjoy teaching them, and working with them, and he must be able to derive genuine pleasure from seeing them progress. Secondly, a good teacher must be a compulsive worker. If he has a bad dose of the Protestant ethic, so much the better! Teaching is a time-consuming task, and one of the rather interesting facts that has emerged from the time sheets that I have kept over the years is that the time required to prepare for each hour in class has not diminished perceptibly.

Liking and respecting students implies, for me, the everyday courtesy of knowing their names. It is important to students that they be more than simply a number on a computer printout. They need to be identified as individuals, and they need to feel that they have the friendship of their professors. Given the rising enrolments in our universities, this may become increasingly difficult. It is no problem with a group of twenty, or fifty. I am a great believer in roll calls, not because I want to compel students to comply with the University's regulations that require them to attend fifty per cent of all classes, but because a roll call is the most efficient technique I know of for learning who students are. Parenthetically, I might add that I do not like compulsory attendance rules in university courses because I think that they deprive an instructor of important feedback. If students are free to attend or not as they choose, then the instructor has a day-to-day indicator of how he is doing. If students "vote with their feet" then the instructor should look rather seriously at the kind of teaching job he is doing. To return to the question of getting to know students: the problem becomes difficult when groups have a hundred or more students in them. Obviously nobody wants to waste half of the period calling a roll. Yet I believe that it is important that *someone* know these students by name; if the instructor himself cannot learn them, then his conference leaders, who act as his stand-ins when large groups are split up, must do so.

I think that a teacher who cares about his students will make himself readily available to them. He will maintain an open door, or at least there will be known periods of time when his door is open, so that students feel welcome to come in and discuss their problems with him. Sometimes he may need to chase after those who are not performing as well as he feels they should, in order to persuade them to discuss the problems they are having with his course.

It has been my experience that those teachers who like students and respect them derive pleasure from watching their progress. But as a corollary, they find it discouraging when, for one reason or another, students do not make the progress that might have been expected. It has also been my experience that good teachers feel a strong responsibility for those whose progress does not measure up to their potential. A good teacher is likely to regard those who fail to meet his criteria as a reflection on his own ability as an instructor; he is most unlikely to regard them as a group of stupid individuals who should never have been allowed in his presence in the first place. Of course, one can carry this too far: there *are* students who, in spite of the best efforts of a teacher, simply will not work. There are those who will dislike an instructor, and who are unlikely to be motivated by him regardless of his techniques. There seem to be some for whom a particular body of knowledge appears to be totally incomprehensible, regardless of the form in which it is presented. I do not suggest, therefore, that an instructor will manage to bring all of his students up to an acceptable standard. What I do suggest is that a good teacher will quite likely look to his own methodology, techniques of presentation, and his own shortcomings before he blames the students for their failures.

Liking students, respecting them, deriving enjoyment from teaching them was the first of my cardinal rules for good teaching. The second—hard work and careful preparation—is even more important, I think. There are two parts to preparation: the mastery of the subject matter, and developing the techniques of presentation. As to the first, it goes almost without saying that a good teacher should know his subject and should keep up to date on it. This can take a great deal of time. It does not involve making original contributions to knowledge in the subject. Instead it means keeping up on other peoples' contributions, finding relevant examples, checking newly-published sources. It involves what one rather tactful individual, trying to bridge the gap in the perennial academic teaching-versus-research battle termed "research for students." This kind of work was contrasted with "research for colleagues," which comprised what is normally considered to be the scholarly research of academics.

It is in the techniques of presentation of the material, however, that the art or science of teaching lies. Preparing material for presentation is a time-consuming task. My own rule of thumb is rather an elastic one: proper preparation time for me ranges from two hours for each hour in class, to about eight, depending on the complexity of the topic in question, and the amount of graphic material I prepare. One of the facts that I have already noted is that my preparation time now differs very little from what it was when I began teaching some years ago. I cannot walk into a class "cold" now, any more than I could when I first started teaching a particular course. Since other people whom I regard as good teachers find that the same thing is true of them, I am hopeful that this failure of preparation time to decline is not merely a matter of Parkinson's law, the Protestant ethic, decreasing efficiency, or increasing senility.

I suppose that I really learned the lessons about careful and detailed preparation when I gave Introductory Economics as a credit course for our evening students on open-circuit television in a cooperative venture between Sir George Williams University and the CBC. There were fifty-two lectures in the series, each one 29 minutes in length, give or take no more than 15 seconds. For these, virtually every move was planned, from the blackboard to the podium, or from the magnetic board to the cellomatic. While this is somewhat extreme for the normal classroom, it clearly demonstrated the efficiency of planning. The television experience was exhausting but instructive, because at the same time I was teaching a "live" section in the University. I was in the classroom for three fifty-minute periods a week for twenty-six weeks; the series was on the air for two half-hour periods a week for twenty-six weeks. I was hard pressed in the classroom to keep up with the television series.

That series achieved a peak of organization that I have never again achieved, though it is an objective that I always bear in mind. First of all, students started out with an index of lectures. In addition they had a printed outline of each one, including copies of graphs that were difficult, plus a statement of the required reading for each lecture. They also received a set of mail-in assignments—about twenty in all, as well as certain supplementary reading materials. I have issued these fairly detailed outlines to all introductory classes that I have taught since then, and they have proved to be valuable teaching aids. In one year in which I was slow to issue them, I discovered that a flourishing under-the-counter market existed in a nearby coffee shop for a version of my TV notes. They were selling at a price that, had I ever had the nerve to charge it, would have enabled me to retire at an early age.

All of this preparation had to be done well in advance of the lectures themselves, and this ensured careful planning for each unit of the series. It went much further than planning, of course, because each lecture had not only to be planned, but timed with extreme care. I felt that I had to rehearse the lectures, not only in the studio prior to the live-taping session (in which there is no possibility of correcting errors) but also at home. Our playroom used to be set up with two small chairs for my young daughters who learned to sit still and not to giggle too frequently at Mother's performance, and an ever-patient husband with a script in one hand and a stop watch in the other. Obviously that kind of preparation is impractical for normal classroom teaching, and it was one of the factors that made that series a more time-consuming operation than I would have believed possible. I religiously kept time sheets, and I calculated that writing the script, preparing graphics, outlines, and assignments, plus the time involved in running around to get scripts typed, shuttling back and forth to the CBC graphics department, showing up at the studio, cost me an incredible 34 hours for each half-hour script, and cost my economist husband over three, making an average expenditure of time, according to my records, of 37⅗ hours per 29-minute script! *That* is preparation—and I wouldn't want to repeat the performance for every lecture (or when would I ever get my committee work done!).

The greatest value of the series, I think, was the lessons I learned about how effective graphics are as a teaching device, and what a variety of them can be employed by an instructor prepared to spend some time exploiting their use. As a result of that series, I have abandoned the blackboard in favour of the overhead projector. Some of my colleagues assure me that this may be all right for economics, but it will never work in their particular subject. So I shall confine my observations to my own discipline. Economics—particularly economic theory—is a visual subject. One of the most common explanatory devices is the graph, and the use of pre-prepared transparencies on an overhead projector, perhaps with the aid of overlays and of copies run off on a duplicating machine for each student, are helpful teaching aids.

Overhead projectors are becoming so common in educational institutions today, from the elementary grades on up, that it is unnecessary to list their advantages over the blackboard—such advantages as always being able to face a class so that you can watch for the puzzled expressions on students' faces when you have said something they haven't understood, or the quick questioning arch of the eyebrow of a good student when you have said "*in*elastic" and you should have said "*e*lastic."

Being able to predraw diagrams is another great advantage. Predrawn diagrams work out. When I was making extensive use of the graphics department of the CBC, or of our own instructional media centre, one of my favourite devices was a series of overlays that enabled me to build up a diagram step by step. The first layer of the transparency frequently contained nothing but the framework of the graph; then at a certain point, one hinged overlay was folded in from one side, adding the next step to the process, then another and another, until the complex diagram was all set up. This device is much superior to the illustrations that appear in textbooks, which usually show only the finished product, without all of the various steps by which it was built up.

Sometimes it is much easier to rely on one's own artistic ability than to depend on the help of graphics departments, which have a habit of being busy when you need them most. Here again technology has come to the teacher's aid. One can, of course, simply predraw graphics with special pens and pencils on clear sheets of acetate and project them. The problem is that such drawings are not permanent: they are easily smudged and a moist finger can do irreparable damage. One advantage of them is that they can be done in a number of colours. The problem of nonpermanency and the inadvertent erasure can be met by making a pencil drawing of the material, putting it through a thermofax with a special transparent acetate, and the diagram emerges, sharply and permanently etched, ready for projection in conservative black and white.

One very useful device, to my way of thinking, is a film master on which one can type, trace, or draw. This master, which ultimately is projected on the overhead, may first be run through a duplicating machine, so that both the instructor and the students start off with the same basic diagram—the students with one on paper, and the instructor's projected on the screen over his shoulder. Then the instructor, working on a clear sheet of acetate placed over the original film master (to save the master for the next go-round), and the students can build up the diagram together step by step.

The reason I like this device so much is that it gets students actively working on the problem. When they are participating, the toughest part of the learning battle is won. They do not mechanically take notes; instead they are forced to think through a problem, and not merely watch the instructor think through one for them. They find out immediately whether or not they understand what is going on; there is immediate feedback of the kind that can be derived from a programmed text, which makes a student respond, and then tells him in the next frame whether or not his response was correct.

I find this device particularly useful in teaching economic theory, which is highly structured and very logical, and which therefore lends itself admirably to this technique. I have found that teaching economic policy presents me with a different kind of problem, and I am not yet satisfied with my techniques. Economic policy, at the level at which our course is offered, is a more conversational subject than theory—less structured, less logically appealing, and open to a good deal more waffling. It is more difficult to get all students participating, and I find myself sometimes, at the end of a session, rather frustrated because the period has turned out to be more of a lecture than I would have liked.

Diagrams play a much less important role in policy, but even so I still find the overhead projector a useful teaching aid, though it serves a somewhat different function. Before information can be presented in a logical, clear form, or before a discussion can be kept within the bounds of relevance, it seems to me imperative that there be a good outline. Such an outline helps one develop a topic in a rational manner, and if it is transcribed onto a series of graphics, the rationale is made evident to students who watch it emerge, point by point, on the screen in front of them. This device is a first-rate source of discipline for the instructor because it makes him take the time and give the forethought necessary to get his material into such a logical form.

Another benefit of such a graphic is that it guides the teacher and helps to eliminate any need for notes. This permits him to concentrate his attention on his students and on their expressions, which are the clearest signal of comprehension or lack of it. Definitions and key words projected at appropriate intervals are also helpful in this regard. Even where such an outline is predrawn for the overhead I find that I still need a good deal of time to work through the outline and the related materials before I am ready to meet a class. One of the most valuable periods of time to me, and one that I am most reluctant to relinquish to anyone for any purpose, is that last quarter or half-hour before a class. In those few minutes I can work through my outline just once more, making sure that everything is in order.

In Sir George Williams, where we have both a day and an evening university, and where it is customary for instructors to offer their courses in both divisions, I find myself teaching on, say, Wednesday night the material that I have already taught to day students in two or three separate periods during the week. Even though the material is likely to be relatively fresh in my mind, I still find that my performance is much improved if I take plenty of time to work through the outlines and the material once again. By the time one adds to this review time the hours necessary to read some recent contributions in a subject, or to check a new source on an old topic, and the time to do a graphic or two for the overhead, it is not surprising to find that anywhere from two to eight hours may have slipped by in the preparation of materials for tomorrow's class.

Getting active student participation, one of my major goals, is relatively easy with some kinds of material (I have already mentioned the device of building up diagrams together) but much more difficult with others. Perhaps the most common method of getting participation is the question and answer method, which works well when students have completed their reading assignments. It is then possible to have discussions and to elicit from the students a large part of the material necessary to build up the outline. The instructor's summary at the end, with the outline being developed as he goes, can then serve to fill in any gaps and to put the entire discussion in a logical form.

This system works fairly well with groups of up to fifty and it is not impossible with up to one hundred. Thereafter the problem begins to get out of hand. My largest class was a group of 325, and I think that it was probably the greatest source of discouragement I have had in teaching. In two previous years I had handled classes of between 150 and 200, but the problems there seemed to be less acute. Perhaps it was the particular room I was in, although it was equipped with the latest gadgets and I had a large library of graphics. One source of discouragement was that I was able to get to know a smaller absolute number, and hence a much smaller proportion of that class, than I had in my previous large classes. Since I work best when I know my students, it was almost inevitable that I found the large group rather unsatisfying. The method I used ended up as the lecture method; the lectures were highly organized, thoroughly prepared, and called for the use of many graphics on the overhead. However, given the size of the class, save for a brave minority who were not afraid to ask questions or make contributions, it turned out to be largely a one-man (in the "broad" sense of the term) show. Perhaps we have become too sensitive to criticism of the lecture method as an instructional device. There are places—large classes being one of them—where its use seems to be almost inevitable, though I am intrigued by the various experiments going on in teaching introductory courses in different disciplines to large numbers without any lectures at all, relying on study guides, assignments, programmed instruction, and other forms of instructional capital.

Testing and marking are other time-consuming occupations of a teacher. I consider examinations to be useful, both in providing students with feedback on how they are doing, and in telling the instructor how *he* is doing, and I am not sure at this point which is the more valuable contribution. I think that a well-constructed test that makes a student apply the tools he has learned, or organize the knowledge he has acquired in class and from his reading into a logical response, is a valuable learning experience. Prompt and frequent feedback is important, so that it is vital that the instructor should correct papers as quickly as possible and get them back to students while the questions are still fresh in their minds. I think that a student needs to know how he is doing and where he ranks in his class, and a test or examination is about the most objective way (or at least it *can* be) of providing him with that information.

A device that I have used for a number of years in an intermediate theory course is the unannounced quiz which is given in the first 15 or 20 minutes of a class. I warn students at the beginning of the year that I use this method frequently to ensure that before they show up for any class they have reviewed the previous day's work. I also cheerfully admit that it is not the most popular form of testing and that if I am quietly "done in" some time, the finger of suspicion will point at them. I am surprised at how cooperative the students are: they freely admit that it keeps them working steadily; misunderstandings and errors are promptly corrected because one of the rules of the game is that these papers must be marked and returned to them the next period. I also find out where their difficulties lie and whether I have succeeded in getting across a complicated concept.

Another source of information for an instructor about how well he is succeeding is the evaluation form that is filled out by students. I am aware that such forms are not held in high esteem by many, who regard them as popularity contests, or say that students are incapable of judging the merits of an instructor or his material until they reach a much higher level of maturity. My own feeling is that this is to underrate the ability of students. There is available for the voluntary use of instructors in Sir George Williams University an evaluation form that was worked out a few years ago by a faculty committee on instructional problems. I find it very helpful to have students answer this questionnaire and to give them the opportunity to make anonymous comments if they wish. Some remarks, admittedly, are facetious but most are helpful. The questions give the student an opportunity to express his opinion on such matters as whether or not he understands the objectives of the course, whether the instructor is well prepared, whether he spends too much or too little time answering questions, whether the student would recommend the course to others, and so on. I think that we as teachers, if we are not to get out of touch, need this kind of feedback on our own performance. Students are our customers, and they are in a better position than anyone else to inform us about the quality of our product. It is not pleasant to have to face criticism but I think that a teacher can learn a great deal from such evaluation.

Preparing for classes, seeing students, testing and marking—all these require a great deal of time, and one of the major obstacles to being a good teacher in an institution of higher learning is the competing demands on a faculty member's time. First there is the pressure to publish: the "publish or perish" doctrine and the statement that universities need good teachers strike me as being somewhat incompatible principles; it is simply a question of the allocation of that scarcest resource of the university teacher—his time. This is not to say that good scholars cannot be good teachers; obviously this is not true. But it is difficult for scholarship and teaching to be simultaneously-produced products unless the scholar's teaching load is very small. There are just not enough hours in a day to accomplish both.

The other source of heavy pressure on an academic's time is the burden of administrative duties imposed by the increasingly democratic organization of universities. Committees have a habit of encroaching more and more on a faculty member's time, leaving him less and less able to maintain an open-door policy for his students, less able to spend the time he needs to prepare outlines and graphics, to mark tests and assignments, and to do the necessary research for his students. Such demands also make it more difficult to keep up with what is happening in the field of teaching itself. In all disciplines there are experiments and innovations taking place that teachers should know about—programmed instruction, self-instruction, team teaching, and learning cells, to mention only a few. These new techniques fascinate me and I would like to try a number of them. I think a teacher needs to try new methods in his classroom; it keeps him interested and enthusiastic about his profession. That is why I am looking forward to reading the other essays in this collection, so that I can discover techniques which others use, and which I can adapt for use in my own classroom—just as soon as I get off some committees and find the time to try them!

MURIEL ARMSTRONG

Muriel Armstrong took her first degrees, Bachelor of Arts and Bachelor of Education, in her native province of Alberta, taught high school there, and later studied economics at McGill University and the University of Manchester. She was awarded the degree of M.A. in economics by McGill in 1954.

For the next three years she was a research economist with the Newfoundland Royal Commission on the Revision of Terms of Union between Newfoundland and Canada. From 1957 to 1960 she was a part-time lecturer at Sir George Williams University and also a freelance news commentator for the CBC, on Trans-Canada Matinee. She became assistant professor of economics at Sir George Williams in 1961 and professor in 1969. During the year 1973–74 she acted as chairman of the Department of Economics and associate dean of arts.

She was a member of the executive of the Canadian Economics Association from 1968 to 1971 and is chairman of the Association's committee on education. She has served as a member of the Social Science Research Council of Canada and has been a member of the board of directors of the Montreal Metropolitan YMCA.

With her husband, D. E. Armstrong, she contributed "Third Party Intervention in the Alberta Coal Industry" to Patterns of Industrial Dispute Settlement in Five Canadian Industries, *edited by H. D. Woods (Industrial Relations Centre of McGill University, 1955). She is author of* The Canadian Economy and Its Problems *(Prentice-Hall, 1970). Her research interests include attention to teaching methods, especially with respect to the teaching of economics.*

"Cheerful" was a word which recurred in the notes Professor Armstrong's former students wrote about her. She was pleasant, youthful, zestful, enthusiastic, inspiring, they said.

She knew her subject and presented it clearly, making effective use of visual aids—charts and graphs shown by an overhead projector, for example. One graduate noted that Mrs. Armstrong had been teaching the same course concurrently on television and apparently was using some of the same materials and techniques in the classroom with good effect.

Her thorough planning of the course and her conscientious preparation for each class session was evident, and greatly appreciated. This characteristic seemed to be related to her genuine interest in her students, her concern that they should understand, her readiness to search out answers to questions they raised, and her care in commenting on the material they wrote for her inspection.

Summing up much of what graduates said were these remarks by one of them: "Mrs. Armstrong . . . had the power to communicate enthusiasm; she was invariably thoroughly prepared. . . . She had the gift of inspiring students to go away and study for themselves. . . . She was always thorough in every sense of the word, and in every aspect of her job."

The Problem of Authority

Leon Getz

This short essay is written in response to a request for "a thoroughly personal account of your philosophy of teaching and your approach to it." It is of course for others to judge whether what follows qualifies as a "philosophy of teaching." In fact, I doubt that it has any greater significance than a centenarian's recipe for longevity; but then, it is offered not as a guide to the perplexed, for I am among them, but rather as an account of what I think I am trying to do, and why. If it is a philosophy, I hope it also determines or at least influences my conduct as a teacher. Samuel Butler once remarked of some English church-goers that "they would have been equally horrified at hearing the Christian religion doubted, and at seeing it practised." I hope there is no comparable gap between my profession and my practice, though I am not too sanguine about that.

Let me begin with some general points. I see a distinction between teaching and education. The former seems to me but one among a variety of means of attaining the latter. Education as I understand it is a process by which one attempts to develop and perhaps reformulate his understanding of the life lived around him, and his relationship to it. Most of us do not bother to think much about that relationship, for it is in general more comfortable not to. We require some sort of stimulus or provocation before we will do so. The job of the teacher is to provide the stimulus for the effort at understanding. But the effort must be that of the student. In other words, I see my task as that of provoking my students into educating themselves. In the process, I too expect to be provoked—and to be educated.

Secondly, I should say that in my opinion the only appropriate posture for a university as an institution to take on social issues, is one of disinterested neutrality. The dominant North American concept of the university as a service institution is, to me, an abomination. It is no more the function of the university to train lawyers than it is to train warriors in the war against poverty or against Communism. In particular, I deplore the widespread tendency to treat education as an extension of the economic system, and students as potential factors of production to be processed in the interest of maximizing the growth of the gross national product. I recognize, of course, that the realities of university financing make mine an increasingly utopian view, though I see no more reason to applaud this development than I do to resort to crime because the evidence indicates that it is on the increase.

Disinterested neutrality on social issues is not, however, an appropriate position for a teacher, as a teacher. To begin with, it is a pretence. We all have opinions, if only as to the relative importance or interest of different questions. To conceal these opinions is dishonest. Moreover, to argue that teachers should not, as teachers, express their opinions, is to argue that one requires a licence to speak freely—a notion that I reject. I do have opinions, and if they relate to issues falling within the scope of my work as a teacher, I feel bound to disclose them without prevarication or ambiguity. More than this, I feel bound to assert and defend my opinions as forcefully and eloquently as I am able. I feel this obligation for two reasons. First, my opinions are important to me, and I would like others to share them. Secondly, the process of disclosure and defence seems to me sound educational practice, at least to the extent that it may stimulate my students to attempt an evaluation of my opinions and, in the process, to reconsider and refine their own. If this objective is attained, it should produce corresponding responses on my part. What all this amounts to is that I believe in the value of what is now rather faddishly referred to as the "Civilization of the Dialogue."

A number of consequences follow from this view of my role as a teacher that have practical implications for me. First, since I believe education to be a dialectical process, my effectiveness as a teacher should depend upon the persuasiveness of my arguments, rather than upon any allegedly authoritative position that I, or others, might think I occupy. Secondly, I believe that education is a co-operative process demanding reciprocal investments of time and energy from all involved. Thirdly, there are or should be no passive participants in the process; and fourthly, the dialectic can only be successfully carried on in a disciplined or, in the current argot, a "structured" form.

Let me try and explain first my view of "authority," since it is central to my understanding of my responsibilities.

There is, I think, a temptation for teachers to believe that they have a monopoly on wisdom and understanding, and to behave accordingly. In part, no doubt, this may be attributed to some special elements in the psychological make-up of a teacher. A large part of the explanation, however, lies in the fact that the community expects teachers to behave in this way. We have all been propagandized into believing that education is a process by which something is done to a student, over which he neither has nor, as many would hold, should have any control. Students come to universities to be taught, to learn, not to be educated. There seems to be a community expectation and understanding as to the nature and purposes of education which posits a completely dependent relationship between student and teacher, and involves something in the nature of a physical transfer of "knowledge" from one to the other. The teacher in this model is thus cast in an authoritative mould, and the student becomes merely a passive recipient of whatever the teacher chooses to give. This general view infects us all, and influences our perceptions of our roles.

Quite apart from this community expectation about education in general, however, there are special elements in legal education which produce an even more accentuated notion of the authority of the teacher. Lawyers, perhaps more than any other group in the community, hold closely to the view that the long continuance of an institution is evidence of its perfection. In part, this reflects the conservatism of a profession with a continuous historical tradition. But it is as well the product of a rather special view of the nature of law, held by lawyers and laymen alike, and of the somewhat special reverence in which "authority" is held by lawyers.

The method of the common lawyer is essentially historical. He looks for past analogies—precedents—to provide guides to the solution of present problems. There is a good deal to be said in favour of this method. I personally find it attractive, not only because it embodies a proper degree of caution in responding to social change, but also because it offers certain defences, albeit minimal, against caprice and arbitrary power. Unfortunately, however, the method has for a variety of reasons become perverted and distorted. What is properly a wise rule of conduct has become transformed into something akin to a biblical injunction which, affirmatively, requires a lawyer to look to the past, and, negatively, precludes him from looking elsewhere. The result is that solutions devised in other times and places are, or are said to be, completely dispositive of present problems. Lawyers cling desperately to the authority of precedent, and sanctify this perversion with the Latinism *stare decisis*—stick to what has been decided. Legal rules thus acquire an authority and an influence totally unrelated to the original reasons for their emergence, or to any content of wisdom that may inhere in them. Precedents become a substitute for thought, rather than a stimulus to it.

I recognize that the above description is in many respects a caricature. Nevertheless, like all caricatures, it contains a central core of truth. Lawyers do have an exaggerated reverence for the authority of precedent. This leads them to believe that "the law" is a body of rules of fixed and certain content which can be reduced to writing in a way which renders those rules dispositive. From this, it is but an easy step to the conclusion that the rules can be learned, and hence taught by whoever knows them. The person who knows them is thus invested with an authority almost as great as that of the rules themselves. Lawyers expect law teachers to teach the students the rules, and the students expect to be taught the rules. This misunderstanding of the nature of legal rules is a pervasive one, and is widely shared by the lay community.

It need hardly be said that this view of the nature of law is one that I totally reject. At the same time, it is important to recognize that it is a view that has a profound effect upon the expectations of law students about their legal education, and the perception which law teachers have of their roles in it. It accentuates the notion of the teacher as authority, which in any case is a seductive one to most of us, me included. It also lends support to a subservient view of the role of the student. It fosters an attitude of submissive resignation on the part of students towards their legal education, and relegates them to a passive role in it. The role that the teacher is expected to play in all this offers him a good deal of emotional security, by providing him with the comfort of an uncritical acceptance of his views. Not surprisingly, therefore, teachers are tempted to play that role for all they can.

I hope it is apparent that this view is quite hostile to the aims of education as I understand them. To my mind, it is critically important to counter the effects of the concepts of authority that I have tried to outline. My conduct as a teacher, therefore, is directed towards that objective.

It is a little difficult for me to describe what I do in this attempt, since much of it is sheer gimmickry—voice modulation, gestures, and other "bits of business" as the actors say. My style is, I think, flamboyant. I wish to communicate my own fascination with my subject. Law is fascinating to me, and legal study an exciting pastime. Moreover, I find teaching a marvellous occupation. I cannot imagine any other that could give me more pleasure. It caters to all my delusions of grandeur; it appeals to my vanity, gives me a platform for my opinions and an outlet for my verbosity and bombast. I love an audience. Teaching provides me with one. It also offers some satisfaction of my desire to do something that I think is socially useful. I try to behave myself as a teacher, therefore, in ways that maximize my own satisfactions.

All of this might be regarded as an exercise in pure self-indulgence. Perhaps it is. At the same time, however, it is central to my understanding of my role as a teacher. Some years ago the students in my department, as part of a course evaluation, described my classes as "dripping with melodrama" and me as "opinionated." I have no idea how these comments were intended. I took both as tributes. It seems to me quite unreasonable to expect others to show an interest in, or enthusiasm for, matters about which I am only half-hearted. I want to persuade my students to share my fascination with law. I therefore try to provoke, irritate, annoy, and entertain them into a sense of involvement with the subject. If they can be persuaded into doing this, whether out of annoyance at my opinionatedness, or pleasure in whatever entertainment value they may derive from my performances, they will be making a commitment to their own education. That is critically important, for it should lead them to accept the major responsibility for their education, and to recognize the necessity to assume an active role in it.

The more theatrical elements of my method are directly related to my concern for the destruction of the notion of the teacher as authority. I do not wish to be taken as asserting by this that a teacher neither has nor should have any authority. What I do intend to convey is my conviction that this authority should in the final analysis derive from his persuasiveness, not his position. It should be demonstrated, rather than completely assumed. Nor do I wish to be taken as saying that there are no differences between teachers and students, for I do not believe this. If nothing else, I have had something approaching two decades more experience than my students in studying and thinking about legal problems. That, it seems to me, entitles my opinions to at least initial respect. It does not, however, entitle them to uncritical adherence. I try to make it plain to my students that the views that I hold today are not those that I held yesterday, and that there is no more reason to assume the validity of my current opinions than my former ones.

I am aware of a certain danger in this general approach to the problems of stimulating student involvement in their education. Some years ago a colleague remarked that there are teachers who are popular for the right reasons, and those who are popular for the wrong reasons. It is difficult to articulate the difference precisely. Broadly speaking, however, I think he was making the point that very often questions of style are confused with matters of substance. I understand that I am regarded as a reasonably popular teacher, or at least that I am not regarded as an unpopular one. I worry a good deal whether this is because students find me entertaining, which I would regard as a "wrong" reason, or stimulating. I have no guarantee that the latter is the case, and I do not think I can get reliable answers by asking the students. All I can do is hope that I have a sufficient concern for matters of substance that the cultivation of style does not become an end in itself.

To some extent, of course, matters of style are related to matters of substance, and it is in connection with the latter that I am concerned with the rather special notion of authority held by lawyers and others in relation to law. Let me give a simple illustration. It is frequently asserted by courts that they have no jurisdiction to decide what are referred to as "hypothetical questions." There are innumerable cases reported in the law reports in which courts have refused to decide on precisely this basis. I could offer this proposition to my students as an unquestioned "rule" of law, and, in time-honoured lawyers' fashion, cite four or five cases in which it has been "authoritatively" stated. But this would tell them almost nothing of value. The information itself is actually quite trivial. For one thing, it tells one nothing about the nature of an hypothetical question, and in any event, it is highly unlikely that exactly the same questions would arise again in precisely the same form. Moreover, the information is misleading, for there are an equal number of reported cases in which courts have indeed answered hypothetical questions. The addition of this latter information at least indicates that courts differ over what constitutes such a question. It may also indicate that the so-called "rule" is not as authoritative, or at least is not so clear and certain in its content, as might have been hought.

But even a "definition" of the essential characteristics of hypothetical questions would be of little value, assuming such a definition were possible. It may help us to discriminate between questions which are and which are not hypothetical. It would tell us nothing, however, about why the legal system elects to deny access to its facilities to persons with some kinds of questions they wish answered, while granting access to others with different kinds of questions. That sort of issue raises immense and fascinating problems about the functions and purposes of courts, the nature of justice, and the organization of the system of government. An attempt to deal with these problems is, in my view, a proper and necessary concern of legal education. They are much more important, and much more interesting than any asserted "rule."

It may be that as a result of an approach to these problems, one might conclude that the so-called "rule" can be satisfactorily justified. It will then seem to be a persuasive rule. But its persuasiveness will be seen to rest upon its wisdom, not upon the fact that it has been repeated four times with appropriate incantations by black-robed gentlemen sitting under a Royal crest, or by its assertion in stentorian tones by a teacher posing as their apostolic delegate.

It is of course quite possible that a totally different conclusion will be reached. The "rule" may be found thoroughly unwise. That is beside the point. The point is that the participants in any discussion of that rule will have arrived at a conclusion that is authoritative to them because it is their own conclusion, not because of any arbitrary authority attached to the rule itself, or to their teacher. That is what education, in my view, is all about. I should also say that, whether or not the rule is thought by everyone to be wise, the process of analysis and consideration must lead to some understanding of the way in which society is organized. It should also, and this is important to me personally, heighten the respect for law, and thereby, one hopes, maximize what has been called its "moral impact."

I have a feeling that much of what I have written is very trite. This was probably inevitable, since I am sure that almost all teachers of law, certainly all whom I know, would share the general approach I have outlined. The differences among us, I imagine, relate largely to matters of taste and style. Such matters relate directly to variations in individual temperament and personality, rather than to educational objectives. It may be significant that I feel much more at ease standing in front of either a large group of students or talking to a single person, or perhaps two or three, than I do with a group of ten or twelve sitting around a seminar table. I have a sense that I am more effective when I feel at ease. I do not know the critical points at which I lose and regain that sense of ease. There are some groups I find too small to justify a full-scale performance, and some too large to talk quietly to. This probably indicates that my style is theatrical, outgoing, and exhibitionist. But that is almost certainly the way I am as a person. The correspondence should surprise no one. Other teachers prefer other environments.

If there is a connection between a teacher's sense of effectiveness and his effectiveness in fact, then it seems to me one of the tragedies of the way in which most universities are organized, that they do so little to provide opportunities for teachers to develop a sense of effectiveness. We are all expected to conform to a rather narrow concept of what a teacher is, and to operate within forms of organization that reflect that concept. I am fortunate in that my temperament enables me to fit within some of the existing forms. Others are far less fortunate. This does not mean that they are bad teachers—simply that they do not fit within conventional moulds. That, I think, is inevitable, given the existing community understanding of the aims of education, and given also the fact that modern universities are dominated by a very direct notion of service to the community. The result is that educational considerations are subordinated to totally extraneous pressures in the organization of universities. That may be inevitable. It is not for that reason any less a tragedy.

I wish to make one final point. The qualities of a good teacher are not in any significant sense objective. They are the product of an incredible and bewildering mixture of time and place and attitude, most of which are beyond the control of any individual. It is possible that for some students I am a good teacher. It is certain that for others I am an impossibly bad one.

LEON GETZ

A native of Cape Town, South Africa, Leon Getz took his B.A. and LL.B. degrees at the University of Cape Town. From there he proceeded to the London School of Economics where he obtained an LL.M. degree, and then to the Harvard Law School as a Ford Foundation Fellow. He qualified for a second LL.M. degree at Harvard in 1962 and in that year was appointed an instructor in law at the University of British Columbia. He became a full professor in 1970. Three years later he was appointed professor in the Faculty of Law at the University of Toronto.

His scholarly interest in corporation and commercial law is reflected in articles published in Canada, the United States, England, and South Africa. He was a member of the Federal Government's Task Force on Corporate Law Reform, 1967–69, and of a three-man group which prepared the final report and recommendations to the Minister of Corporate and Consumer Affairs in 1971. His interests have recently extended into the machinery of justice (especially civil justice) and judicial administration.

During the year 1970–71 Professor Getz was on leave from UBC to act as counsel to the Law Reform Commission of British Columbia.

Reports from his UBC students indicate that Professor Getz was appreciated as a "sympathetic, much-travelled, understanding individual," always available for private discussion. He had a grasp of and interest in his subject, a rational and logical approach, clarity of speech and precision in delivery, and was always prepared for his lectures.

He placed heavy emphasis on the social development of law, referred frequently to decisions and trends in other jurisdictions and countries, and stressed the overall effect of the law on society in general rather than its effect on the legal profession alone. Related to this was his interest in current social problems and the solutions offered by legal institutions. "His research on any point of law which concerned him was exhaustive and well documented."

In class he was informal and encouraged discussion, even in large groups. He made effective use of the Socratic style of teaching.

Le métier est parfois ardu

Jacques-Yvan Morin

L'enseignement universitaire est un "métier" en lui-même, quelle que soit la discipline professée. J'entends par là que tel excellent ingénieur ne fera pas nécessairement un bon professeur de Génie, ni tel grand avocat ou juge un bon professeur de Droit, quoique l'exception vienne parfois confirmer la règle. L'ingénieur et l'avocat doivent entretenir des rapports quotidiens avec des clients et, à l'occasion, persuader une société ou un tribunal de la justesse de leur point de vue, tandis que l'enseignant de niveau universitaire doit *communiquer* ses connaissances à de jeunes hommes et à de jeunes femmes dont certains sortent à peine de l'adolescence, dans le but non seulement de les *informer*, mais surtout de leur *former* l'esprit.

Le professeur universitaire, s'il veut exceller, doit donc, avant tout, posséder naturellement, ou acquérir, une certaine tournure d'esprit, une aptitude à établir des contacts spontanés avec un milieu jeune et à s'adapter à l'évolution de plus en plus rapide de ce milieu. En second lieu, il doit trouver les méthodes pédagogiques qui conviennent le mieux à la discipline qu'il enseigne. Bien sûr, il doit également faire autorité dans son domaine et même se tenir à la pointe du savoir, mais toute la science du professeur, fût-elle la plus profonde, ne saurait être communiquée de manière efficace, même au niveau universitaire, sans ces dispositions naturelles et ces qualités pédagogiques. Telle est du moins la leçon que m'ont appris vingt ans de vie universitaire au Québec, en Europe et aux Etats-Unis, dont une quinzaine en tant qu'enseignant.

Ce n'est un secret pour personne que la vague de contestation qui a secoué les universités depuis deux ou trois ans ne visait pas seulement l'institution elle-même et la société en général, mais également, dans biens des cas, les professeurs et leurs méthodes d'enseignement. On a même vu des groupes d'étudiants réclamer l'abolition de tel enseignement en particulier, pour le motif que, selon eux, la matière était "inutile" ou sans intérêt. Certes, les remontrances étudiantes étaient le plus souvent adressées aux professeurs en tant qu'administrateurs de facultés ou départements et représentants des autorités, mais il est arrivé que les étudiants prennent à parti les programmes, le contenu d'un cours, les méthodes pédagogiques, les examens, et même les personnes. Pour certains enseignants, tout a paru remis en question, y compris leur présence à l'université, et les désillusions engendrées par ces critiques n'ont épargné ni les professeurs chevronnés ni les jeunes universitaires.

La contestation étudiante n'avait point l'université pour seul motif ou objet. Dans certains cas, il semble bien qu'on s'en soit pris aux enseignants parce que les étudiants n'avaient personne d'autre sous la main. Les professeurs ont quelquefois été perçus comme les symboles de la société contestée parce qu'ils étaient le plus directement en contact avec les jeunes et qu'au demeurant, ils étaient relativement sans défense; il suffisait qu'ils parussent accepter un peu trop passivement les défauts de la société pour en devenir les porte-parole aux yeux du monde étudiant. On ne saurait donc mettre un terme aux difficultés actuelles dans l'université en modifiant seulement les méthodes pédagogiques ou le contenu de l'enseignement. Néanmoins, je suis convaincu, pour avoir vécu les événements des dernières années dans plus d'une université, qu'on eût pu améliorer sensiblement le climat entre étudiants et enseignants et même faire profiter l'ensemble de la société de tous les éléments positifs que recelait la contestation, si les universitaires avaient eu une conception plus claire et plus dynamique de leur rôle social, des attitudes plus ouvertes à l'endroit des étudiants et une pédagogie mieux adaptée aux circonstances nouvelles.

Dans le monde vers lequel nous nous dirigeons à grands pas, toute fonction sociale, économique, ou politique et toute position d'autorité, devront constamment être justifiées, tant sur le plan des objectifs poursuivis que sur celui de la compétence de la personne occupant la position. L'autorité ne se suffit plus à elle-même, elle devient essentiellement fonctionnelle. Or, cela me paraît vrai dans l'université comme dans toutes les sphères de la vie collective. Qui plus est, ce phénomène se manifeste d'abord à l'université, avant d'envahir la société tout entière. Il appartient donc aux universitaires de comprendre sa signification et tout le renouveau qui peut en découler pour peu qu'ils sachent aider les étudiants à transformer leur refus plus ou moins cohérent du système socio-économique et politique en une volonté raisonnée de changement. Cela me paraît d'autant plus important dans une faculté de Droit, où le conformisme le plus béat peut succéder aux élans rénovateurs les plus généreux, dès que l'étudiant entre dans la vie professionnelle. Ces considérations nous ramènent aux dispositions naturelles et aux qualités pédagogiques que doit posséder l'universitaire enseignant.

Parmi les dispositions "naturelles" les plus importantes, je compte celle qui consiste à aimer se trouver en compagnie des étudiants, sans la moindre affectation de supériorité. Cet attachement pour le milieu étudiant, qui est une forme de respect, n'est malheureusement pas le fait de tous les universitaires; quant à la condescendance, les étudiants intelligents ne peuvent la souffrir et, à mon avis, ils ont parfaitement raison. J'ai connu des enseignants qui méprisaient plus ou moins consciemment leurs auditoires étudiants et ceux-ci le leur rendaient. Dans l'enseignement, l'autorité a peut-être appartenu, dans le passé, à ceux qui jetaient des foudres, mais aujourd'hui, elle ne peut tenir qu'à la compétence du professeur, à l'intérêt, voire à l'enthousiasme, qu'il témoigne pour sa discipline et à la sympathie qui s'établit graduellement entre son auditoire et lui-même. Combien est subtile cette influence dont jouit le professeur auprès de ses étudiants. Elle ne repose point sur l'emploi de grands mots ou le port de la toge (il y a bien longtemps qu'on ne la porte plus que pour les portraits officiels et des cérémonies qui se font de plus en plus rares). Même le piédestal sur lequel sont élevés les professeurs européens n'impressionne plus guère.

Je me rappelle très bien les qualités qui m'ont frappé chez mes propres professeurs: la compétence, certes, mais aussi la sensibilité aux facteurs métajuridiques, une attitude d'accueil à l'égard de nos questions, fussent-elles maladroitement énoncées, enfin l'indépendance d'esprit qui n'excluait point l'engagement devant les problèmes sociaux et politiques de l'heure. L'un de ces professeurs, un Anglo-Canadien, soulevait beaucoup d'intérêt, tant par ses leçons sur le droit constitutionnel que par ses digressions, et l'ascendant qu'il avait pris sur sa classe était considérable. Il nous élevait à la hauteur de ses vues, nous montrait des horizons plus clairs, emportait notre adhésion par des appels à la raison empreints d'une fougue contenue. Son autorité, en fin de compte, tenait au fait que nous en arrivions inconsciemment à nous identifier à ce genre d'homme, même si parfois nous ne pouvions partager telle ou telle de ses idées. Mon admiration pour ce professeur demeure profonde après vingt ans, même si nous en sommes venus à défendre des thèses opposées au sujet de l'avenir politique du Québec. Nous avons eu, à l'occasion, des explications assez vives sur la question, mais rien ne saurait altérer le fait que je lui dois sans doute pour une bonne part ma vocation d'enseignant.

L'autorité morale du professeur n'a rien à voir avec la complaisance envers les étudiants. Certains enseignants qui éprouvent des difficultés avec leur auditoire pensent conjurer le sort en se montrant moins exigeants ou en transformant leur cours en une suite de galéjades. Bien sûr, une plaisanterie qui tombe à propos peut détendre l'atmosphère, mais le genre est difficile. Rien n'est si sournois que le rire des complaisants et il n'en manque jamais dans le sillage d'un enseignant. Si certains universitaires pouvaient entendre les commentaires de leurs auditeurs au sujet de leur "esprit" et s'ils savaient le mépris qu'ont les étudiants pour les cours “faciles” (même s'ils ont quelque fois la faiblesse de les rechercher), ils tomberaient des nues.

Il est vrai que le métier est parfois ardu, voire ingrat, surtout lorsque les classes comportent un trop grand nombre d'individus qui ne sont pas encore sortis de leur rébellion contre le père. Il suffit alors qu'un enseignant soit un peu terne pour voir se retourner contre lui toutes les révoltes inassouvies de l'adolescence. Il faut en prendre son parti, puisqu'aussi bien les nouvelles structures de l'enseignement nous valent un rajeunissement permanent du milieu étudiant. De surcroît, on voit maintenant arriver à l'université toute une génération de jeunes pour lesquels la télévision a été un moyen d'éducation quotidien. Ils ont pris l'habitude de tourner le bouton lorsque le programme ne leur paraît pas suffisamment intéressant. De là à faire sentir à leurs professeurs le peu d'intérêt qu'ils portent à certains cours, il n'y a qu'un pas, lequel est franchi plus rapidement aujourd'hui qu'il y a dix ans.

Pourtant, la quantité des connaissances qui doivent être transmises ne fait qu'augmenter et toutes ne se prêtent point également à des exposés “vivants.” C'est alors que les dispositions naturelles de l'enseignant ne suffisent plus et qu'il faut faire appel aux ressources de la pédagogie. D'une manière générale, le nouveau climat exige que les cours s'effectuent le plus possible sur le ton du dialogue, “les yeux dans les yeux.” La lecture des notes doit être confinée aux définitions les plus ardues, aux passages qu'il convient de citer textuellement—et encore! Un cours lu est un cours mort et il vaut mieux avoir recours à la polycopie pour les textes essentiels.

La préparation d'un cours exige sans doute plus de temps qu'autrefois, du point de vue de la présentation. J'ai connu un collègue qui se vantait de n'avoir point à relire ses notes avant chaque leçon; il se contentait de débiter textuellement chaque année ses savants commentaires. A l'époque, il se tirait d'affaire, mais il y a trois ou quatre ans, il sentit de lui-même que le moment était venue de quitter l'enseignement. Naguère, nous nous scandalisions du manque de préparation d'un professeur, mais nous nous résignions à le subir, quitte à nous payer copieusement sa tête; les étudiants d'aujourd'hui n'ont plus cette patience et je ne suis pas prêt à leur donner tort.

Il ne sert à rien de tempêter, quoique l'explosion de colère d'un professeur respecté puisse à l'occasion produire quelque effet. Il y a d'ailleurs toutes sortes de chahuts et j'en ai connu de fort sympathiques. A quel universitaire n'est-il pas arrivé de glisser dans sa leçon une idée insolite, voire saugrenue, dans le but de provoquer ses étudiants? Le vacarme qui s'ensuit prouve au moins que ceux-ci sont attentifs et si, par hasard, l'idée était proposée sérieusement, le professeur sait qu'il doit la retourner davantage. . . .

Dans toute classe, il se trouve inévitablement quelques individus dont on se demande ce qu'ils font là. Il y a celui qui lit son journal dans la vingtième rangée, ceux qui se remettent de la veille, celui qui étudie minutieusement ses voisines et, parfois, celles qui ne demandent pas mieux. Tout ce petit monde est vite répéré par l'enseignant qui n'a pas les yeux rivés sur ses notes. Quelques regards soutenus suffisent généralement à rétablir la communication avec les esprits égarés, surtout lorsque l'auditoire sait par expérience que le professeur n'hésitera point à se saisir de la première occasion pour se payer la tête des récalcitrants. Cela exige évidemment une certaine présence d'esprit car il faut toujours avoir les rieurs de son côté en de telles circonstances. D'autre part, il faut se garder d'un humour blessant car tel étudiant qui se laisse aller à la rêverie n'est pas nécessairement le plus bête, ni le moins intéressé à la matière. En fait, il convient de n'intervenir que si un étudiant dérange ses voisins.

L'idéal serait de connaître personnellement chaque étudiant, comme cela était encore possible il y a une dizaine d'années. L'augmentation des effectifs, conséquence nécessaire de la démocratisation de l'enseignement, nous donne maintenant des classes de trois à cinq cents étudiants, que nous divisons en deux ou trois groupes, selon le nombre d'enseignants disponibles. Les leçons se donnent devant cent cinquante ou deux cents étudiants que nous ne voyons que pendant un semestre ou deux, au niveau de la Licence. Pour peu qu'on doive s'occuper également d'une vingtaine d'étudiants de Maîtrise, il devient impossible de suivre chaque étudiant de Licence et de l'aider dans ses difficultés propres, à moins que les professeurs ne se partagent le groupe. Quoique l'on fasse, on se trouve toujours devant la nécessité de capter durablement l'attention de personnes que l'on connaît peu.

Néanmoins, la chose est possible, même devant un auditoire de deux cents étudiants, si le dialogue peut être établi. Pour qu'il en soit ainsi, la première condition est que l'enseignant puisse regarder chaque étudiant dans le blanc des yeux. Rien ne m'est plus pénible que ces amphithéâtres sans fond où l'on distingue à peine les figures des étudiants assis dans les dernières rangées. L'expérience m'a enseigné, même, que l'on communique difficilement avec les esprits errant au delà de la quinzième rangée, surtout dans nos sombres amphis modernes, pour lesquels on a poussé le souci du vase clos jusqu'à supprimer les fenêtres. Je n'ai résolu cette difficulté qu'en faisant semblant d'accrocher des yeux à peine visibles. Peut-être cela suffit-il, mais la technique en est malaisée.

Les yeux étant captés, le dialogue peut s'engager. A mon avis, il faut consacrer le quart ou le tiers de chaque leçon aux commentaires et aux questions des étudiants, en prenant soin d'exiger que l'intervenant se fasse entendre clairement de toute la salle. Loin d'être une "perte de temps," l'interruption, dont les étudiants savent d'avance que je n'y donnerai suite qu'après avoir terminé l'énoncé d'une idée, stimule l'intérêt et valorise son auteur; lorsque les étudiants prennent confiance, elle tourne souvent à la conversation, les mains se levant à gauche et à droite. Lorsque deux ou trois étudiants tirent d'eux-mêmes les conclusions ou soulèvent les questions auxquelles je veux en venir, j'estime que je n'ai pas perdu mon temps. Ceux que la timidité empêchent de participer apprennent du moins des autres à penser par eux-mêmes; on voit souvent à leurs yeux qu'ils n'ont rien perdu. Il n'est d'ailleurs pas rare, après quelques semaines, de voir intervenir, timidement au début, de nouvelles figures. Quelquefois, il faut susciter l'intervention: "Mademoiselle, visiblement, vous n'êtes pas d'accord . . ." Il m'est arrivé de provoquer ainsi de véritables déflagrations d'opinions.

Certes, les questions soulevées ne sont pas toujours du plus grand intérêt, mais elles sont rarement sottes. Il faut prendre soin de souligner les interventions heureuses: "Voilà une observation juste, une bonne question." Pour les autres, il suffit de répondre en une phrase, sans commentaires; tout le monde a saisi à demi-mot, y compris l'intéressé. Après deux semaines de ce régime, la qualité et la pertinence des interventions s'améliore nettement. Si elles se font trop nombreuses, il ne faut point hésiter à les limiter. Quand le dialogue s'est vraiment instauré dans une classe, le professeur peut manifester ses exigences et celles de son programme sans la moindre difficulté.

Il en est de mon enseignement, qui porte sur le droit international, comme de plusieurs autres: il risque d'être fort abstrait si l'on n'y prend garde. La reconnaissance *de jure*, la succession d'Etats, la théorie des compétences, la clause *rebus sic stantibus*, et la querelle entre les tenants de l'universalité et ceux de l'intégrité des traités sont des expressions peu familières aux étudiants de première année. Aussi faut-il avoir recours à des définitions faites de mots communs et à de nombreux exemples. L'actualité en fournit constamment un bon nombre et ces références sont d'excellents moyens d'habituer les étudiants à se tenir au courant des événements internationaux et à comprendre les rapports entre le droit et les faits, entre la matière étudiée et le monde réel. Les plus actifs arrivent bientôt au cours avec des découpures de journaux qui constituent à l'occasion d'excellents points de départ pour la discussion.

L'enseignant doit être au courant des tout derniers développements dans sa discipline. Il prend un grand risque s'il se contente de répéter le cours de l'année précédente. Quelle déconvenue que celle du professeur à qui l'étudiant laborieux fait observer que la jurisprudence qu'il commente a été renversée en appel le mois précédent! Toutes les parties d'un cours ne peuvent être aussi fouillées les unes que les autres, mais chaque année doit amener quelques coups de sonde plus profonds dans diverses parties de la matière. A cet égard, rien ne m'a valu les écrits par lesquels j'ai tenté de faire le tour de quelques aspects fondamentaux de ma discipline. Les heures passées à lire et à refléchir comptent, en rétrospective, parmi les plus importantes de ma vie d'universitaire. Il n'y a point d'enseignement fécond sans recherches constantes.

Dans cet ordre d'idées, il me faut dire deux mots de l'année "sabbatique," qui fort heureusement commence à s'implanter dans nos facultés. Il y aurait beaucoup à dire en faveur de l'extension de ce congé à toutes les sphères de la société, mais il me suffira de constater qu'il est essentiel à l'universitaire après quelques années d'enseignement. Professer signifie transmettre un patrimoine d'idées et d'interrogations, donner à l'étudiant tout ce que l'on a pu découvrir. Aussi l'universitaire ressent-il le besoin de "faire le plein" après quelque temps, surtout s'il assume un programme chargé. En ce qui me concerne, je sais, pour en avoir bénéficié, tout ce qu'une année passée dans une université étrangère peut apporter de renouveau dans la pensée et dans l'enseignement.

Sur plus d'un point, j'ai découvert pendant ce congé fécond, que mes idées et mes méthodes tombaient en désuétude. J'en suis revenu avec des préoccupations plus vastes, un programme de recherches sur les rapports entre le progrès technique et le droit ainsi qu'un nouveau cours pour mes étudiants de Maîtrise. Que mes collègues de toutes les disciplines n'hésitent point à prendre un congé sabbatique, si possible à l'étranger, même s'ils craignent de n'y point trouver tout le confort dont nous avons l'habitude dans ce pays. Leurs étudiants seront les premiers à en bénéficier à leur retour.

Nul plus que l'enseignant, sans doute, n'éprouve le sentiment d'être une charnière entre les générations. De nos jours, la transmission des connaissances devient un métier constamment plus complexe et plus exigeant, mais qui n'en propose pas moins des satisfactions profondes à ceux qui acceptent ce rôle de charnière entre la vieille sagesse et les interrogations toujours renouvelées de la jeunesse.

Le contenu des programmes changera et les méthodes pédagogiques évolueront, mais le rapport enseigné-enseignant sera toujours nécessaire au progrès, tant moral que scientifique, de l'humanité. Dans la sphère bien réduite du savoir qui est la mienne, j'éprouve le besoin de contribuer au progrès de la société dont je fais partie, quoique j'admette que mon travail ne soit pas spectaculaire et ne puisse porter fruit qu'à long terme. Si je n'avais le sentiment de remplir ainsi un rôle essentiel, je ferais autre chose.

JACQUES-YVAN MORIN

Jacques-Yvan Morin est né à Québec. Il a préparé son baccalauréat au Collège Stanislas, relevant de l'Université de Paris, puis il a fréquenté l'Université McGill, où il a été reçu "Bachelor of Civil Law" (B.C.L.) en 1952. Il a obtenu sa Maîtrise (LL.M.) du "Law Institute of the Americas," (Dallas) et de l'Université Harvard. Il a obtenu le "Diploma in International Law" de l'Université de Cambridge. Il fut admis au Barreau du Québec en 1953.

M. Morin est entré en 1957 à la Faculté de droit de l'Université de Montréal, où son enseignement porte sur le droit international public. Il était professeur invité à l'Institut des Hautes Etudes internationales de l'Université de Paris en 1961, 1967 et 1970, et à l'Institut Européen des Hautes Etudes internationales de Nice en 1969–1970. De 1963 à

1967 il fut membre de la Cour permanente d'arbitrage, à La Haye.

Parmi ses cours publiés figurent L'État fédéral en droit international *(1962),* La pollution des eaux en regard du droit international *(1967) et* La pollution des mers et le droit *(1970). Il est rédacteur en chef adjoint de* l'Annuaire canadien de droit international *pour lequel il a écrit de nombreux articles. Il a collaboré autrefois à la revue* Cité Libre *et, plus récemment, à la revue* Maintenant.

De 1966 à 1970, M. Morin fut président des Etats généraux du Canada français et dans la campagne électorale en 1970, il fut (sans être élu) candidat du Parti Québécois. En annonçant sa candidature il déclara:

> *Toute mon action depuis quelques années a été inspirée par cette sorte de patriotisme qui veut préserver la nation en tant que moyen d'accès à l'universel. Pour cela, j'ai milité, depuis les bancs de l'université, pour les droits individuels et collectifs, ainsi que pour une véritable démocratie économique. En entrant au Parti Québécois, loin de renoncer à ces idéaux, j'y ajoute une idée qui donne une dimension nouvelle à toutes les autres, parce qu'elle constitue le moyen privilégié de les mettre en oeuvre; l'indépendance du Québec, complétée par une vigoureuse participation à la société internationale.* (Le Devoir, *23 mars 1970*)

A l'élection du 29 octobre 1973, il a été élu dans la circonscription montréalaise de Sauvé et il est devenu Chef de l'Opposition à l'Assemblée Nationale du Québec.

Ses anciens élèves ont commenté la connaissance étendue qu'il possède de sa discipline, à l'importance de laquelle il croit profondément. Il a un "style oratoire de premier ordre" mais il "ne devait pas sa réputation de professeur brillant seulement à son éloquence séduisante. Il se sert de son magnétisme personnel pour capter une attention soutenue de ses étudiants."

Selon les diplômés, ses cours étaient bien structurés et logiques, et d'une préparation soigneuse. Les exemples affluaient. Son cours de Droit international public devenait aussi une leçon d'histoire contemporaine; "il tenait à nous inviter à la vie internationale." "Il recherchait constamment des solutions nouvelles aux problèmes politiques, sociaux et juridiques."

Le professeur Morin "nous inondait de bons textes, ce qui nous forçait à lire." Il admettait volontiers les questions et respectait les opinions des étudiants, et "il avait le sens de l'humour, en plus d'être un excellent pédagogue."

Gambits and Gimmicks

Jan W. Steiner

It is difficult to analyse my lecture technique, because I have become convinced over the years that this is the least rewarding and effective method of instructional communication. If, indeed, my students considered me adequate as a lecturer, I must attribute this to my theatrical talents and antics and the receptiveness of the audiences whom I confronted, rather than the content of my lectures. I can make this assertion justifiably, because I have given the same lectures to audiences who responded little, or not at all, to the presentation. This brings me then to my initial conclusion: unless a rapport exists or rapidly develops between audience and lecturer, the outcome is likely to be a fiasco. A chance remark in small group teaching often creates empathy. For example, when talking to a group about a condition known as hourglass stomach, I was asked what the cause of the condition was and I replied promptly: "Eating sand." Understanding between this group and myself was established from then on.

For large group teaching, I usually try to invent an incisive or dramatic opening gambit. I never enter a lecture hall without making sure that my dandruff is brushed off my shoulders and my zipper fastened. I first give the audience for at least a few minutes a chance to adapt to seeing me on the podium—the shock might otherwise interfere with our communication. When I confront an audience of 200 twenty-one to twenty-three year-old students I might start by saying: "All right boys and girls, can we begin?" If I have knowledge of a love affair between two students, I might begin with: "Silence please. Would Mr. Jones kindly avoid making such loud smacking noises when kissing Miss Smith." Apparently a mild insult or a slightly amusing remark on a topic of common knowledge in the class creates an atmosphere which is immediately receptive. The jokes may be puerile, but they attain the desired goal.

It is worth stressing at this point that, whereas mild insults serve their purpose, certain comments are taboo. For example, I have found that I could not make a disparaging remark about doctors to an audience of students aspiring to become physicians. I interpret this to mean that no insult, however trivial and inconsequential, directed toward the pristine pivot of a student's motivation, is permissible. I have found, for example, that in administering autopsy material to a group and remarking on the butchery of a surgeon who brought the patient to his demise, I encountered deaf ears, and at times, an incredulous or even hostile reaction, although my allegation may have been correct. However, once I have established good rapport with a class, I can make such remarks with impunity and often to advantage.

I watch my audience very carefully for signs of restlessness which I interpret as evidence that I am faltering in my presentation and not holding the attention and interest of my class. If I notice students turning to look at the classroom clock, fidgeting, or engaging in surreptitious conversations, I take immediate corrective steps. I might say "Are you becoming aware of your ischial tuberosities?" or "I see you are getting tired. Do you wish me to stop now?" I have yet to find a class who answer in the affirmative. A joke, if successful, might break the monotony sufficiently to allow me to resume without a recurrence of the problem, for perhaps as long as half an hour.

I have found great advantage in using archaic or anachronistic terms or proverbs. To indicate indignation I use the phrase: "My hackles quiver." I use metaphorical mixers to spice the presentation: "I warn you that what you will hear from me is only the distant rumbling of the handwriting on the wall." "When you boil it right down to brass tacks" or "If you continue believing this nonsense, I will give you a look which you can pour on a waffle." I will even descend to doggerel in order to make a point: "A lisping lass should not be kissed, lest you get infectiouth mononucleothith."

I use visual aids extensively, since the material I present lends itself readily to this approach. I draw on a blackboard, often in a bizarre manner, until the whole surface is covered in hieroglyphics to the point that I cannot find my way around in the maze. This has become my hallmark to such an extent that I will sometimes demolish a blackboard before I even start my lecture and announce to my students that I have done so to save time. In other words, the blackboard serves as a backdrop rather than any useful purpose. I often project 35mm. slides. Habitually, I will insert a picture of a naked woman in a suggestive posture in the middle of a presentation on liver disease and then blame my wife for having interfered with my filing system.

I feel that, in part at least, my success is based upon a careful preparation of each lecture. I often try out lectures for size on audiences who should understand what I am trying to say. Other members of my department have often been subjected to this ill-treatment. In general, this approach tends to sharpen my perception of the weaknesses of the presentation. I often treat my wife to this narcissistic display. I gauge the success of such presentations by her reaction; if she appears bored I know the presentation is up to my usual standard.

I have three essential requirements which I consider the sine qua non of success:

1. I love working with students and I consider it truly worthwhile to instruct them. This makes for an appreciation of their problems and enables me to communicate with them better.
2. Enthusiasm for my discipline seems an essential prerequisite. I believe that I have something worthwhile to present to a future doctor, even though I know that much of what I am presenting is, in fact, rubbish and likely as not to be untrue within a very short time.
3. I try to preserve my sense of humour in front of an audience in any circumstances, however traumatic. Under no conditions do I show my devastation when my audience decides to boo me.

JAN W. STEINER

Jan Steiner was born in Moravia. His medical studies at Charles University in Prague were interrupted by the German invasion in 1939, and for the next two years he served in the French Army and the Czechoslovak Regiment of the British Army. After being invalided out of service, he continued his studies at the University of Liverpool and qualified as a Doctor of Medicine in 1943, the degree being awarded by the University of Oxford on behalf of the Czechoslovak universities.

He took postgraduate training in pathology and then practised for ten years in England before emigrating to Canada in 1955. He became a fellow of the Royal College of Physicians of Canada in 1966.

His first appointment at the University of Toronto was as a fellow in pathology in 1957. He became pathologist at the Toronto General Hospital in 1964, professor of pathology at the University in 1965, and associate dean of the Faculty of Medicine a year later.

An active research worker throughout his career, Dr. Steiner's investigations during recent years have dealt largely with various aspects of experimental liver injury. Research articles of which he was joint author have appeared in the leading medical journals of North America and Europe. He received the Starr Medal for Medical Research at the University of Toronto in 1962. He is a member of the editorial boards of Chemico-Biological Interactions *and* Virchow's Archives.

Pathology was his teaching field during the period covered by graduates' comments. In both 1964 and 1966 he won the Silver Shovel, an award given annually by the Undergraduate Medical Society of the University to the professor judged to be the best clinical teacher of the year.

Dr. Steiner's former students used such words as these to describe him: vivid, enthusiastic, energetic, vigorous, dynamic, magnetic, dramatic, flamboyant, unorthodox. He impressed them with his extensive knowledge of his subject, his clear, systematic, spontaneous presentations, his emphasis on essentials (leaving students to look up the details), and his ability to synthesize masses of information—some of it conflicting.

His sense of humour was mentioned over and over again. It permeated his lecture sessions. Some of his jokes were said to be corny, but they helped him to make his points. "One actually can visualize in one's mind a particular lecture to recall a fact, and I can still do so for some," testified one practitioner. "When today I see a patient with hepatitis I hear his words explaining the liver structure," reported another.

Most of the graduates' comments were about Professor Steiner in the lecture room before a large class, often using diagrams and slides. In small seminars, though, he was effective in "relating pathological specimens to the signs and symptoms in clinical medicine." In this setting he taught "by questions as much as by talking."

He treated students as "reasonably mature" adults and had good rapport with them. His sincerity was convincing. "If he had one aim it appeared to be to create a more knowledgeable, efficient Canadian physician."

Education Is a Love Affair

Douglas Waugh

It has been said by some anonymous sage that whenever a scientist does not understand the interrelations of complex phenomena, he disposes of the problem by writing them all down and drawing arrows between them. This gives the illusion of both profundity and simplicity that allows him to live with his problem and even to appear to understand it. Here then is my diagram of the essence of teaching:

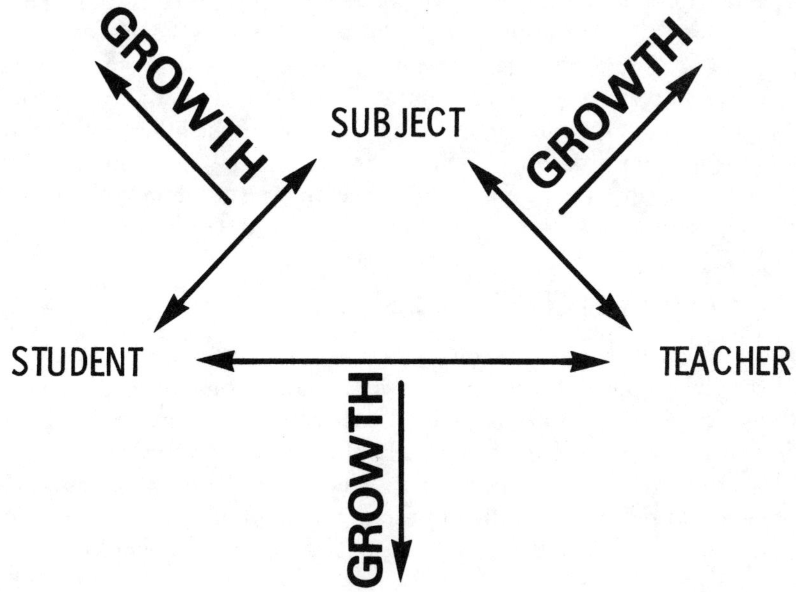

Viewed this way, the educational process is really quite simple and easy to understand. The student, teacher, and subject each react with one another and, if the reaction is successful, each of the three relationships acquires the capacity for independent growth.

As I ponder my diagram, it brings into focus a number of aspects of the teacher-learning process of which I may have been dimly aware, but never saw with any clarity before. The first is that the whole process, if it is to be effective, should ideally be one of centrifugal and symmetrical growth, i.e. the relationships must remain more or less balanced.

Growth of course implies a system that is animate rather than inert. In this respect it should be noted that each of the apices of my educational growth triangle is (or should be) alive and constantly changing. Subjects, as well as teachers and students, can grow and metamorphose with great rapidity or may suffer atrophy, or even death.

The three-way relationship thus becomes one involving complex and partly independent variables, each subject to both external and internal influences. This is more easily perceived if each corner of the triangle is seen as part of another triangle, and so on *ad infinitum*. Such a complex of semi-independent variables conspires to make symmetrical growth unlikely and places a burden of responsibility on both teacher and student to maintain a balanced relationship with each other and with the flexibility of their subject. It thus becomes a major responsibility for the teacher to foster and catalyze the development of adaptability in the student while accepting the need for this quickly to become an independent process. To achieve any success in this (and success will always be limited) he will need every resource at his disposal and must be prepared to exploit every bit of luck that comes his way.

While most educators look upon the relationship between student and teacher as the very essence of the educational process, good teaching is unlikely if there is not also considerable three-way interaction between teacher, student, and subject matter. This interaction should in each case be one where each derives some benefit from the other two. I want to proceed now from this broad outline to an analysis of some of the factors I consider important in the development (or inhibition) of each of the relationships I have outlined.

The Teacher-Subject Relationship

Ideally a teacher should be on terms of intimacy with his subject. This is not always possible and some of my unhappiest moments have been those occasions when I have had to teach relatively unfamiliar material. In general, the greater the teacher's familiarity with and affection for his subject the better he will perform. It is no coincidence that poets reach their lyrical best when writing of their loves, and so it is with teaching. I am wary of the man who says, "I don't care what assignment I'm given,

I'll be able to handle it." He is like one who sleeps only with prostitutes and never learns about love.

The ideal relationship between a man and his subject is one in which he is an active participant in its evolution. In science this is likely to be by way of research, although it may also be achieved through writings, or the development of better curricula or by some other means. However it comes about, such a man is likely to be a better teacher than one who only takes from his subject and gives nothing in return. Alas, in most of our professional schools there are far too few of such teachers and much teaching must be done by those who are not participants in the field of their teaching. An opposite type is also too common—the "teacher" who is so preoccupied with his researches and scholarly activities that he has no time for or interest in teaching. It cannot be expected that students will become excited about a subject if they are thus shielded from those who are part of its dynamism. Unhappily, even if all of our researchers and writers were active in teaching, there would still not be enough of them. Academic administrators and granting agencies could however do more, on the one hand to foster scholarly pursuits and on the other to ensure that those so engaged are selected at least partly on the basis of their interest in teaching.

It does not of course follow automatically that a researcher will be a successful teacher. If he is unable to perceive that minutiae that are important to him may have little relevance for students, if he is excessively cynical about his scientific colleagues or if he gives the impression that only his great brain can truly comprehend so complex a subject he will win no popularity contests and may turn student interest away from the subject.

I do not mean to suggest that a teacher should *never* deal in minutiae or be cynical or be occasionally impressed by his own cerebration. Indeed, lapses of this sort if not too frequent can perhaps better display the human imperfections of the teacher and allow students to see him as a creature of foible even as they know themselves to be. This sort of thing is a delicate matter and probably cannot be contrived. The total effect of the teaching process whether or not it includes exposures of the teacher's human frailties must reflect a clear understanding by the teacher of the place of his subject in the broad context of his students' needs and aspirations. Only in this way can teaching and the teacher have relevance.

A few teachers are able to sense their relevance instinctively and with great accuracy. A great many more believe they have this ability, or that they "know best what is good for the student." It is rare, I believe, for such teachers to be correct in this attitude which has the unhappy effect of convincing them that feedback from students is unimportant.

This brings me to another phase of good teaching that I consider an essential ingredient. This is the need for the teacher to *know* the impact of his work. I do not mean that he should merely note class performance on his examinations, although this is part of it. He must also learn from his students how the things he does affect their learning, whether they feel needs he is not meeting and whether they see irrelevancies not apparent to him. If he is to do this effectively, he must be prepared for criticism as well as praise and must find ways of putting his students at ease when they approach him with problems. This they are likely to do if he is willing to discuss matters with them in rational terms, argue when appropriate and acquiesce gracefully when students are able to present a case with more logic than his own. Probably in the majority of instances, the teacher's view will prevail or at least it should if there is any validity to the view that universities exist because some people know more than others. More often than not, though by no means always, it should be the teacher who knows more.

The Student-Subject Relationship

The interaction between the student and his subject may seem to have little to do with the role of the teacher, yet if it doesn't exist both learning and teaching will be inhibited. Many students are enrolled in courses in which they have had little or no prior interest and in such cases the student's only objective is to get rid of the subject by achieving a passing grade. In medical school such attitudes are common and usually derive from the student's estimate of the practical value of the subject in relation to the kind of career he is planning for himself. Thus the budding surgeon may decide that laboratory classes are of no use to him, or the embryo psychiatrist may find little to interest him in his surgery or pathology courses.

While the correctness of such assumptions can be argued, this serves little purpose. It is clearly asking too much to expect all students to fall in love with, or even be attracted to, all subjects. In a professional faculty such as medicine, all that can be assumed is that all students are attracted to *some* of the subjects. The acceptance of this simple assumption by teachers can help to clarify their role and also to reduce their frustrations.

As I see it, the teacher's role in the context of the student-to-subject relationship is that of facilitating mutual attraction, of providing a suitable environment for seduction, while recognizing that other unions may prove more attractive to the student. Such a teacher will be aware of the need to present his subject as favourably as possible, yet in such a way that it appeals to both the committed and the uncommitted student. His success in this can be measured in part by shifts in students to the committed group, but also by the reactions of tolerance or interest he arouses in those who remain uncommitted.

The good teacher must recognize and accept the fact that not all (or even a majority) of his students will embark on a love affair with his subject. If he shows lack of interest in or resentment toward students who fail to be attracted, or directs his teaching only to those who are, he is likely to enjoy only limited success with a small group of students. Those who cannot be lovers should at least be friends and the teacher must show as much interest in the latter group as in the former.

The Student-Teacher Relationship

This is the focal point of most discussions of the education process and has obviously been part of the foregoing discussion. If we are given a situation where the teacher is active in the growth and development of his subject and where students approach it with interest or even a willingness for involvement, then the successful outcome of the educational process is largely determined by the interaction between student and teacher. *This is one of the most delicate and precious relationships in human society and indeed upon it rests the very survival of society.* If all students and all teachers could accept the implications of this statement, the overall quality of both teaching and learning would improve immeasurably. By this I mean that each should accept responsibility for knowing and understanding the other in their relationship to the subject and each must recognize that the other has something to teach him. Where each, for whatever reason, regards the flow between them as being mainly or exclusively one-way there will be little growth and that which occurs will be parasitic.

To say this is not to advocate academic anarchy or even revolution but rather to press for the reversion of the University to its traditional pattern as a community of scholars (both teachers and taught) rather than as the information delivery system it is too rapidly becoming. If students and teachers are to share responsibility for learning a subject together and for learning from one another, at least some of the requirements for this can be defined.

It should be obvious that a satisfactory mutual learning situation is most likely to develop where there is bilateral respect and relative freedom from inhibition. The respected teacher is likely to be one who knows his subject and his students' needs and whose sincerity and integrity are apparent. He will also be one whose students do not fear him. These attributes are easier to define than to acquire although it is possible to suggest some guidelines.

To learn of students' needs, a teacher must find ways of knowing the students themselves. This he may do by joining with them socially, and many are more successful than I at this precarious manoeuvre. Something can also be learned by noting postgraduate activities of former students and by learning the backgrounds of students being admitted to the school. The teacher must also learn and stay abreast of social changes taking place within the age-group he is teaching. Some of this can be picked up from the media but much must also be learned from the students themselves. This takes time and demands the teacher's accessibility, but without it the generation gap grows wider. In this I feel I may have some advantage over many of my colleagues in the accident of being childless. At least I notice that many of my confreres with children appear to expect from their students the manners, behaviour, and respect that they regard as a parental right.

A teacher who feels this need to support a parental establishment when he deals with other people's children is bound to have difficulty communicating with his students. Most university students are in an age group that is highly sensitive to the strictures of parental authority and will instinctively resist anything they sense to be in this class. This is not to deplore the generation gap, or to say that it doesn't affect me, but rather to emphasize the need, particularly in learning situations, for free communication across it. It would be as wrong for me to expect students to agree with my attitudes that began to evolve in the thirties as for them to expect me to share their involvements in the seventies. While an analysis of the generation gap is not germane to this essay it is essential to recognize that in most university teaching situations the student and teacher must communicate with one another across that gap.

While the importance of the teacher's recognition of the communication problems that result from the generation gap may be obvious, it is equally true that students must identify their responsibilities in this regard. I have had the experience of giving teaching assignments to an outstandingly qualified and enthusiastic teacher only to have student delegations confront me with demands for his removal because they found him difficult to understand. The most distressing aspect of this demand was the students' insistence that they would be happier with a man of lesser talent but who made their job of note-taking easier. In discussing the matter I referred to the need for students to understand and respect their teachers, but also made it a point later to advise the instructor that had he not appeared too aloof students would have approached him rather than me. In this case, reason and understanding prevailed on both sides and I later learned that good rapport had developed between the teacher and his students.

It is an extension of this theme to emphasize again the need for teachers to learn from as well as with their students. If this need is recognized ways will be found to meet it. At Dalhousie Medical School we evolved in the Department of Pathology a number of formal and informal approaches to this. One of these was the use of questionnaires to get class opinion on a variety of aspects of our program. When their anonymity was secure, students gave us valuable advice as well as pungent commentary on many topics. The student responses were required reading for all members of the department and led to major changes in the program, in line with our unofficial dictum, "Popular teaching is not necessarily good teaching, but unpopular teaching cannot be good."

Another program developed in this department has been called, "Preventive Education."[1] This assumes that students admitted to medical school have the ability to succeed and that therefore academic failures should be preventible. Part of the prevention program is the provision of a faculty advisor to assist each student with his problems in the course. This together with a program of examination analysis aids in identifying specific weaknesses of individual students and has led to the establishment of remedial instruction programs that run for six weeks prior to final examinations.

While neither the use of questionnaires nor of preventive education programs assure better teaching they do have the effect of increasing the informal contact between student and teacher and of providing a basis for mutual learning. Similarly effective contact took place in 1968 when Dalhousie students and department staff took part in a combined video-tape study of that standby of medical education, the oral examination.[2] The results of the study were a devastating indictment of a hitherto sacred cow as a result of which such examinations were immediately abandoned by the department.

These and other approaches to educational problems can only succeed if there is an atmosphere of trust and respect between student and teacher. The initial and essential step for the teacher in establishing trust is to indicate clearly at the start of a course what is expected of the student, how he will be assessed and the objectives and orientation of the program. These must be made clear to students and staff alike and should not be tampered with except in extraordinary circumstances. In the few instances (such as the abandonment of oral examinations) where we have found it necessary to change the ground-rules of the course in mid-year, this was done only after lengthy discussion with class representatives. The establishment of integrity in one area of course accomplishes nothing if it is not matched in all. Thus trust cannot grow (or even take root) where examinations are used (or appear to be used) as instruments of discipline rather than of evaluation or where students are insulted or ridiculed before their peers. Neither can it develop where student problems go unrecognized, untreated, or ignored.

Although trust and respect generally go together, a trusted teacher can lose respect in a variety of ways. He can do this merely by being well-intentioned but dull, in which case there may be little hope of salvation for him. An otherwise good teacher can lose respect by failure to attend to the little housekeeping details of his craft. This can occur because his dress is sloppy to the point of distraction (I have heard of a teacher who wears no trousers beneath his lab coat!) or because he always gets his slides mixed up. These and other faults usually result from inadequate preparation and few things can be more insulting to students than the idea that their teacher thought so little of his responsibility that he did not make himself ready for them.

Students will also be insulted if they find in their further study of a subject that their teacher has either misinformed them or been out of touch with recent progress in his subject. This need only happen a few times with a few students before the teacher's credibility is seriously and often permanently impaired.

I do not think it essential that a good teacher be also entertaining although a little of this can be helpful. Entertainment when it occurs in a teaching session is likely to be most effective when it occurs as a spontaneous recognition of incongruity rather than as a prepared joke. Too much entertainment can interfere with teaching and all of us know teachers whose primary focus seems to be on their performance rather than on its results.

When I was asked to write this essay I responded with enthusiasm, feeling sure that I had something to say. After a few thousand words, it is time I got to the point and delivered myself of the grain of sand that, handled appropriately, could become a pearl: Good teaching is a love affair between the teacher, his subject, and his students in which each participant must be terrified of failure.

DOUGLAS WAUGH

Born in England, Douglas Waugh grew up in Winnipeg, took his premedical studies at the University of Manitoba and went to McGill University for his professional education—M.D., C.M., then M.Sc. and Ph.D. in pathology. In 1954 he was certified as a specialist in pathology by the Royal College of Physicians and Surgeons of Canada.

He served in the Royal Canadian Army Medical Corps from 1942 to 1946, then returned to Montreal for research at the Pathological Institute of McGill. After a brief period on the staff of the Faculty of Medicine at the University of Alberta he joined the Faculty at McGill. From there he went to Queen's University and later to Dalhousie University where he became professor and head of the Department of Pathology—the post he held when he was invited to contribute to this collection. Subsequently, in 1970, he was appointed dean of medicine at Queen's University.

Dr. Waugh's research in pathology and in medical education has been reported in more than sixty publications. A number of his articles on aspects of medical education have appeared in the Canadian Medical Association Journal *and others.*

Pathology has been his teaching field and in 1967 he was given the Professor of the Year Award at the Dalhousie University Medical School.

As a lecturer, said his former Dalhousie students, Dr. Waugh was well organized, concise, clear, understandable. He was effective too in seminar and small group discussion, "being able to keep a lively discussion going in the direction he desired." Competent, modest, sincere, honest, fair—these are the kinds of adjectives used to describe him. He was enthusiastic about his field and about teaching it, but saw it in perspective.

"Dr. Waugh established a new system of assessment during one year," reported one graduate. "This enabled lecturers to assess their effect and students their progress. His prime method here was multiple choice questions at frequent intervals." He showed keen interest in students, treating them as individuals "but not as equals or buddy-buddy." "He was quick to praise and faster to encourage."

NOTES

1. D. Waugh, "Preventive Education: A Positive Program to Reduce Academic Failure and Poor Performance," *Canadian Medical Association Journal*, 98 (1968), 669–73.

2. D. Waugh and C. A. Moyse, "Oral Examinations: A Video-tape Study of the Reproducibility of Grades in Pathology," *Canadian Medical Association Journal*, 100 (1969), 635–40.

From the Known to the Unknown

Jaroslav Havelka

Being confronted with the task of answering the question, "What makes a good teacher?", I sensed a trap. Then it dawned upon me that this might be actually a shrewd form of provocation; namely, to lead me into a passionate disputation in defence of my beloved and permanent hobby. Here then is the rub: although the question remains formidably tough and the ensuing image of a "good teacher" spotty and grossly hypothetical, I am foolish enough to attempt an answer. And this I can do primarily because of a grateful memory.

I suppose all of us old enough to be subject to nostalgia remember a teacher who made the difference. I was lucky: I had two such teachers. The first one was my uncle. He was my elementary school teacher in a not too large, one-room country school in Czechoslovakia. I remember few of the facts he taught me (although I'll remember forever the drama of the battle of Austerlitz, never exceeded by Tolstoy's description of it). The thing I remember most about him was his ability to make everything he taught profoundly interesting and exciting; his reading of *King Lear* was unforgettably mysterious. The second one was Amato Masnovo, Professor of Philosophy at Milan University. His learning was enormous, his intellect subtle, precise, and strangely warm. His "amor intellectualis" for St. Augustine was full of tender humour and reverent disagreement. His philosophical arguments were developed with continuous attention to our youthful aspirations, for he loved us like his sons. He knew the secret of spiritual joy; time and again he gave forth sudden rays of wisdom, then became abruptly humble as if ashamed of himself in front of his admiring audience. He was a master of quodlibets, a form of student cross-examination of the teacher, in which he displayed a brilliant capacity for synthesis ranging widely beyond his specialty. In him the "what to teach" and "how to teach" became an inseparable unit of mental activity resulting in the highest degree of intellectual culture. What he knew and what he did "made the difference."

Ante Omnia

How do you train such teachers? How do you prepare them? The real question, as it has been since Aristotle began to teach, is what is the proper balance. It is not primarily a detailed division of lectures, discussions, laboratory work, and examinations, supposedly forming the backbone of the teaching task. Proper balance in teaching is a tendency and capacity to impart the known and to foment in the receiving mind a desire to know—what the teacher does not yet know.

To open to the student's mind the possibilities of as yet unstructured elements of knowledge requires confidence in the teacher's competence, wisdom, and dedication to ever reaching beyond. This balance is flexible, fluid, and subject to transformation in a fast-changing world. It is a profoundly intellectual awareness that accumulated knowledge and the predictably knowable form a continuum without which there is neither culture nor civilization.

The Art of the Great Fugue: Andante sostenuto

The horizon is not a fixed line but a changing imaginary boundary. In this notion is contained the nucleus of responsibility a good teacher should assume. He knows that the best minds in science and the humanities offer him their results in the firm belief that they have guessed right. He knows also that although the truth-bearing passion is there it is far from infallible; and that every discovery he has absorbed and understood has already made its impact on his interpretation of the world.

The puzzle has disappeared, the problem is no longer there. A new guess must be made, a new question formulated. Here then is the unique and beautiful occasion for teaching: to move from an established discovery into the quest of further approximation of the truth. No doubt, the application of existing principles is very practical, but it does not usually advance knowledge; the magic of originality requires further guessing, further approximations, new visions of natural and ideal reality.

Here the teacher can be at his best. He can excite his students more with the awesome prospects of possibilities than with the cataloguing of inert discoveries and reports. Rather than boring them with rules and principles which they can learn from their basic books, he invites his students to glimpse problematic probabilities which he or other minds still seek to fathom. However, his stern demand for knowledge of the established before one predicts and guesses further is absolute and implicit in his earnest and passionate approach. Before he invites his students to a fascinating game of prediction and hypothetical constructs, he wants them to know the ground-rules. The good teacher is demanding, knowing that improvisation is the noble art of the informed. Any interpretative act has a prerequisite of knowledge, and in that form it appears to be the teacher's essential subject matter, whatever his specialty may be. For him to be merely an instructor of textbook facts is a flagrant betrayal of his intellectual vocation.

In the midst of his students, a good teacher should insist with the fervor of his conviction and integrity that the sublime beauty and truth of any great argument rest in its promising tentativeness: in what it eventually can be, not in what it merely is now. This is creative probabilism which is based on faith in an expanding cognitive universe and avoids cynical relativism. Sceptic and cynic also know the provisorium but find it a matter for despair. A good teacher finds a way to pass beyond that despair—by choosing a commitment. And in this characteristic probably lies his attractiveness for young searching minds. Their youthful idealism delights in the prospect of infinite progress punctuated by the assurance born of conviction.

Commitment is certainly an attitude of risk, as every love is. But commitment is also an announcement of profound confidence in the living strategy shaped by values inherent in culture. Commitment is a vision of a value worthy of adherence. Commitment is also a proper understanding of any value: its practical changeability within the limits of its ideal meaning in human life.

To whom then should we assign the responsibility of teaching in terms of values at our universities? To cynics and sceptics? They do not believe in any values. But if the natural answer is: leave it to a good teacher, there still remains a hard question, namely, how is he going to do it. After all, a value is in Whitehead's terms a "matter of importance," as contrasted with a matter of cold facts governing student curricula. Let me approach the problem of value teaching in this way: living is an urgency; it plunges us into chaos and randomness if we do not hurry to organize our existence; life does not wait for our organizing efforts but if we are courageous and insistent enough it eventually appears to have meaning and sense; culture at its best is that organizing principle and because it originates in the sphere of life-explaining ideas, it is similarly urgent and coercive. Thus any culture's urgency is a commitment and a value.

Almost intuitively a good teacher senses that his commitment is primarily to life and its ideal, value-oriented interpretation, culture. He understands its urgency but simultaneously he notices the placidity and unhurried procession of facts, discoveries, and reports barely touched by the passage of time. A unique occasion arises to put his talent to work.

He chooses an approach which I would call a convergent punctuation: as he surveys a static array of facts he becomes alert to subtle possible correlations with an existing and unfolding sphere of values to which he is particularly sensitive. His talent lies in recognizing the fertile potentialities of objective principles to be lifted into the region of relevancy by value-interpretation; he transforms isolated data from the subject matter of instruction into value-influencing and thus culture-determining functions of education.

He interprets the "matter of importance" for living as he passes and precisely notices the marble garden of facts. For him the facts to be learned must go, whenever possible, through a vital process of focussing on value-relevancy. Education for values takes place only when the teacher is committed to interpret the facts of his discipline through the aspirations he stands for. His enthusiasm and excitement, contagious to his students, is the product of his unwavering persuasion that knowledge and its principles make sense only in the dynamic and committed framework of significant living.

At that moment he has found a contact with the central efficiency of his vocation: to educate for value through teaching. It is one of the most rewarding aspects of teaching, one which cannot be really planned but only hopefully anticipated, until it happens. In that sense teaching is a creative act; it should be what Koestler would call a "bi-sociation," a bringing together of the formerly unconnected, thus forming a wholeness which contains a new significant quality instrumental in our lives. Any subject matter, however abstract, has this value-potentiality.

Summa cum laude: Noosphere

What is intellectual excellence? And is it only intellectual? Do we need it in this troubled world of ours? Does education aim at it? These and similar questions the young men ask; and they call them relevant questions. We mature ones naturally want the highest degree of excellence in functions that are crucial to our efficiency and creativity. We examine and pass judgment on the quality of it. The outcome is, more often than not, that instead of excellence we are satisfied with an agreeable standard. And since we do not have a clear vision of it, we relegate its spurious measurement to our ever-present statistician.

Are we not confusing a capacity for holding and replicating information, usually measured in terms of scores, grades, class standing, and degrees, with proper intellectual eminence? Here then is the dedicated teacher's further invaluable role: to search for such eminence and witness it. The task is to sense superior intelligence as a radiant quality fast developing into increasingly complex interpretative comprehension, until it unfolds into a passion to understand in the universe its own emerging.

The gifted young face us with an almost pitying attitude, in the knowledge that we may initiate but never can complete the process of discovery their minds are capable of. Intuitively they trust their own inferences more than ours and, sometimes pathetically, want us to understand why they do. They ask for an unusual sort of mental discipline: trustingly expecting us to guide their tentative approximations, while assuming that their competence in terms of facts must be tested. They are delighted if we accept their game rules: "We know the facts—but who cares—we want to know what has not chanced yet to be known." They are disappointed if we force on them our conclusions. They need and value our intellectual curiosity and excitement—but after that they drive on on their own super-highway of the intellect. They sense our intelligence; trust it, but challenge it. Thus they often reverse the role of teacher and student— and treat us with amused tolerance for permitting it. Indeed, they are formidable children.

Let us not burden them with too many standard problems and questions. Their responses may be painfully slow (as contrasted with the speed of the quiz-kids) because in each problem they detect a universe of possibilities. Yet all the time these agile minds are searching for some sort of reality, overriding other realities, which when discovered will have universal validity. In that sense they display an admirable and often precocious passion for cognitions and values yet to come but already potentially pertinent to modern man's dilemma.

Their focus then naturally shifts from intellectual insights into a fiercely progressive moral, interpersonal, and social consciousness. In that complementarity they are really superior minds and there they need our assent and encouragement. For that, in turn, the most gifted among our students will call us relevant teachers.

The remainder of this essay is an uneasy and reluctantly formulated appendix to what I have said above. To expose and explain certain intangible aspects of my profession-vocation is difficult and can be painful. If teaching is an art, it is unique; and to explain uniqueness could mean its destruction. Yet there still remain some points of strategy which may have general validity.

In the first place, I take care to make a distinction between instruction and teaching. This distinction could help to clarify the controversial issue of any teacher's effectiveness. What is often assumed to be teaching is actually instruction, which can never substitute for teaching. An instructor communicates basically an array of data, facts, and reports, presented in such a fashion that the emphasis is on a coordinated sequence of discoveries, presumably indispensable for the understanding of any specific branch of human knowledge. It is primarily a reproduction and reviewing of categorized knowledge leading eventually to logical conclusions and theoretical assumptions. In this respect instruction alllows the student to become familiar with the main factual body of the discipline.

Only then can the student be taught how to use complex inferences, interpretations, new hypotheses, and theories which should eventually lead to an enriched contact with the sphere of human values. And that is already the domain of teaching proper; there the fascinating task is to stimulate and encourage the student to penetrate beyond that which is already known and initiate him into the intellectual function where understanding and creativity merge. In that sense teaching becomes a "subversive" activity, distinctly favoring the abandonment of the already established and aiming at the reorganization and expansion of knowledge.

I recognize this distinction by structuring my undergraduate and introductory courses as follows:

Phase A. The student is introduced, as soon as possible, to an abbreviated but cohesive network of important data, principles, and basic theories which form the objective backbone of my discipline, psychology. This is a period of instruction which the student is expected to follow for about two months. Usually an up-to-date textbook is chosen and trimmed to a digestible body of information. The student is asked: a) to read a chosen section; b) to attend lectures that follow the text but frequently add new data and their interpretations; c) to take part in a weekly discussion-lecture devoted to the clarification and reinterpretation of the presented material (attended if possible by both the senior and the junior instructor; here the junior instructor should gain his primary teaching experience); d) to attend a short series of lectures designed to give a general understanding of scholarly and scientific strategy and interdisciplinary philosophy; e) to write examinations on the material covered in these two months. (Even at this stage the objective examination, e.g. multiple choice, should be avoided since it introduces a wrong emphasis and minimizes intellectual involvement.)

Phase B. In my opinion, this is the most important in terms of teaching. It is introduced by a series of more detailed inquiries into the already presented data, with emphasis on the distinction between the formal technicalities of a routine work and the intellectual and creative potentialities in it. The sequence of topics treated in Phase A is preserved but the task of the student changes. The textbook is now dropped and a number of papers introduced, each representative of one topic. The student is expected to read and prepare comments on these for a lecture-discussion period. The lecturing is now more restricted and the discussion sessions given greater emphasis.

The accent is slowly shifting from examination of the established factual content to the exercise of inferences, hypotheses, and their critical examination in the light of already known facts. The generally cognitive and theoretical aspect is increasingly stressed, and possible relationships between various branches of knowledge investigated. This is a period in which I introduce a variety of personal preferences and biases related to my own value commitments. The students are encouraged to examine these new premises and interpretations and subject them to criticism.

Phase C. This phase is primarily devoted to encouraging the student to become more familiar with and develop his favored areas of interest. The emphasis here is on self-determination of his interests, freedom from the teacher's direct support, and at the same time maturing reliance on the teacher's wider experience. This should not be a period of premature specialization but a quest for intellectual autonomy, a most potent ingredient in the student's motivation. He will read in his chosen area almost exclusively and in it will write a major paper that will be examined orally in a tutorial session.

From the beginning of this threefold general program optimal structuring is needed. I feel that my first task is to restrict and simplify the information base of the course. Furthermore, structuring is related to the problem of relevancy. The term "relevant" has two meanings for me. A fact or datum is relevant if it advances our understanding so significantly that it cannot be omitted or disregarded in our quest for knowledge. The second aspect of relevancy relates to the realm of human values. Students sense acutely the need for relevancy but are not always sure about its meaning and direction. They take it as invariably and directly related to the social and political problems of our times. No doubt those are relevant, but teaching at its best should aim at a much more radically expanded domain of relevancy, namely the examination of the widest spectrum of man's understanding and aspirations —that is, his spirituality. In my teaching I try to reject the narrow range of relevancy and urge the students to adopt the wider interpretation of it.

Thus Phase A should be a period of lecturing with an emphasis on structuring; it should be one of fast and concentrated digestion of basic material, where questioning is free but limited to content. Inquiries should be to the point and frequently criticized as to their cogency. The pace is naturally brisk, and curiosity should be stimulated by examples, applications, and even anecdotes. (I have found that Pavlov's classical conditioning becomes more interesting to the bored student when I mention his political unorthodoxy and his relationship to Lenin.) At that time the feeling of a growing intellectual commitment should materialize; the best evidence of it is the student's willingness to become self-critical, and thus for the first time be ready for any sort of examination. I think that his growing involvement should naturally elicit a rather delicate decision, to welcome a scrutiny of his own intellectual progress. That decision should come spontaneously and so the examination routine should not be forced upon him but be adopted primarily at his request. The lecturing at this stage should be concerned with factual competency; committed to relevancy, enthusiastically lighthearted, witty, exact, and nondefensive; suggestive of a game and relying very little on the reading of notes. (Sometimes I memorize even statistics and graphs, and that not in order cheaply to impress but to suggest that a high motivation is the best ally of a good memory.)

In both Phase B and C the student is expected to be already acquainted with a skeleton outline of his subject matter. The lecturing, although now less extensive, becomes actually more important as it slowly evolves from information-communication to interpretation-communication. Now each lecture is expanded into a prolonged discussion in which the teacher becomes adviser, interpreter, moderator, and a critic of the exposed material, of the student's reaction to it, and even of his own interpretation. When an impasse is reached, the teacher attempts to preserve the continuity of the argument and give further information or expert insight where necessary.

The main emphasis now is on the developing capacity for spontaneous generation of ideas, their control, completeness, and chaining, and on the relentless pursuit of inferences, discovery of discrepancies, contradictions, hidden connections, symbolic validity, and spiritual significance. The teacher introduces the student both cautiously and confidently into the realm of abstractions and the nuances of symbolic language. The good feeling of disciplined commitment, intellectual grasp, and penetration is frequently tested and encouraged. The best criterion seems to me to be the student's progressive enjoyment of independent thinking, wider inferences, greater economy of expression, more controlled and yet daring predictions, and a tolerant interaction with other students and the teacher.

In conclusion, let me comment on the atmosphere of the relationship between the student and his teacher. I see my essential task in teaching as enriching and edifying personality and encouraging responsible subversion. The first task is self-explanatory, and as far as the second is concerned I hope that my position is not misunderstood as studiously existential or romantically nihilistic. What I mean by subversion is this: to rely in my discipline on established knowledge as merely a natural background which my teaching should transcend, expand upon, enrich, and possibly contradict because of its imperfection and tentativeness. Intellectual evolution is in every respect progressively subversive. This I tell my students and invite them to the responsible and disciplined joy of dethronement and rebuilding rather than destruction.

At the same time I make it quite plain that the rebuilding is an outcome of my unique experience and ideas, and that for a while they had better listen to me, because I am going to call the signals of the game, whether they like it or not. Furthermore, I intensely dislike a hastily programmed democratization of the student-teacher relationship. I suspect its facile leveling, premature arrogation of rights without responsibilities, conceited, smug, and even vindictive disregard for natural individual differences. I still proudly cherish the deeply aristocratic nature of some important aspects of life, without which culture, civilization, and spiritual involvement is unthinkable. I do not enter the classroom to promote any homogeneity of intellectual and personal growth, or any standard of socialization. I do realize the subtle and sometimes profound differences in terms not only of obvious capacities but especially of latent potentialities among those young people I face.

The moment I greet them, I become all sorts of things to them, from a tortured king to a nuisance, from a source of some specific datum to, perhaps, a unique and joyous stimulus which may in some instances endure for a lifetime. Not one of those young men and women sees me as a standard image. Why should I see them otherwise?

Before I attempt anything in my teaching task, I must instill in them the notion that they are worthwhile individuals, with whom I have the unique privilege of sharing a profoundly fascinating exchange of ideas, aspirations, and values. This eager anticipation they must sense in me, otherwise I am a dead duck to them, and a subject of contempt to myself. They must feel that teaching has for me an aura of inexplicable magic, the preservation of which should be the fundamental criterion in a hopeful revival of our tiring civilization. They must respect me in my role of Socratic midwife, of a disciplined and sometimes wise anarchist, and as a dependable source of encouragement when youthful melancholy becomes too oppressive. They must be taught that life is rarely self-evident but is a deeply mysterious and significant event, and that that lesson is worthy of being propagated.

Epilogue

There may be a way to add a brush stroke to the incomplete and evasive Teacher's portrait. Like a ghost of the Wandering Jew he accompanies an endless procession of the fascinated, disappointed, and grateful young. He can change his mask and yet in each disguise I recognize him:

- Don Quixote, a valiant man of honour and lofty ideals, he imagines himself called upon to protect them against the whole insensitive world; he has his wits turned by inordinate study but remains nonetheless sane and profound in his poverty and loneliness; his integrity is manly and his kindness is childlike—he is a teacher.
- Hamlet, a complex and a concave mind, reflecting the void of human existence and fighting it desperately; a sceptical contemplator and a haunted believer—he is a teacher.
- Faust, an intellectual and symbol-maker; a relentless seeker and builder of transcendental models which imperil his emotions but allow him to commit himself to the unattainable and find peace in it—he is a teacher.
- Don Juan, seductive, graceful, and elegant; a victim of his own insatiable desire for love and admiration; a tragic actor, a pretender, and

yet deeply concerned about the intangible human ties from which he is exempted—he is a teacher.

There is in each good teacher a fragment of each of these.

JAROSLAV HAVELKA

Jaroslav Havelka was born in Czechoslovakia. During the German occupation, when Czech universities were forcibly closed, he studied at the Conservatory of Music and Art. After the war a grant from the Italian government enabled him to continue his studies, in philosophy, art, and psychology, at the University of Milan. Following a short sequence of posts as tutor, salesman, and translator, and with the equivalent of a master's degree from Czechoslovakia and a doctorate from Italy, he emigrated to Canada. He is now a Canadian citizen.

During his first years in Canada he worked as an assembly-fitter for Canadair, then as a lecturer in slavic literatures at l'Université de Montréal. He became a graduate student (and animal caretaker) at McGill University and, in 1954, qualified as Master of Science in physiological psychology. For an additional three years he remained at McGill as a research assistant in psychology. His interests at that time centred on the study of neuropsychology, language and bilingualism, and problem-solving, and resulted in publications in these fields.

In 1957, Dr. Havelka joined the staff of the University of Western Ontario as an instructor in psychology. He was promoted to the rank of assistant professor in 1959 and associate professor four years later. In 1969 he was named professor and head of the department of psychology of King's College, an affiliate of UWO. In 1974 he was one of those chosen to receive an OCUFA Teaching Award.

His major work is The Nature of the Creative Process in Art *(M. Nijhoff, The Hague, 1968). In recent years his orientation has been toward the psychology of personality, cognitive and creative functions, and the development of humanistic psychology. Professor Havelka says that his most rewarding current project is interdisciplinary work leading to the restoration of the recognition that the inner life of man and his creativity are psychologically by far the most important variances characterizing his unique quest for authentic existence.*

During the period under review Professor Havelka taught psychology to arts as well as nursing students. The following summary of graduates' comments draws on the responses of both groups.

His broad knowledge and experience of his own and related fields gave him an unusual perspective, according to his former students, and he was able to relate theory to practice—and his subject to life and to the problems of individual members of his classes. His enthusiasm for his field was evident. Because he usually had large classes he used the lecture method, but encouraged questions and discussion as well.

Several graduates referred to his habit of walking about the lecture hall as he spoke. One reported that "Dr. Havelka would walk throughout his lecture—first up one aisle, and then the other. This was not a distraction; rather it was felt as an effort to involve and include the student more individually." He was thoroughly organized and it was his habit to lecture without notes. He was flexible, too, being willing to deviate from his planned topic to discuss one the students were currently anxious to explore. He used humour to enliven his classes and "was capable of keeping a lecture hall in a continued state of merriment or in deep shock over some of his tales."

Several graduates mentioned Professor Havelka's speech. One who met him just after his arrival at Western said, "He was brand new to the department . . . and his groping with the English language won us immediately to his side. We all tried very hard to understand very clearly so that we might help him express himself with greater ease." Another called his accent charming rather than distracting, and a third suspected that at times he thickened his accent to make students pay more attention.

Not all adjectives applied to him were equally complimentary. By one or another he was said to be intense, unconventional, eloquent, dramatic, vibrant, moody, witty, opinionated, energetic, dynamic, relaxed. He was referred to as a stage hypnotist, an exhibitionist, an artist, a poseur, and a wise, compassionate, and highly civilized human being.

There was agreement, though, about his respect for and interest in students and their welfare. He teased them, bantered with them, listened to them, and was approachable and available. He told them what was expected of them, took their intelligence for granted, and demanded excellence.

The Teacher Has No Proxy

William H. Fowler

Despite the rise and fall of exercises for the mind, ungraded systems, programmed learning, and other "sure-fire" methods, I suspect that teaching has had the same function all along—that is, to help students form accurate knowledge and interpretations of their world. The power to achieve coherent understanding and timely responses resides in the inner mechanisms of the individual's mind. The teacher can neither think nor act for the student, although many teachers perform their role as if they had student proxies to carry out these processes. The teacher as an external agent in the learning process can do no less than help supply perceptual fuel for the engines of the mind. He may do more if he understands the amounts and grades of input that will satisfy the student's need, development, and inclination. The teacher can also provide each student with opportunities of actually experiencing and working with the objects of his mind. Lastly, he can help students assess what they have done, always with the prospect of doing it better the next time. These are the ways and the approximate sequence by which the teacher may help the individual create a conscious order in his own special sphere of life. Some of these conditions may be enhanced by the technical conveniences in our classrooms; some may be hampered by the rigidity and systemization of the school day. In the final analysis, teaching is still very much a practising art that relies heavily on the personal ingenuity and integrity of the teacher.

In addition to the abbreviated points related above, I have been drawn to three questions which I felt compelled to answer with a degree of satisfaction, at least to myself, in preparing this paper. I have made special reference to the study of physical education in pulling these questions together. First, in relation to the infinite stores of knowlegde available to man, what constitutes the infinitesimal domain of knowledge in physical education? Secondly, it seems apparent that the prospect of living, let alone teaching, without being conscious of the existence of meaning is a glaring discrepancy of fact that tugs and pulls at our daily lives. If there is some truth to this surmise, what purposeful meanings and causes give dimension and vitality to the study of physical education? Thirdly, how can one mobilize and elevate the personal worth of each constituent in the learning situation? The first two questions deal with the depth of expertise and communion a professor holds with his subject material. The latter question touches on the psychosocial forces of the student-teacher relationship. If I have treated the so-called "tricks of the trade" less than might be expected, it is only because I view them as secondary credentials for the professor in higher education. The real "trick" in university teaching is to develop and combine a sound theoretical posture toward one's field of study with an empathetic approach to the totality of each student's consciousness.

As for knowledge, I am inclined to support Northrop Frye's observation that every field of knowledge is the centre of all knowledge. This notion kindles the belief that the roots of specialized knowledge run deep in the fertile ground of all knowledge, and the further one investigates his own field, the more he tends to tap the deposits of information in other fields. For many years the student of physical education received anemic doses of knowledge from such diverse and established disciplines as anatomy, physiology, mathematics, physics, chemistry, psychology, and history. In addition, the student was instructed through "method and materials" courses on how to deal effectively with various classroom situations. At best, this educational design produced ill-raised hybrids, more or less superficially funded with scientific concepts and liberal ideas, and at the same time more or less vaguely prepared to handle the realities of the teaching profession.

Fortunately, over the past few decades physical educators attending to such areas as kinesiology, exercise physiology and fitness, motor development, motor learning, play, recreation, and sport have formulated and shaped a body of knowledge which is truly unique to physical education. Consequently, the art and science of human movement may be identified clearly as the theme of study in physical education today. The study itself seeks to reveal and advance the behavioral qualities which undergird all varieties of purposeful human movement, and it discloses a commitment to specialization in the developmental and expressive uses of movement. Having opened a vein in the cross-section of knowledge, the physical educator is now in an improved position to give theoretical sustenance to the applied concerns of his study. Until recently, backing for physical activity programs has relied solely on the measure and weight of experience. Experience cannot be ignored in an applied study such as physical education, but I am inclined to believe that the practical is rooted in the theoretical, and only because of this is it knowable and worthy of scholarly attention.

To those who teach in the more established disciplines, these dispositions have already been settled and are respected by the academic community. To the teacher of physical education, however, these newly acquired theoretical bases represent advances that are bound to improve the quality of instruction and research. The professor who is marked as a master of his subject has a backing of trust and confidence that no other feature of personality or presentation can approximate.

In conveying factual information to students, I feel there is still a place for lecturing, provided that it is precise, brief, and logically sequenced in the course; verbosity conditions the learner to expect many things which are not worth hearing. There is also an unfortunate tendency in academia to conjure up all kinds of mysterious nomenclature to explain various phenomena. The object of any communication in learning is to reach the mind of another person, not to "bounce abstractions off his dome." There is one final point which bears mentioning, and it is related to the organization of lecture material. While there are a great many thoughts which could be exposed in the classroom, there are usually only a few key facts or concepts that deserve direct, vocal countenance in a course of study. In this sense I evaluate annually the courses I teach, with a view to eliminating trivia, updating and vitalizing information, and rescheduling lecture presentations.

Purpose is for everyone a vital element in learning. Why is he emphasizing that? What about this view? So what? These remarks, and all attempts to derive something more out of a course than what is merely found in the textbook, are expressions of the student's need to connect meaning to factual findings. There are many advocates of the "disinterested pursuit of truth," and I support their claim. Specifically, I am supporting a description of a scholarly method of investigating knowledge; as a statement of philosophical import, however, it can hardly be regarded as much more than an idyllic dream of an educational "pie in the sky." The smallest modicum of knowledge contains a purpose that begs to be expelled and used at the appropriate time. A student remarked to me recently, "What we need is a moratorium on the advancement of new knowledge while a search is made for better ends for the knowledge we have already disseminated." The spirit, if not the reality, of this point is well taken. Knowledge, the glorified end of education, has proliferated in word and print over the past few decades, largely without comment or debate, and the students of our nation have reacted unkindly and abruptly in this atmosphere of acquiescence.

In determining what is good about what we know, the argument "from experience" may not be very convincing, but it represents the only pliable substance available from which value judgments can be fashioned. Adult values are different from the values of young people because they are based on different experiences. In this sense, there is a credibility gap between one individual and another. Relevant teaching is largely a matter of providing opportunities for people to share their experiences, and this can only happen if and when all parties have had a reasonable chance to work with the subject under scrutiny. Many seminars I have attended are nothing more than "mini" lectures. One student is sent forth to investigate a body of knowledge, and like a good dog he smells out the bone, retrieves it, and presents it to a collective group of ignoramuses which often includes the professor. I personally like the open-forum approach or the inquiry method of presentation, particularly when it is employed immediately following a class-directed set of readings or assignments. This method is also applicable towards the end of the term when more ordering, synthesizing, and applied problem-solving is desired. No person, whether he be professor or student, has any right to call himself a scholar unless he speaks out. Quantification is the function of computers and teaching machines; qualification is the main function of human intellects. If education is to make any impact on mankind, it must permit the integrity and the primacy of the individual to display itself.

Physical education provides an interesting case of a study which may be on the verge of losing its main thrust despite an increasing command of the parameters of knowledge that sustain the science and theory of human movement. From early antiquity physical education, like fine art and music, has been experienced and revered as a special human resource essential to man in his search for a life accentuated by vitality and dignity. Physical education, as noted, is an applied study, and the profound meanings inherent in its character rarely emerge unless the individual runs, throws, swims, or just plain sweats. To the bespectacled professor who gleans knowledge through quiet reflection on a page, physical efforts often seem childish and unbecoming to an institution of higher learning. There could be a trace of truth in this sanctimonious stand, as no effective and enduring change of behavior is likely to take place without action and awareness in the higher nerve centres. Lest we forget, however, movement is one of the oldest forms of learning, and like human speech, it is the happy result of a discovery of the mind. Without the sensations that arise from the alternating rhythm of stressful and relaxing exertion, the conceptual world of the physical learner would be naive and incomplete. Physical activity in the forms of exercise, sport, and dance are central to the study and practice of physical education, and if these manifestations appear too crude and technical for the university mind, then I would prefer a different setting for our study. Abstractions will never rightly form the basis of learning in a "doing" phenomenon, and I would challenge any mad rush for academic respectability that meant sacrificing these important experiential lessons.

I conclude that purpose is steeped in human values; whether something is good or bad, meaningful or trite, must not only be pondered and questioned by teachers and students alike, but it should also be woven authentically into the fabric of learning particular to each study.

The learning situation embraces human beings as well as content and things. "Ay, there's the rub;" for I have heard that in the school of the professor's dream there are no students, just a library, a laboratory, the lamp of learning, and a caretaker to turn out the lights. Students represent human variables that somehow defy all the nice little laws of nature, and to counter these, the masters of higher education have used essentially one of two procedures. One way has been to put everyone through the same mill. All students take the same lectures and examinations, and everyone is treated the same until, of course, the grades are handed out. Fear of failure is sprinkled liberally in this kind of system, but it helps to reduce the variables of behavior; teachers teach, and students learn how to answer examination papers in one way or another. Those who get out of the groove find themselves out of school. In the other method, teachers have tacitly agreed that their presence only confuses independent thinking, and besides, there is more important scholarly work to be done "back in the lab." A liberal and permissive environment is established, and the student is encouraged to do his own "thing." There appear to be very few disagreements with this system because anarchy and academic specialization look after their own interests very well. As there is an ungraded system of evaluation, nobody fails; only those who can't handle the night life drop out.

To use contemporary phraseology, both of the methods described above are "cop-outs." Both try, in different ways, to circumvent the learner and his problems; both debase the mind and spirit of man. It should be obvious that human potential and dignity are fulfilled primarily through learning. As teachers, we need to know how people learn, and especially how people learn how to elevate and refurbish their own spirits.

There are few principles of behavior that have been the subject of more research and discussion than reinforcement, and the student who receives an "A" on a term paper, or a word of praise from the teacher, undoubtedly gains the appropriate benefit from this important tool of teaching. Gratification of this kind, while necessary at times, is not exactly what I had in mind for those in the advanced stages of education. It is based on the Freudian premise that people are desperately holding on to each adjustment of life; they are also viewed as being too negative to venture forth without constant support and reinforcement from others. I am not in the mould of the experimental psychologist, but from my own observations, I would say that the deficiency-need motivated syndrome of behavior has been grossly over-generalized, and I suspect that the overall gains derived from this manner of dealing with situations are much too restrictive and transient to be of real value in the learning situation.

Most healthy-minded individuals I have encountered reach out for self-expression and self-improvement; their accomplishments in life, no matter how small, breed increased motivation and excitement rather than decreased tension. They also seem more concerned with the prospects of being and becoming than with the probabilities of merely coping. Individuals are this way, I gather, because they perceive themselves to be acceptable in the eyes of others, not as brilliant or useful agents of society but as love-worthy human beings like you and me. The fundamental source of reinforcement for the student is the realization that he is acceptable to the teacher as an individual with potentialities for growth and expression.

The teacher manifests acceptance by identifying and familiarizing himself with the student as best he can, and by giving the student a variety of opportunities to display his abilities. The student reveals himself to the professor in many ways: past performance, classroom participation, assignments, and personal consultation are but a few of the avenues open to the discerning teacher who is interested in identifying with the students he teaches. The important thing is that without these direct observations, the teacher cannot return with any degree of objectivity to his own reality to complete the understanding. I hasten to add that the teacher cannot afford to be unduly swayed by the intensely emotional atmosphere of another person's situation; for it is at this point that empathy backs down and flimsy sentiment enters the picture. I don't mean to imply that one should walk away from another's dilemma; it's just that extreme feelings tend to distort what is really obvious about what we observe.

As everyone does something a little better one way rather than another, it should be evident that one single measure of a person's ability, such as the standard examination, is hardly worth the paper it is written on when it comes to evaluating a classroom full of potentials. Even from the standpoint of feedback or the confirmation of learning, the final examination is too little, too late. Diversification of courses is only one way of providing equality of opportunity. The main responsibility for equating opportunities among students, however, rests with the teacher, who must assess as closely as he can each student's capability of benefiting from various types of learning experiences. In the realm of achievement, one's degree of performance will never rise above one's perception of demand. Here, too, the teacher may be instrumental in fostering situations where need for advanced performance is seen by the student as an integral part of a larger learning experience.

The academic course I teach attempts to investigate and interpret the motivations and nuances of participation in various kinds of organized and unstructured play, game, and sporting activities. Evaluations are based on four major assignments rather than a final examination. The assignments are designed to give the student direct and varied learning experiences and challenges; they range in nature from subjective reflections about critical incidents of child play to an in-depth field study of a particular play group or an actual sporting event. Group endeavours are planned along with independent study assignments. The student receives a written evaluation and a letter grade (A to D) for each assignment. At the end of the year, the four assignments completed by each student are ranked in the order of their respective letter grades. The top assignment is granted a total weight of 40 marks, second ranked–30 marks, third ranked–20 marks, lowest ranked–10 marks. The letter grades are then converted into equivalent numerical marks to establish the student's final grade out of 100 marks in the course. This procedure is followed, on one hand, to reduce the apprehension students may have regarding the infallible control teachers sometimes demonstrate in assigning grades. More important, I would hope, is the fact that the results of one's performance are vital to the learning process, and somehow these confirmations must be internalized. The student, in this case, can realize his shortcomings without serious penalty, while at the same time reinforcing his own best efforts. What talents he lacks in preparing one assignment may be more than made up for in the creation and expressions of a different assignment.

I must finally and reluctantly admit that nothing I have said is new. Much of it has been assimilated silently and unconsciously, I'm sure, from the handful of exceptional teachers I have had. The rest paraphrases the thoughts and writings of a very profound humanitarian and psychologist, Abraham Maslow. If my successes in teaching outweigh the failures, they attest to the reciprocal interaction of perceiving the worthiness in others. The failures have served to keep me honest; for if the achievement of the teacher is measured by enlightened and distinguished acts of learning, it may also be calculated by the sense of proportion it brings to the teacher.

WILLIAM H. FOWLER

A graduate of the University of Western Ontario, the Ontario College of Education, and Springfield College, Springfield, Mass (M.P.E.), Professor Fowler taught in an Ontario secondary school 1956–61 and was director of its student activities program during the last two of those years. He began his university teaching career at McMaster University in 1961, was made an associate professor in 1968, and was chairman of the Department of Physical Education from 1967 to 1970. He has been the University basketball coach for twelve years.

In addition, Professor Fowler has served on the board of management of the Hoover Park Y.M.C.A. and the board of directors of the Hamilton Y's Camp Wanakita, the editorial staff of Canadian Coach *and the Fitness and Amateur Sport Directorate's committee on the development of a sport involvement model for Canadians. He has played many leadership roles in camp and recreational planning, and is director of the annual Geneva Park Athletes and Coaches Camp.*

During the period covered by graduates' comments he taught, at various times, courses on health theory and design, recreation theory and design, psychological and sociological foundations of physical activity, and play, sport and leisure. In addition, he has been involved in monitoring and analysing action and interaction modes in a broad spectrum of games, sports, and psychomotor play activities.

Professor Fowler's former students said he was a dynamic person, sometimes a clown, but obviously dedicated to his field and his role as a teacher. He was well read in his subject, prepared carefully for class sessions, "was punctual and hardly missed a class all year," and related theory to practice with many pertinent illustrations.

In addition to lectures, he made effective use of seminars and group discussion. One type of assignment which was appreciated was research undertaken by pairs of students, with subsequent reporting in oral form to the group and in written form to the instructor. He was highly organized, his lectures were relaxed but obviously well planned, the projects he proposed for the students were meaningful. He was a good disciplinarian, demanded excellence, and was fair. Professor Fowler was emotionally involved in his work, graduates said, took a personal interest in his students, and marked their assignments thoroughly and helpfully.

The Quiet Life!

J. C. Gilson

Universities are facing one of the most exciting and, at the same time, one of the most trying periods in their history. Demands on the university are increasing, with corresponding pressure on teaching staff, academic administrators, budgets, and building space. Fundamental changes are being called for in the curriculum, and methods of instruction are being adjusted to meet the needs of the new generation of students coming forward from the high schools. Undergraduate life on the campus is in a high state of tension. Graduate student training and research are claiming a growing proportion of the staff members' time and energy. At the same time, the general community expects greater service and attention from an academic staff already preoccupied with internal claims and responsibilities of the university.

This is the exciting, rapidly changing, and complex environment in which the university teacher now finds himself. Apparently this has not always been the case. Professor Frank Underhill, a distinguished Canadian educator, turned to the play, *A Man For All Seasons*, for the traditional view of the teaching profession:

> Let us go back for a moment to another revolutionary age, that of Sir Thomas More. In the first act of Robert Bolt's play, *A Man For All Seasons*, young Mr. Richard Rich wants Sir Thomas More to help him to a good job. More advises him to put aside his ambition for a career which will bring him prestige, wealth and power and to settle down to a quiet life as a teacher. His words embody the classical consolations of the teacher in all ages.
>
> More: Why not be a teacher? You'd be a fine teacher. Perhaps even a great one.

Rich: And if I was, who would know it?
More: You, your pupils, your friends, God. Not a bad public that. Oh, and a quiet life.[1]

Teaching in the contemporary university is far from a quiet life. University professors have many claims on their time and energy besides teaching. Indeed, some observe that teaching has become one of the peripheral responsibilities of the university community. The more cynical suggest that a university would be a good place to work if there were no undergraduates.

Several hypotheses have been advanced to explain the apparent decline in the prestige of the university teaching profession. The dominant theme of Professor Barzun's book, *The American University*, is that the university has become so preoccupied with the needs of society that teaching can no longer be the central concern of its members. In Professor Barzun's words, "the nearest equivalent to what the university is becoming is the medieval guild, which undertook to do everything for the town. . . . The only thing that the guild used to provide and we do not is Masses for the dead, and if we do not it is because we are not asked."[2]

He suggests that teaching has not become less important in the mid-century university; it is only that educators have had wished upon them a variety of tasks formerly done by others or not done at all.

Another writer, Professor Arrowsmith, suggests that the universities have failed as teaching institutions because research has developed greater academic respectability. He argues that university professors have abandoned their Socratic pretensions and traditions and have turned their attention to publication and the prestige of the research laboratory. In his opinion, the conflict between research and teaching cannot be resolved by reconciling them, but only by divorcing them altogether; reconciliation, he suggests, can only occur at the expense of teaching.[3]

After almost twenty years as a university professor, the author recognizes the difficulty of maintaining a perspective on the long-run rewards to be gained from teaching when the benefits of research and public service appear to be more immediate and tangible. However, there is one fundamental consideration which cannot be ignored. There can be no question that teaching is a primary responsibility of the university. If teaching is not a basic function of the university, then it follows that the whole *raison d'être* of the institution is denied. A university without students is inconceivable; it might possess the best research facilities in the country but without students it has no unique claim as an institution of higher learning.

Cardinal Newman argued that, "If the objects of the university were scientific and philosophical discovery [only], I do not see why a university should have any students." A university is different from an industrial science laboratory or a government research station because it has the responsibility to teach. This is not to say that teaching is the only legitimate function of the university but rather to emphasize that teaching is its unique and important responsibility.

There are signs that teaching will regain its former position of importance in the university community. An increasing number of administrators, teachers, and students have begun to examine critically the long-held assumption underlying the nature and organization of teaching and the learning process in the university. The good teacher is being recognized for his contributions to the academic community. The "publish or perish" doctrine is not the only criterion being used at the present time to evaluate the worth of the university professor. University teachers themselves are becoming more aware of their responsibilities as teachers, and many are taking deliberate steps to improve their performance in the classroom. Students are becoming more conscious of the need for good teaching and they are making their wishes known in clear and unequivocal terms.

What makes for effective or successful teaching? This is a question which pedagogical experts have pondered for years. Most will agree that there is no one formula which can be followed with predictable success by the university professor. Teaching is a highly personal experience with the result that there are as many ways of effective teaching as there are successful teachers.

What follows then is a personal account of a highly pragmatic approach to teaching—an approach which has been modified and shaped by several years of classroom experience.

My only credentials at the beginning of my teaching career were twenty years as a student and the influence of outstanding teachers under whom it was my good fortune to study. I was one of those described by Professor Arrowsmith as having no formal preparation for the profession other than what could be "picked up" on the job. It must be said, however, that graduate training was the necessary starting point for my university teaching career. Without a prolonged period of study in some discipline or field of specialization, teaching in the contemporary university would simply not be feasible, pedagogical preparation notwithstanding.

If I were asked to list the two most important factors involved in the teaching process, they would be the following: complete mastery of the subject being taught and adequate preparaton for each lecture. In my several years of teaching experience, I never found a reliable way of disguising an ill-prepared lecture. Lack of preparation, or incompetence in the subject matter, cannot be hidden for long, no matter how enthusiastically the lectures may be delivered. My experience suggests that three hours of homework and preparation for every 50 minutes of lecture time are necessary if the students are not to be better advised to spend their time in the library. Incidentally, this amount of preparation time is as necessary after several years of teaching experience as it is at the beginning.

A well-prepared lecture, however, does not guarantee a well-delivered lecture. Students do not expect teachers to be orators or actors, but they have a right to expect effective communication. Effective communication does not compensate for incompetence in the subject matter but, without it, lectures are generally far from enjoyable or inspiring. I discovered from experience that a teacher can suffer badly from "over-exposure" after 50 to 75 lectures, unless a conscious attempt is made to vary the style and pace of the lecture. Standing on one's head for the occasional lecture may be a welcome relief from the more stereotyped blackboard presentation. In addition, many university teachers might benefit greatly from speech training or a course in public speaking as I did at the beginning of my career.

After some experience it became apparent to me that too much time was consumed in the classroom in the dictation and transcribing of notes. Fifty minutes filled with note-taking leave little opportunity for the lecturer to stimulate constructive thought and interest, or to generate involvement of students through class discussion. The parallel may be seen in Gulliver's visit to the grand Academy of Lagado where he found the professor standing in the middle of the room commanding six-and-thirty lads to crank out bits of information on an educational contrivance which he had invented and dictating the results to four remaining boys who acted as scribes.

If students are not to become mere scribes, lecture notes should be reproduced whenever possible and distributed at the beginning of the term. I found a remarkable change in the classroom environment when I began to adopt this practice.

While students appreciate some degree of humility in their teacher, they expect him to be their intellectual leader in the classroom. I concur with Professor Barzun's observation that "A good teacher will tolerate a certain over-confidence in undergraduates—that is part of pedagogy—but to make believe that their knowledge and his are equal is an abdication and a lie." I am certain that Professor Barzun would not have students sit at the feet of the master but he does say that the teacher has the responsibility and the obligation to make his lectures intellectually challenging and worthwhile.[4]

My experience suggests that a balanced diet of research and teaching is essential if boredom and irrelevance are not to destroy the teacher as the years go by. Nothing should be more disturbing to the student than the teacher whose notes are obsolescent and whose original set of examination questions has survived many years of asking. Nothing so refreshes a teacher each year as an on-going program of research. A teacher who is not constantly exploring new ideas through scholarship and research is not in a position to explore new ideas with his class.

Finally, it is my personal feeling that greater emphasis should be placed on the use of the course and teacher evaluation questionnaire. The quality of teaching should be of as much concern to the university as the quality of its research programs. There are few professional journals which will accept articles for publication before they have been properly assessed by a panel of expert reviewers. It is no less important that the teacher should be willing to accept a systematic evaluation of his course and teaching performance. It is amazing to me that students have not made greater use of the evaluation questionnaire. After several years of experience with the teacher evaluation questionnaire, I have never felt that I had received an unfair assessment of my performance in the classroom. When criticisms were made they were generally fair and constructive.

These are the lessons which I have learned from my experience as a university teacher. I recognize, however, that the past is only a prologue of what is to come. There will be radical changes in the university curricula and in the methods of instruction. The conventional wisdom may prove to be completely inadequate for the future. Some educators believe that, by the end of the present decade, universities will become true learning centres where teachers will be advisers, independent study will replace the lecture, and the final course examinations will be abolished and the student will sit for a comprehensive examination whenever he feels ready to present himself as a candidate for a degree. In Professor Paschal's words, "It will make the professor not a purveyor of information, but rather the senior scholar in a joint intellectual adventure, and the advisor who helps direct the student's organization of his learning."[5]

University teaching in the future will not be for the timid nor for those unwilling to change or innovate. It will be neither a quiet nor an easy life. But it will have its unique reward. The reward will not be in power or prestige or wealth but in the deep personal satisfaction which comes in helping to liberate the minds and hearts of young men and women.

J. C. GILSON

Dr. Gilson was born in the Manitoba town of Deloraine. He studied at the University of Manitoba for the degrees of Bachelor of Science in Agriculture, and Master of Science, and took his Ph.D. in agricultural economics at Iowa State University. He held scholarships or fellowships through most of his career as a student. In 1966 he was elected a fellow of the Agricultural Institute of Canada.

He worked for the Canada Department of Agriculture and the Manitoba Department of Agriculture for several summers while he was a student. In 1954 he joined the staff of the University of Manitoba, rising to the professorship in 1963. Subsequently he became head of the De-

partment of Agricultural Economics and Farm Management (1967), dean of the Faculty of Graduate Studies (1968), and vice-president (research, graduate studies and special assignments) (1971).

His record of service to his profession of agricultural economics and to his community (local, provincial, national, and international) is extensive. He was economic and statistical consultant to the Manitoba Royal Commission on Crop Insurance; councillor, vice-president, president of the Canadian Agricultural Economics Society; chairman of the agricultural advisory group, Committee on Manitoba's Economic Future; member of Canada's Task Force on Agriculture; and member of Canadian delegations to international agricultural conferences (OECD, Paris; United Nations, Geneva). He has been chairman of the Manitoba Crop Insurance Corporation for more than twelve years, and a member of the Science Council of Canada for three years.

Professor Gilson has published more than seventy articles, both technical and popular, in journals ranging from the Canadian Journal of Agricultural Economics *to* The Country Guide. *In addition, he has presented more than 160 papers to seminars, meetings and conferences or on the air.*

According to his former students, Professor Gilson knew his subject, organized his material well and at a level suited to his students, and was an excellent and interesting speaker. His treatment of the subject was enriched by his own wide experience and his involvement in practical policy issues and problems.

He was interested in his subject and his students, and evidently enjoyed teaching. After-hours discussions were common. Frequent mention was made by reporting graduates of the extent to which students were involved, immersed, in his courses, by means of discussion but also and especially because of his emphasis on research and term papers as assignments. It was said that he was particularly effective in small classes at the honors level.

Another characteristic noted by several graduates was his imagination, his foresightedness. "His lectures were filled with projections and visions of the future," said one.

NOTES

1. F. H. Underhill, "The Scholar: Man Thinking," in *A Place of Liberty*, ed. George Whalley (Toronto: Clarke, Irwin, 1964), p. 61.
2. Jacques Barzun, *The American University* (New York: Harper and Row, 1968), p. 11.
3. William Arrowsmith, "The Future of Teaching," in *Campus 1980*, ed. Alvin C. Eurich (New York: Delacorte Press, 1968), pp. 116–33.
4. Barzun, *American University*, p. 91.
5. Elizabeth Paschal, "Organizing for Better Instruction," in *Campus 1980*, p. 227.

Student-Centred Teaching

Eleanore Vaines

> Whatever we do in teaching depends upon what we think people are like. The goals we seek, the things we do, the judgments we make, even the experiments we are willing to try, are determined by our beliefs about the nature of man and his capacities. It has always been so . . . . The beliefs we hold about people can serve as prison walls limiting us at every turn. They can also set us free from our shackles to confront great new possibilities never dreamed of before.[1]

It is often assumed that young people will automatically abuse freedom. Given the chance, runs this type of thinking, today's student will always take the easiest way, learn just what he has to, indulge himself, fake it, dazzle his teachers with footwork and escape scotfree with a degree he has done nothing to deserve—most probably becoming a political radical and a drug addict in the process. And doing it on his father's hard-earned money.

I believe that such attitudes and practices are less likely to prevail under a program that encourages the student to be a responsible person. Such behavior is more likely to be the rule where young adults are treated as untrustworthy children from the beginning, and learn first to beat the system by its own rules.

I believe that, given an atmosphere which favours learning, students will take that responsibility and they will grow and enjoy it. Such freedom can be heady at first and there are problems. But as the student has opportunities to make choices and see the consequences of his actions, such opportunities are cherished. That is as important a part of a student's education as the subject matter studied.

This essay is a statement of what I believe about people in general, and specifically about people as students in the microcosm of the classroom. My beliefs arise from the experiences I have had with people and the written records about man to which my mind has been exposed. The ideas to which I am dedicated are dynamic, changing concepts about the world, the human condition, and me. Because these thoughts are the antithesis of static, I reserve the privilege of being able to benefit from tomorrow's experiences. It takes a full lifetime of growing to be a human.

I love to teach. I love to learn. Both processes are sources of great pleasure for me. I hope to engage in those activities in sound and imaginative ways for the rest of my life. Teaching and learning in their broadest terms are fascinating and deserve my most devoted attention. If the learning process consisted only of acquiring knowledge, then on today's educational scene a teacher might well be a liability. But I believe a teacher, present in person, has a role to play in facilitating the mysterious process of learning.

Many questions surround this complex interaction, and it is further complicated by the North American context. What is an education? What constitutes a university education? What is a teacher? What is an effective teacher? What is learning? Are there prescribed roles for administrators, teachers, students, and parents? What are the conditions which facilitate learning? Can learning be measured? If answers come quickly, then the problems are not understood. These and many more are value-laden enigmas that, to my knowledge, have eluded consensus.

What happens to college and university undergraduates during that important slice of their lifespan which four years or more of college represents?

> Critical examination of several studies of freshmen and senior responses to questions about their college experiences reveal that comparatively few changes occur in the personal characteristics of students and that even these few, while widespread among students on different campuses, are neither universal nor radical . . . some of these changes occur in young people regardless of whether or not they attend college.[2]

It is usually assumed that the whole student will be affected by university, but in fact changes in him as a person appear to be minimal. What are the implications?

Teaching and imparting knowledge might make sense in an unchanging environment. But modern man is living in a world that is continually undergoing change. The knowledge that a student will receive today will be out of date or modified within a very short time.

Education must aim for a more subtle goal: the facilitation of change and learning. The educated man is the man who has learned how to learn; the man who has learned how to adapt and change; the man who has realized that no knowledge is secure, that only the process of seeking knowledge gives a basis for security. In our fast-changing world reliance on process rather than upon static knowledge is the goal for education that makes sense.

The teacher or facilitator is, of course, intimately involved in this process. As a facilitator, he must deal with a number of variables. What is to be taught? How is it to be taught? Who is to be taught this content in this setting? Who is qualified to teach this student? What is the process whereby meaning is transferred? What kind of environment or learning climate is most conducive to learning? A basic underlying question that persists is, who besides the facilitator should deal with these variables?

There are trends emerging from inquiries in each of these areas that are sources of excitement and stimulation. The challenge is not only to keep up with these, but to absorb these findings. To be what I say I am, what I believe, what I know, and what I am—all at the same time—is difficult. On one hand I am forced by conventional rules and tradition to conform to stereotype expectations. I am expected, for example, to know answers, to give grades, to prescribe acceptable activities, and even, in some rare cases, to discipline students.

Beyond these and many other prescribed functions in a sometimes over-prescribed context, I am "free" to experiment with curriculum, techniques, students, learning, and the environment. Some of the limitations are real and some are fancied, for the system tends to perpetuate its good as well as its evil. The fact that there is no agreement on the meaning of basic terms such as "learning," "teacher," and "education," is both a restriction and an asset. In this schizophrenic setting, therefore, consistency is impossible. But being a real, human, loving, accepting person is feasible.

The whole concept of the "teacher" is clearly changing. The very word as we now define it will be inadequate to describe the variety of people and skills that will be needed to serve in the approaches to education that are becoming possible.

Student-centred teaching (SCT) is one approach. It is a variety of leadership-in-learning that is appropriate in an ever-changing environment, while meeting some of the new goals for education. The characteristics and the philosophy of student-centred teaching were described by Carl Rogers in his book, *Client-Centered Therapy*.[3] He has been a major source of inspiration from which other teachers and I have gleaned and refined ideas. I am indebted to Rogers for my belief that the student, not the teacher and her performance, should be the centre, the focal point, of the learning process.

> It may avoid needless misunderstanding if it is clearly stated at the outset that education which embodies the principles of client-

centered therapy has relevance for only one type of educational goal. It is not education which would be relevant in an authoritarian culture, nor would it implement an authoritarian philosophy. If the aim of education is to produce well-informed technicians who will be completely amenable to carrying out all orders of constituted authority without questioning, then the method we are to describe is highly inappropriate. In general it is relevant only to the type of goal which is loosely described as democratic. . . .

This would seem to mean that the goal of democratic education is to assist students to become individuals

who are able to take self-initiated action and to be responsible for those actions;
who are capable of intelligent choices and self-direction;
who are critical learners, able to evaluate the contributions made by others;
who have acquired knowledge relevant to the solution of problems;
who, even more importantly, are able to adapt flexibly and intelligently to new problem situations;
who have internalized an adaptive mode of approach to problems, utilizing all pertinent experience freely and creatively;
who are able to cooperate effectively with others in these various activities;
who work, not for the approval of others, but in terms of their own socialized purposes. . . .

Whether this goal is appropriate to our current culture is a question which each reader must decide for himself. Since our culture to a very large degree is organized on an authoritarian and hierarchical basis and only partially upon a democratic basis, it may seem to some that education should reflect this ambivalence.[4]

I believe in student-centred teaching because its goals are consistent with what I believe institutions of education should strive for: the development of the responsible individual. The role of the teacher is vastly overrated: a teacher only facilitates learning. The learner only learns what he really wants to learn in terms of rewards to the self. To focus on the teacher or on teaching is to emphasize the wrong questions. To facilitate change towards democratic goals the student and the learning climate should be the focal point. Full achievement of these ends is not feasible within the present structure of the university. However, there is a degree of compromise that one can tolerate and still seek these objectives.

The Facilitator

The facilitator in student-centred teaching is the initiated leader who has some tools to aid the students in setting their goals, analysing information, and making available human and material resources. Some roles of the facilitator include his ability to motivate and direct; to know each student for whom he is responsible, and by name; to care about them as people and to encourage the individual and the group to develop their potential. Choosing methods, audio-visual aids and techniques for the classroom experiences that involve the learner are important functions of the facilitator. As a result, if the student is genuinely interested in learning, the role of the leader is to aid the individual in reaching *his* goals.

This role emphasizes the process of learning and techniques of how to learn. To most important questions there are no definitive answers. The facilitator helps the learner learn how to learn, to ask important questions and apply some standards of critical thinking to the analysis of such questions. In order to accomplish these goals, the democratic leadership of the facilitator must be highly flexible. The facilitator is more actively involved than in a conventional authoritarian setting. He must listen carefully as well as speak. He must be prepared not to read a lecture but to discuss not only the facts but the worth and merit of the information. He too is a learner. He is a resource. He is a risk-taker. He is a stabilizer. He is a Person.

The Student

The student and the facilitator have much in common. The essential difference in student-centred teaching is that the student is uninitiated. That is to say, he usually lacks the experience or the knowledge that would qualify him for the role of the facilitator. In student-centred teaching the student is responsible for his education. The student's involvement and interaction with his environment, with other students, and with the facilitator are important aspects of that responsibility. Cliché-ridden as it is, it must be repeated that the student will only benefit from the resources that the university has to offer to the degree that he is willing to take advantage of them for his total development as a person.

In practice such development is usually a cumulative process. As the student becomes more involved and responsible for his education, the more rewarding he finds the experience, the more he tends to immerse himself in the opportunity. He is free—to come and go, to read, to explore with other learners, to meet his needs. The facilitator, the classroom, the other students, the available resources become adjuncts to his education and not the centre of the student's educational experience.

The Atmosphere for Learning

The climate of student-centred teaching is of great significance. As has already been implied, the university setting is only an arrangement of resources and tools that a student uses in order to learn and gain an education. The student's attitude concerning his education is at the heart of any revolution that student-centred teaching might create. Nothing should or can stand in the way of that education if the student feels that in a total sense it is his responsibility and to his benefit. In addition: "The essential principle might perhaps be the following: Within the limitations which are imposed by circumstance and authority, or are imposed by the instructor as necessary for his own psychological comfort, an atmosphere of permissiveness, of acceptance, of reliance upon student responsibility, is [to be] created."[5]

With the onus on the student for his education, the experience has the potential of being a vital, volatile, ecstatic one, combined with the elation of personal achievement. Education is not just a matter of courses, classes or teachers, but a matter of growing, exploring, changing, reformulating, and renewal.

Student-centred teaching is one means to the ends of democratic, ongoing education. It can help the individual in a world of changing needs and changing roles. It is an approach that can have a lasting impact. It is, after all, what the real world is all about and reflects the human condition.

The physical and psychic world that we live in cries out for people-involvement—for responsible citizens with feelings of self-identity and worth. I believe with deep conviction that student-centred teaching is one experience that can help people become informed, concerned, compassionate members of society. I believe that student-centred teaching is an experience that can have an immense and lasting influence for good on the lives of the participants.

The pragmatism of pedagogy is the bridge between the romanticized realms of conjecture and the realities of the classroom. It is entirely conceivable that what I think I am doing and what is actually learned by the students may bear little relationship. Let me outline briefly what I think takes place in the course entitled "Communication" for which I am responsible.

Home economics in higher education is an applied discipline that draws its subject matter from many different areas of study. Flossie M. Byrd has defined it as "the study of the human and material forces affecting homes and families and the utilization of this knowledge for the benefit of mankind."[6]

"Communication" is designed to help undergraduate students of home economics to pass on knowledge they have acquired so that other people may be helped to help themselves. It is also hoped that the course will help the student to gain some insights about herself. There are three sections of the course required of all fourth-year students enrolled as Dietetic or General Family Science majors in the School of Home Economics at the University of British Columbia. One section affords opportunities to practise prepared oral presentations with the aid of video-tape feedback. In another, students are required to practise interviewing in a clinical setting. I coordinate these sections and am directly responsible for the third, which is described in the calendar as follows: "Group Process as it relates to Home Economics, with special emphases on oral expression, nonverbal language and levels of human interaction. Some implications of mass communication are explored." The course varies from year to year so what follows is not an exact description of any one year's experience. Students entering the course have diverse backgrounds, with the social sciences as well as the physical sciences represented. To my knowledge no student has entered with any previous experience of a formal course in communication.

The objectives of the course are outlined according to Bloom[7] and Krathwahl's[8] levels of learning in two domains, the cognitive and the affective. They are: to understand a broader definition of communication, to gain some understanding of five related concepts, and to become aware of the interrelationship of these concepts. In thirteen two-hour sessions approximately seventy students explore five concepts and accompanying sets of generalizations as they relate to communication. The concepts are as follows: Man in a Mass Media Society, Man in Groups, Man to Man: The I-It Relationship, Man to Man: The I-Thou Relationship, and Man and his Human Potential. To help the student visualize the interrelationship of these concepts, a systems approach is used, that is, a way of thinking about a total system and its components. The one used with the "Communication" class is referred to as a microcosmos—simply a visual or graphic aid for the purpose of clarifying the relationships of the five major concepts and their interrelationship with sub-concepts.

The learning experiences are planned to help the student become personally involved in the content. The exercises and activities that are chosen are as important as the content. Techniques and methods which require the students to interact in varying degrees of depth are carefully outlined in sequence for each two-hour session and build from the known to the unknown, the concrete to the abstract, and so forth. This logical progression is planned to help the student understand the objectives and content of the course and to see possibilities for further study when the course is completed.

The first two sessions are used to acquaint the student with the course requirements and procedures, and to provide some opportunities for interaction within the class. Students are encouraged to learn each others' names and use them.

I outline during this stage a set of rules, and make it clear that they can be negotiated at any time if they are found to be unacceptable. Some in use at present are:

Notes 1) Please do not take notes, listen and mimeos will be given to you throughout the term that will summarize the major ideas. An extensive reading list is provided for your convenience.

Books 2) Books are provided in the reading rooms and libraries on campus and may be purchased at the bookstore. I do not lend my personal copies.

Punctuality 3) You must be on time for this class; the door will be locked when the bell rings.

"I" 4) Please use "I" when discussing issues or presenting ideas. It is a symbol of your responsibility for what you contribute to this class. Please do not use phrases as "everybody knows," "most people think," and so forth.

Process 5) There are no "right" answers in this class. The important thing is the thought and logic that you use in order to reach YOUR answer.

Feedback 6) Please practise the technique of clarifying the ideas you hear. Be sure that what you hear is what the other person actually said.

The rules are only guidelines. Some are student-centred; several are for my own comfort and convenience.

The actual teaching-learning sessions will not be outlined in detail. Here, however, are some of the experiences that the students have said they found particularly meaningful.

To clarify the phenomenon of Man in a Mass Media Society, I ask the students to bring for analysis a bag of garbage—one of the media of their society. We use money and credit cards for that purpose as well. As background for the first few sessions the students write graffiti on sheets of paper taped to the walls. Marshall McLuhan's film, *The Medium is the Message* (National Film Board), is a thought-provoking presentation that helps to pose some questions concerning Man in a Mass Media Society. The students ultimately explore the extent to which the individual is programmed in a mass media society. This is a controversial subject and stimulates further reading and discussion. There are structured assignments that are planned to help the students observe, describe, and interpret these mass forms of communication which surround them.

The possibilities for exploration of the Man in Groups concept are endless. There are many educational games and exercises available to help the student gain insights into the behaviour of groups and individuals in groups. In the course, attention is directed to experiences that deal with optimal group size, group tasks, and leadership as it relates to group behaviour. Increasing the group size over a controlled period of time while attempting to solve a specific problem is one way used to illustrate some simple facts about the ability of a group to accomplish a task in relation to the number in that group. Group consensus problem solving is an exercise that involves the students in a task that requires decisions about the priorities of issues presented to each group. For example: What is most important and what is least important of the seven attributes of a counter-culture that offers hope for a better quality of life for Canadians? This problem requires the group to work closely together for the task is not complete until every member of a group of six agrees on the hierarchy.

Role playing is used in an exercise in which each of the six members of a group acts out a specific leadership style while the group is involved in discussing an issue. After the group has experienced these six different styles, the effects on the behaviour of the group are discussed and each group is asked to arrive at some generalizations about leadership and the function of a leader. Is a "good" leader a product of the needs and functions of a group, or are leaders born?

Man to Man: The I-It Relationship is introduced by having the students interact while wearing masks. There are practical problems in this exercise. Some masks are difficult to breathe in, for example, and some are warm to wear for long periods. In general the students do find this a revealing experience. What are some of the advantages and disadvantages of wearing a mask? Whom did you talk to most and to what kind of mask were you attracted? With whom did you interact least? What masks made you feel isolated? How did you feel about the way others treated you? Do you think people wear masks and for what reasons? Do you ever wear a mask?

The I-Thou Relationship is a deep and fascinating topic for most of the classes to which this concept has been presented. For man to aspire to and attain such an intimate level of communication is discussed from many different viewpoints. Love, joy, and empathy are three emotions that are specifically explored. These are approached in an eclectic manner, through the writings of such men as Martin Buber, Rollo May, Carl Rogers, Abraham Maslow, and Gordon Allport. Small group discussions, situational flash cards and photos, circular response, interviewing, and visual aids that depict common stereotypes are some of the methods used.

The concluding session on this concept is a session devoted to listening—a multi-media experience in which use is made of records, short films, concept loops, film-strips with and without sound, objects that must be identified by listening to the descriptions, taped stories that must be retold after hearing them once. These activities encourage an understanding of listening as an active process, as a vital aspect of communication and as an important link in the I-Thou Relationship.

Man and his Potential is the final concept that is explored in the course. Films, such as Roman Polanski's *Two Men and a Wardrobe* and the National Film Board's production, *Angel*, are used, as well as lecture-discussions with opportunities to experience how perceptive each person's senses of sight, sound, smell, and touch are.

In the last class session I use half of a large blackboard to write down the objectives that I had had for the course. The students are asked to fill in the other half of the space with what they feel they have gained from the course. This is usually an exciting period. The students' responses cover the gamut and are often quite different from the ones I have outlined. It is revealing to discover how many and varied are the experiences the students have had.

A large group discussion is centred around defining the "Unreasonable Man." This final exercise is meant to help the student look with fresh insights into this phrase in relation to their potential for seeing the new and exciting world about them. In Shaw's *Man and Superman* one of the characters is the author of "The Revolutionist's Handbook," from which this maxim is taken: "The reasonable man adapts himself to the world: the unreasonable one persists in trying to adapt the world to himself. Therefore all progress depends on the unreasonable man."

Evaluation

The evaluation procedures and instruments for the course are in the process of development. One in use as an experiment is called a grade contract. The goals to be achieved and the evidence to be shown in order to earn a grade of "D" are stated explicitly. So also are the additional goals and evidence for a grade of "C", with still more, equally clearly stated, for a "B" and, likewise, for an "A". Thus a student can choose her target, low or high, and be assured of the grade indicated if she fulfils her part of the contract. Students have been enthusiastic about this scheme.

This essay is a brief statement about some of my ideas and attitudes and some examples of how I practise student-centred teaching. It is a philosophy about people that is ever-changing. As I grow with the students the interrelationships and possibilities are inexhaustible. I believe that the facilitator is the key to the effectiveness of the student-centred approach and I also feel that the facilitator is dispensable. My ongoing challenge is to be who I say I am and who I say I want to be.

Learning in groups requires thinking, feeling, choosing, and acting out. Traditionally, education has been concerned most often with verbal learning, less often with growth in the ability to express feelings and least often with what people actually do. Ideas, values, principles, attitudes, feelings, and concrete behaviour patterns are involved in whole-person process-product learning. I believe that student-centred teaching has great potential as *one* approach for guiding students in higher education toward understanding and becoming involved in higher levels of learning. I feel that sound and imaginative ways of educating are vital forces in a democratic society, and I have just begun to fathom what a helping relationship with people can mean.

ELEANORE VAINES

Eleanore Lund Vaines was born in the State of Washington and attended Wenatchee Valley College and the University of Washington (B.S. in home economics education). Later she qualified as a Master of Science in home economics education at Cornell University, and expects to complete work on her doctorate at Michigan State University in 1974. She taught home economics in high school in her home state, at the American College for Girls in Cairo, Egypt, and at Cornell before joining the staff of the UBC School of Home Economics in 1964 as an assistant professor. She has served also as an extension lecturer at Oakland University and Michigan State University.

Mrs. Vaines has read papers at annual meetings of the Canadian Association of University Teachers of Home Economics, and written articles for the Canadian Home Economics Journal *and other periodicals. She is the author, with Lynda Coluhoun, Lynne Holder, and Melvin Lee, of* The Teaching of Home Economics in British Columbia—A Survey *(British Columbia Teachers Federation, 1970) and her* Trends and Tendencies in Home Economics: Parental Attitudes and Opinion Questionnaire *was published by the University of British Columbia in 1972. She is a member of the American and Canadian Home Economics Associations, the National Council on Family Relations, the International Communication Association, and the American Academy of Political and Social Science.*

According to her former students, Ellie Vaines (they referred to her in this familiar and affectionate way) was a vivacious young woman, full of intellectual and physical vitality, enthusiastic about her subject (communication), and her students. She took pains to know them individually, treated them as friends, and radiated a warmth which was genuine.

The class usually sat in a circle, face to face, but sometimes was subdivided into groups of four or five, or even pairs. Each meeting was a new experience, both of topic and method, according to the graduates. They spoke, too, of the unique experiences arranged during the course: role-playing, preparation of a television presentation, training in interviewing techniques, a "joy trip," a T-group weekend marathon, and others.

She encouraged students to become involved in the class and with each other, respected any opinions which could be effectively supported, and inspired individual pursuit of knowledge beyond course requirements. The testimony of her former students was that Mrs. Vaines was an effective and inspiring group leader—"a true communicator."

NOTES

1. *Perceiving, Behaving, Becoming: A Focus for Education*, Yearbook of the Association for Supervision and Curriculum Development (Washington, 1962), p. 1.

2. Theodore M. Newcomb, "What Happens to Students in College?" *Memo to the Faculty*, No. 41 (Ann Arbor: Center for Research on Learning and Teaching, University of Michigan, 1970), p. 1.

3. Carl R. Rogers, *Client-Centered Therapy: Its Current Practice, Implications and Theory* (Boston: Houghton Mifflin, 1951).

4. Ibid., pp. 387–88.

5. Ibid., p. 397.

6. Flossie M. Byrd, "A Definition of Home Economics for the 70's," *Journal of Home Economics*, LXII, 6 (June 1970), 411–15.

7. Benjamin Bloom, ed., *Taxonomy of Educational Objectives, Handbook I: Cognitive Domain* (New York: Longmans, Green, 1956).

8. David Krathwahl, Benjamin Bloom and Bertram B. Masia, *Taxonomy of Educational Objectives, Handbook II: Affective Domain* (New York: David McKay, 1964).

From Situation to Solution

Jack L. Summers

How do I teach? Frankly, I'm not quite sure. At the beginning of each period I get up before the students and talk for a while; then the students talk for a while. After this I talk some more, and usually ask some questions until the period ends. In this manner we wander through a representative sample of the material which the course is designed to cover. I hope that at the end of the term the student will emerge from this exercise knowing more about the subject than he did at the beginning.

This may appear to be a casual approach to university teaching, and it probably is. When I began university teaching I thought that if I didn't tell my students, they would never know! But over the years I have come to realize that students learn a great deal in spite of their teachers.

Trying to explain how you teach is like trying to explain how you breathe. It is a highly personalized art during which things happen in a natural sequence without too much conscious effort. This sounds terribly smug, but I have taught, trained, and instructed assorted groups of people for more than thirty years. After that length of time at least some of your work should become a natural part of your daily life. For me, teaching is a very pleasant vocation rather than a profound exercise in pedagogy.

I began teaching in the army as a youngster and have been at it in some form or other ever since. I was given some formal training in basic methods of instruction, and a great deal of practice. Though this training was most elementary by any standards, the fundamentals of good instruction which were pounded into me have stood the test of time, and are still the basis of my teaching style and technique. And to answer the question which may have come to your mind—no, I don't teach dispensing by numbers.

It is unfashionable today to say anything good about the army. But I have been subjected to instruction in a wide variety of situations, including postgraduate academic, industrial and military, and I have found that the army provided the highest uniform standard of teaching. In the fields of planning, general problem solving, and decision making, army instruction was outstanding.

I teach in a small professional school, a college of pharmacy, with a total enrolment of some 300 students. Not only does this determine an approach to teaching, but the very fact that I teach at all. I strayed into teaching from economic necessity as an undergraduate, and remained because it was so stimulating. Also, I remained a pharmacist first and a teacher second.

Some contend that professional schools don't belong in the university but with technical schools or other post-secondary vocational training institutions. But the fact is that professional schools are an established part of our universities, and further discussion of the wisdom of this decision is rhetorical.

The approach to teaching in the professional school is different to that of the traditional single disciplines. Eliot Freidson, Professor of Sociology of New York University, describes this difference in the following way:

> By and large, it seems to me that a professional school in a university is concerned with training practitioners of some important art and at the same time with advancing the special knowledge which these practitioners need for improving their art. In the professional school the attempt is made to bring together materials from all the various disciplines which are relevant to practice. In that sense, there is a kind of merging of all the relevant disciplines toward the particular purpose of practice. In contrast, it seems to me that graduate schools of arts and science are more concerned with training researchers or thinkers in various single disciplines, the discipline and its investigation taking precedence over the practice of teaching. These researchers in graduate schools are preoccupied with a very special, hopefully generic field of knowledge within a given discipline —not a variety of disciplines related to a given task of practice, but rather one discipline. This can be so because training is not concerned with the application of knowledge to particular practical tasks—general knowledge which may be used for some kind of practical research or investigation in the future, yes, but not training for the practice of some particular practical task.[1]

There is a very close relationship between the teacher and his students in a professional college. They are members of the same club. From the first day of enrolment the teacher becomes involved with students as individuals who will put into practice the various theories, concepts, and scientific knowledge of the profession rather than as partially vacant receptacles for knowledge. On graduation, student and teacher become professional peers. This relationship prevents the teacher from becoming wound up in his own subject rather than his students. And, frankly, it makes teaching exciting.

Teaching in the professional school has some unique occupational hazards. Upon graduation the product of the teacher is cast upon the profession to be judged by his associates. And your performance as a teacher also is judged. If you have done a reasonable job, or been fortunate in having bright students who survived their academic experience without having their intelligence diminished, or both, you will enjoy a reasonably good reputation among your practising associates. But, if too high a proportion of the unintelligent manage to survive the rigors of the course, and commit some heinous misdeeds through stupidity, or bad judgment, the blame for the catastrophe falls upon your shoulders. And perhaps it should. The teacher in the professional school is the recipient of continuous unsolicited advice from his practising associates on how to do his job. While you learn to receive such gratuitous instruction with a reasonable calm, it is difficult to accept gracefully when given by former students whom you considered of marginal intelligence. It is particularly painful if the graduate has become a resounding success through the sale of beach balls, or some similar activity, which has placed but a gentle strain on his professional competence.

We are expected to attend provincial and national meetings of various professional societies and associations. These meetings take place during the summer months, usually reserved for more scholarly pursuits, and while not always convenient, they do keep the teacher in constant contact with the profession and its problems, and also with his graduates. The splendid isolation of the ivory tower is a luxury which the professional teacher can ill afford. Temporary retreat to such solitude for brief periods may be essential to preserve your sanity, but linger too long and you lose touch with the realities of your profession. When this occurs you risk becoming a detriment to both your students and your profession.

This is the milieu in which I teach.

It is obvious that the teacher's approach and methods of instruction depend upon the subjects being taught. Over the past twenty years I have taught a variety of classes in the field of pharmacy. Some have been applied sciences involving the presentation, explanation, and application of basic scientific principles. At the present time I teach in two areas in pharmacy which might be described as professional practice as opposed to basic pharmaceutical sciences.

My major field is hospital pharmacy management, a full class of two semesters' work in the fourth and final year of the course. Enrolment varies from fifteen to twenty-five students.

The class is designed to teach decision-making at the department head level. It includes material on hospital operations in general, the operation of the hospital pharmacy department in detail, and some basic management principles, applied particularly to departmental management. There is a laboratory period in which students are assigned to work in the pharmacy department of University Hospital for four hours a week. Seminars on specialized topics, and visits to other hospitals, are included as a portion of the laboratory work.

The second area of teaching is history, law and ethics as a basis for professional judgment. This takes the form of a one-semester class of approximately 100 first-year students. This class is designed to give the freshman some knowledge of the background of his profession, the laws which govern the practice of pharmacy, and the ethical and historical factors which will affect his judgment in practice.

As you might well imagine, there are some problems in trying to discuss drug laws intelligently with freshmen who still don't know one drug from another. For this reason, a series of lectures on drug laws is presented as part of a senior class to some seventy students. The series covers the introduction of the legislation, its purpose, its present-day interpretation and actual application to situations in the daily practice of pharmacy.

From the foregoing, it can be seen that I teach the application of concepts to professional practice, rather than in an area of specific scientific knowledge. The object in all of these classes is to train the student to think, and to make judgments.

Like anyone else, my approach to teaching is conditioned by training and experience in the subject area. I served as director of pharmaceutical services for University Hospital for nine years, and assistant director of the hospital for three. During this period I continued to teach a class in hospital pharmacy. Having actually practised hospital pharmacy, and having made decisions at a department level, I find that teaching hospital pharmacy is relatively simple because the subject matter has been a very real part of my daily life rather than gleanings from the experience of others.

Experience of this nature has its dangers. There is a tendency to lean too heavily on personal experience in place of keeping up with newer developments. The experience of other practitioners, often more able than myself, may be discounted, or even ignored. Everyone likes to talk about his own experience, and I am no exception. But such experiences, usually of greatest interest to the teller, are seldom an adequate substitute for a well-prepared lecture. Moreover, there is a hidden danger in using personal experience to illustrate principles because of the tendency to tell about the times you were right. Some of your horrendous blunders in judgment could serve a more useful purpose, but are seldom related.

Association in an advisory capacity with the Food and Drug Directorate for many years has provided an excellent background in federal drug legislation, particularly the intent of the legislation, which frequently is much more important than the letter of the law in the exercise of judgment.

My approach to teaching is based on the premise that I possess some degree of knowledge, experience, and expertise in a particular field. My role is to teach the students what I think they should know about the particular subject. Their role is to listen, to think, and, one hopes, to learn something about the subject from somebody who knows more about it than they do.

I know the subjects that I teach, and they are of great personal interest. There are many recent developments, both in hospital pharmacy and in the laws which regulate the profession, and I enjoy talking about them. These subjects are part of the basic fabric of pharmacy, and are of interest to the students. This makes teaching easy, exciting, and pleasant.

My basic method of instruction is the lecture. By all standards of modern teaching technology, and from the latest results of student opinion polls, this is absolutely the worst possible form of teaching. It has been said that there are few subjects which cannot be taught better by some method other than the lecture, but if one is forced to the reluctant conclusion that he cannot avoid the lecture, the next step is to decide how to make the best of it.

Old-fashioned lecturing is definitely not the "in" thing. But then I am not an "in" person. I don't wear sideburns, and the prime manifestation of revolt against conformity is shaving. But lecturing comes easily. I use the lecture method because it suits me as a person and the subjects that I teach. There is nothing remarkable about my performance. Although of a reasonably genial nature, I am not a comedian and cannot tell funny stories well. I envy the person who can begin each class with an appropriate story. I just don't remember jokes, and get the punch line all mixed up when I do try one on for size. I don't do card tricks or juggle, and am a terrible folk singer, so all that remains is to stand up and talk about things.

Contrary to popular belief, a lecture does not have to be a dull recitation of factual material. There is a bit of the ham in most of us and it's surprising what an impromptu performance can be worked up on occasions. For me, the lecture provides a very flexible method of presenting a subject. Even with relatively large classes it is possible to develop a high degree of class participation in discussion. This, of course, depends on the subject being taught. It is difficult to visualize a scintillating class discussion of Kreb's Cycle. But where the subject treats concepts that involve judgments, it is possible to introduce some basic facts and ideas at the beginning of a period, discuss their application until the class has grasped the particular point, and then proceed with the presentation of the next group of facts. The class can be questioned, or ask questions, at any time during the presentation.

I find it an instructive exercise to assign some of the lectures to the students. This, of course, can best be done successfully in senior classes with a limited enrolment. It provides a welcome break from routine teaching, and one hopes, gives the student a better appreciation of life on the other side of the lectern. Most of the learning accrues to the individual who prepares and presents the lecture rather than to his fellow students, and careful selection of topics and constructive monitoring by the teacher are required to obtain acceptable results.

Having the students teach part of their own course may be tactically sound in helping you to survive the mid-February doldrums, but you run the risk of some of the students doing a better job than the teacher, and this can be somewhat disconcerting.

I make considerable use of handout material as a teaching aid. At the beginning of a class each student is given an outline which includes a statement of the aim of the class, and sets out the work to be covered during the term, organized by subject heading and sub-heading. The outline is supplemented through the course of the lectures by copies of charts, tables, statements of policy, recommendations of national committees and commissions on relevant topics, and appropriate papers from the literature. Note-taking is reduced to an absolute minimum, and more time is available for discussion.

The local news media, newspapers, radio and television provide an excellent ready-made audio-visual aid which requires no classroom time for presentation. It seems that people have an insatiable and morbid curiosity about their own internal workings, and health news in general, and drugs and hospitals in particular, make good news copy and television fare. We begin at least one out of every three teaching periods by discussing some item from the paper or the morning radio news directly related to the field of study. This isn't a delaying manoeuvre, though it can be used as such, but rather a means of making the student realize that the class material does have some relationship to the real world. This is reassuring to both teacher and student.

Generally speaking, I don't use audio-visual aids to advantage. Their effective use requires careful preparation and rehearsal, and I find them a great deal of work in relation to teaching value. Also, there are certain built-in hazards associated with the use of projectors. Darkening the room has an immediate soporific effect, and you have two strikes against you before visually casting the eternal truths before the ignorant. Slides consisting of columns of microscopic print are a sure way of putting a large class into a trance. If you are illustrating a complicated stepwise procedure by means of a visualized flow chart, don't expect more than 5 per cent of the class to be with you at the finish.

Throughout a long career as a student, spanning many years and a variety of learning situations, I was subjected to films on everything from the mechanism of the internal combustion engine to the evils of drink, and managed to sleep through most of them. This experience has warped my faith in the teaching value of films. In spite of this I use films on rare occasions, not as a substitute for a lecture, but to supplement and reinforce basic concepts which have first been presented in lecture form. I prefer to use films with small groups of students, usually as part of a seminar, when the concepts which the film illustrates can be thoroughly discussed and the material reviewed in a critically objective fashion.

In spite of the foregoing, I use one audio-visual aid consistently—the blackboard, or greenboard as it actually is in more modern classrooms. I don't know if it helps or confuses my students, but it sure helps me. If I write something on the board the students come to life and copy it down. The fact that it may be quite irrelevant doesn't seem to matter. This wakes them up and provides a bit of exercise.

The blackboard has several other uses. Sometimes I go chasing red herrings and become thoroughly lost in the course of a lecture. At this point I turn and write something on the board, slowly and deliberately, as if guided by divine inspiration. This gives both me and the students a bit of a breather and a chance to get back on the track.

I find it a useful exercise to write down the headings of the subject to be discussed. This acts as a marker, and if you wander too far off course, you can find your way back simply by glancing at the subject heading on the board. Also, this gives the student a fighting chance in his struggle to determine just what you are supposed to be talking about. The blackboard may be the most ancient of audio-visual aids, but it's helpful, and you can erase your mistakes.

Like all teachers, I find examinations a bind. I'm sure my students do too. But as yet, I have not developed a better way of assessing the student's knowledge of the subject. It may be old-fashioned, but what the students are able to get out of a class is important to me. I am interested in how the student can apply the principles discussed in the class, rather than his precise knowledge of specific factual material. For this reason, and because my classes lend themselves to this technique, my examinations are usually of the case study type in which the student is given a situation and asked to develop his solution.

I have taught courses, such as pharmacology, that were based on factual knowledge, and in these cases the situation type of question has but limited application. But regardless of type, I find the examination a useful teaching tool. This, of course, applies to those tests which can be discussed in class, and for this reason I use mid-term tests despite the anguish of marking them. Also, it is only fair that the students have a trial run. I am not without idiosyncrasies, and half the battle in passing any class is to know the teacher and what he expects for an answer. The student is entitled to learn this before the final exam.

It distresses me that there is little opportunity to go over final exam papers with students. This is particularly true when the student is mistaken on a fundamental point. Challenged on it at a later date, he'll say that Summers told him, and that will make us both look like idiots!

With small classes it is much easier to assess a student's capability through class discussions, seminars, and written assignments. However, in large classes, particularly of first-year students, it is difficult to assess student progress without some form of examinations.

The aspect of teaching that I find most challenging is stimulating the student's thought processes. It is simple enough to impart factual knowledge, or even the mechanics of solving scientific problems, but the task of teaching the student to think is more difficult. However, as the occasional student finds the novel experience to his liking, and begins to exercise his thought process more frequently, it becomes a rewarding experience as well as a trying one.

Like so many other phases of instruction, I find it easier to teach people to think for themselves in smaller classes. In this type of training there is no substitute for learning by doing. And as an essential part of the instructional process is presenting the results of independent thought for the critical review of both teacher and fellow students, there is a real limitation on the number of students that can be handled by a single teacher.

The basic method which I have used is neither new nor original. It is the old technique of assigning a situation problem which the student must work through, make his own judgments, and arrive at a solution. Selected students present their solutions which are discussed and analysed by other class members. The simple factor of available time limits the use of this technique.

In this essay I have attempted to explain my approach to teaching. As approaches go, it appears quite ordinary, and even a little dull. This sobering assessment has restrained me from recommending my approach as a sure-fire method of achieving lasting fame as a teacher. But it has provided me with an effective means of establishing two-way communication with my students, I hope to their benefit, and certainly to the constant renewal of my faith in the young people of our universities.

JACK L. SUMMERS

Jack Summers was raised and educated in Saskatchewan, and began his apprenticeship in pharmacy in 1937 in the town of Wilkie. His pharmacy career was interrupted temporarily while he served in the Canadian army throughout World War II. On retirement from the active army in 1946, he enrolled in the College of Pharmacy, University of Saskatchewan, and graduated with the degree of Bachelor of Science in Pharmacy in 1949. Three years later he obtained a Master of Science degree from the State University of Iowa.

Professor Summers was appointed to the staff of the College of Pharmacy of the University of Saskatchewan in 1949, and has remained a member of faculty continuously since that date. In 1954 he was also appointed to the position of director of pharmaceutical services of the new University Hospital in Saskatoon, and in 1963 became assistant director of the hospital. He resumed full-time teaching duties in 1966 to head the newly created section of professional practice of the College of Pharmacy.

Professor Summers has participated in the work of various pharmacy organizations, serving as president of the Canadian Society of Hospital Pharmacists in 1956–57 and of the Canadian Pharmaceutical Association in 1964–65. His research interests have been in hospital pharmacy organization and management, and in drug distribution systems in hospitals. Over a period of more than twenty years he has contributed a stream of articles to pharmacy journals, and has been editor of The Canadian Journal of Hospital Pharmacy *since 1961.*

Meanwhile his interest in the army and in military history has continued in parallel with his activities in the world of pharmacy. He returned to the militia in 1949, held a variety of appointments and commands, and in 1970 became commander of the Prairie Militia Area with the rank of brigidier general.

According to his former students, a dynamic personality, a sense of humour, and a door always open to students were admired characteristics of Professor Summers, but most of the comments about him and his teaching stressed his wide experience and his way of encouraging learning.

His courses were current and contained no superfluous padding, and he made use of stories and anecdotes from his own experience "to bring points home." He gave the students an outline of the course in advance so they knew where he was going, and went to the trouble of xeroxing and distributing pertinent articles to which students did not have access.

Professor Summers forced students to think for themselves. One graduate described his method this way: "In the third year Law and Ethics course, situation questions, i.e. 'What would you do if . . . ?' formed the basis of the lectures. On the written exams, students had to analyse the best method of approach to a practical problem." Another reported: "His exams were interesting and challenging and did not require a regurgitation of what had been taught. He expected a thorough understanding of the principles he had taught and made use of exams to test the student's ability to apply these principles to situations he might meet in a hospital pharmacy."

NOTE

1. Eliot Freidson, "Social Aspects of the Professions: Their Place in Academia," *American Journal of Pharmaceutical Education*, 34, no. 4 (November 1970).

La préparation est la plus grande partie

Z. *Mézl*

A l'invitation du rédacteur, cet article est basé seulement sur mon expérience et traite de sujets sur lesquels je n'ai fait aucune recherche personnelle.

J'enseigne la pathologie dentaire et buccale surtout par des cours et des travaux pratiques. J'emploie d'autres méthodes pédagogiques, régulièrement, comme auxiliaires. Parfois j'utilise la télévision en circuit fermé, l'enseignement programmé, ou le séminaire comme seuls moyens didactiques.

Je distingue deux étapes successives: 1) La préparation; 2) La présentation aux étudiants.

La préparation des cours

La préparation est la plus grande partie de mon travail. Avant d'enseigner je dois: 1) coordonner et classer mes idées sur le sujet (d'après la terminologie moderne: déterminer les objectifs et la philosophie de mon enseignement); 2) choisir les moyens de transmission les plus convenables pour traiter cette matière.

1) *Classification d'après les caractères du sujet.* Il est facile de trouver de telles classifications dans les manuels. Souvent on les y trouve mais leur approche est diverse. Il faut les comparer, juger, trouver les raisons des différences, et leurs avantages ou désavantages. Parfois, on découvre même cette revue critique dans la littérature.

Il faut finalement exposer la matière en quelques chapitres dans un ordre logique. Il est bon d'étudier chaque item avec un système ordonné (Dans un cas de maladie: causes, évolution, conséquences, complications). Ceci devient stéréotypé et monotone, mais la routine diminue l'effort nécessaire pour apprendre.

2) *Classification d'après l'importance.* Au niveau pré-gradué on peut enseigner seulement une fraction des connaissances actuelles à propos du sujet, donc, il faut sélectionner ce que l'on va enseigner. Mes critères sont les suivants: je choisis 1) cette partie de la matière dont les étudiants auront besoin; 2) des notions théoriques que je juge nécessaires pour développer une bonne compréhension du sujet; 3) des notions théoriques qui permettront de comprendre les problèmes essentiels de la recherche dans ce domaine.

Les cours n'ont pas à fournir l'occasion d'éblouir les étudiants, ni par les accomplissements de la science, ni par les connaissances du professeur. L'étudiant ne peut pas confier à sa mémoire une encyclopédie. C'est pourquoi je supprime les raretés, les curiosités, et les données de la recherche qui ne sont pas nécessaires pour la compréhension du sujet.

Je suis un critique sévère quand je prépare les cours sur des chapitres où j'ai un intérêt particulier et auxquels j'ai pu consacrer des travaux.

Chaque étudiant a son propre système de sélection et de compression de la matière qu'il apprend. Quand on lui présente une quantité excessive d'information, il va comprimer et simplifier d'après son système. Il peut simplifier beaucoup trop, il peut choisir les choses moins importantes et supprimer les choses essentielles. Mon but n'est pas de présenter aux étudiants une grande quantité d'informations. Par mon enseignement, je veux leur montrer les principes par lesquels l'information peut être le plus efficacement coordonnée, comprimée, et simplifiée.

3) *Classification du point de vue de l'étude.* Il y a des notions qu'il faut apprendre parce qu'on en a un besoin constant, comme les termes techniques, les règles élémentaires, et les classifications. Il en est d'autres qu'il faut comprendre, comme certains principes rationnels d'évolution des processus, application des règles, et confrontation à des situations nouvelles et inconnues.

Il y a des faits simples qu'il n'est pas nécessaire d'apprendre, qui ne sont pas d'usage courant et que chaque praticien peut trouver facilement dans un manuel. Dans mon cas ce sont, par exemple, des données numériques, des faits historiques, etc.

Quand la matière est classifiée, il faut choisir les moyens d'enseignement les plus appropriés. Pour certains de mes sujets comme la terminologie, les classifications, le cours me semble le moyen le plus efficace. Pour certains chapitres, quand il s'agit d'observer, percevoir, identifier des phénomènes, les travaux pratiques sont mieux adaptés.

La télévision en circuit fermé est extraordinairement efficace quand on veut montrer à un grand nombre d'étudiants de très petits objets. On peut les agrandir, les projeter sur plusieurs écrans.

Il faut aussi préparer les auxiliaires, surtout les dessins et choisir des transparents. Quand j'ai ordonné mes idées sur les considérations précédentes, je commence la rédaction du cours (formuler le message). Je sépare deux points: 1) la transmission des connaissances; 2) l'enseignement de la compréhension, de l'analyse, de la critique, et de l'application des connaissances.

La transmission des connaissances se fait mieux par écrit. La forme écrite permet à l'étudiant de récapituler la partie choisie avec la vitesse qu'il se choisit. Avec un texte écrit il suffit d'utiliser seulement une partie du temps du cours pour la transmission des connaissances et l'on peut réserver la plus grande partie du cours à un enseignement plus efficace. Il est ridicule de tolérer, pendant un cours, quatre-vingt étudiants prenant hâtivement des notes au lieu de se concentrer sur le sujet: une machine en quelques minutes peut produire tout ce matériel écrit avec une forme beaucoup plus parfaite que les étudiants.

Pour la plupart des cours, je prépare un texte. L'essentiel de ce travail est de simplifier la matière exactement pour le niveau de mes étudiants; donc, au début, pour le niveau des débutants, plus tard pour le niveau atteint par la majorité. Je simplifie 1) la matière et 2) le style.

1) Au début, il faut exercer les étudiants avec les idées les plus simples, expliquer les termes techniques de base, les caractères élémentaires de chaque sujet, les règles générales. Plus tard quand l'étudiant a assimilé les généralités, même les concepts beaucoup plus compliqués lui paraissent à sa portée.

2) J'énonce les connaissances et les idées par des mots et phrases précises, concises et simples.

Un dentiste fait un travail précis et devrait s'exprimer dans un langage professionnel précis. J'oblige mes étudiants à exprimer leurs idées dans un bon langage professionnel. Il faut surmonter plusieurs difficultés: le français par ses règles de style évite l'emploi des répétitions des termes identiques; et trop de ses termes ont un sens figuré qui les rend imprécis. L'anglais distingue mal entre les noms et les verbes, entre l'adjectif et l'adverbe. La presse, la télévision, la radio emploient des termes autrefois précis dans un jargon qui les rend imprécis. J'évite le vocabulaire de profanes, les mots avec un sens figuré et les comparaisons poétiques.

Quand il s'agit d'une constatation de faits et d'une simple transmission de connaissances, un texte détaillé n'est pas nécessaire parce que la matière est bien présentée dans le manuel. Je donne aux étudiants une liste des items avec des noms précis, une classification très claire, et des références détaillées sur les pages d'un ouvrage recommandé.

Quand il faut enseigner la compréhension, le texte est plus élaboré et illustré par des dessins et par des schémas qui montrent l'évolution et les transformations d'un sujet vers d'autres sujets.

Au début de l'année les étudiants peuvent acheter les notes concernant la plupart des matières pour un prix modique. Plusieurs étudiants les lisent avant les cours pour être bien préparés à les suivre. Pour les chapitres ajoutés ou améliorés pendant l'année nous distribuons des feuilles polycopiées au début du cours.

Presentation du cours

Après la préparation, je n'ai pas besoin de lire le cours. Je situe la matière dans le contexte des cours précédents et suivants. J'explique l'importance et les caractères particuliers du sujet. Je discute les relations entre les chapitres qui composent le cours.

Je résume rapidement les faits présentés dans le texte. Il n'est pas nécessaire de répéter tout ce qui est transmis par écrit comme des définitions ou des constatations simples. Mon débit est assez rapide. J'évite la manière cultivée à la radio, à la télévision, et ailleurs, d'énoncer rapidement un fragment d'idée suivi par un long "ah."

Souvent, aux endroits convenables, j'interromps cette transmission de l'information par des commentaires. Je montre aux étudiants comment apprendre cette matière, j'indique les caractères communs et les différences entre les classes, les raisons pour lesquelles le sujet est subdivisé.

Par l'intermédiaire d'exemples simples décrits ou présentés par les transparents, je montre l'application des connaissances que l'on vient de transmettre. Ensuite, je présente des objets ou des situations nouvelles plus compliquées et je pose des questions. Souvent des étudiants répondent. Sinon, j'analyse la situation à l'aide des connaissances nouvelles, comme un débutant devrait le faire. Ainsi je pousse les étudiants à observer et à percevoir les caractères du phénomène élémentaire dans une situation nouvelle, à les comparer avec des choses connues et ainsi classer l'inconnu dans le connu.

De bons étudiants deviennent bientôt capables de noter par quoi un exemple nouveau se distingue des éléments déjà connus. C'est alors que je commence à présenter le chapitre suivant.

Dans ces discussions, des étudiants posent parfois des questions sur des problèmes qui devraient être traités beaucoup plus tard. J'exprime mon appréciation de cet aperçu et j'explique brièvement cette matière anticipée. Je leur donne la référence du cours où elle sera traitée en détail ou dans la littérature. Il arrive parfois dans les classes avancées que l'on me pose une question à laquelle je ne connais pas de réponse: j'avoue mon ignorance et j'invite l'étudiant de faire lui-même une recherche dans la littérature ou à consulter un professeur spécialisé.

Les techniques audio-visuelles

Dans mon sujet, la perception visuelle et tactile sont essentielles. Je me sers souvent des techniques audio-visuelles mais seulement au cas où elles peuvent réellement améliorer mon enseignement. Montrer quelque chose sur les transparents, à la télévision, vaut mieux qu'une description mais il vaut encore mieux montrer la réalité, par exemple une dent malade, et, pour ceci, nous avons des travaux pratiques.

Le film et la télévision en circuit fermé sont les techniques les plus avantageuses pour mon enseignement mais à cause des difficultés techniques, je les emploie moins souvent.

Montrer un fait sur les transparents aide seulement la mémoire. Il faut encore analyser ce qui est montré, exprimer le jugement et la classification. En conséquence, deux choses sont importantes: le choix du matériel audio-visuel et les commentaires qui accompagnent la projection.

Je n'aime pas utiliser les techniques audio-visuelles seulement parce que c'est moderne, comme des coups d'épate pour éblouir par de belles images. Par exemple, pour transmettre la simple idée qu'une chose s'agrandit je ne montre jamais des images de la même chose de plus en plus grandes, ni des courbes, ni des diagrammes. Je ne combine jamais le tableau noir avec plusieurs projecteurs spectaculaires, avec la TV, pour transmettre la même information. La télévision, la presse, les conventions montrent que le langage audio-visuel est très efficace pour convaincre et pour endoctriner, pour faire désirer une marchandise ou admirer le conférencier. Mon sujet est tellement intéressant qu'il n'a pas besoin de truc et la plupart de mes étudiants sont tellement intelligents qu'ils n'aimeraient pas se laisser abuser par du clinquant audio-visuel.

Le dentiste a besoin d'une imagination scientifique; il note les signes d'une maladie et il doit imaginer ce qui se passe à l'intérieur du patient. Notre enseignement doit cultiver cette imagination. On ne devrait pas faciliter la transmission des connaissances à un degré tel que l'étudiant n'a plus besoin d'un effort. La parole et le livre sont encore des moyens importants de communication. Je transmets certaines connaissances et idées par écrit et par audio-visuel, et quand je pense qu'elles sont apprises, je développe leur application par la parole qui force l'étudiant à employer son imagination, par exemple, je montre un transparent; je décris un changement de telle chose; je demande le nom de ceci.

Travaux pratiques

Nos travaux pratiques sont organisés sous forme d'un enseignement programmé, complémentaire et modifié. Les connaissances prérequises sont enseignées dans le cours. Après le cours, l'étudiant arrive avec ses notes et un manuel programmé. Il reçoit quelques pièces anatomiques et coupes microscopiques qui sont accompagnées d'un cahier de réponses. Suivant le manuel programmé, l'étudiant fait d'abord une description simple, ensuite il identifie, classifie, et explique le phénomène étudié à l'aide de termes techniques et des notions qu'il vient d'apprendre dans le cours. Ce travail est programmé en des cadres habituels; immédiatement après avoir écrit une réponse, l'étudiant trouve sa confirmation sur la page correspondante du cahier de réponses.

Après ces travaux pratiques, je présente un ou deux problèmes sans texte préparé; l'étudiant doit lui-même écrire un rapport qui est ensuite corrigé et discuté par un démonstrateur.

La télévision en circuit fermé

Quoique nous employons souvent la télévision comme moyen d'enseignement quand un professeur ne peut pas donner son cours, je considère ceci comme secondaire. J'emploie la télévision comme un support d'enseignement.

La télévision est un moyen excellent pour transmettre les connaissances et enseigner la compréhension d'un sujet qui porte sur de très petits objets avec des changements et évolution. Dans mes cours télévisés, l'étudiant ne voit jamais sur l'écran le visage du professeur mais les images qui développent les idées sur le sujet. Le professeur n'est pas un acteur, je pense que c'est un abus de la télévision de montrer un professeur lisant un texte.

Examens

Une partie considérable des étudiants étudie parce qu'ils doivent passer les examens pour obtenir le diplôme. Il faut donc considérer les examens comme un moyen d'enseignement. Je les prépare et les évalue avec un très grand soin d'après les méthodes modernes. La plupart de nos examens sont maintenant des examens à choix multiples. Les étudiants sont informés d'avance sur le caractère de l'examen et sur la méthode de son évaluation; ils savent que mes examens sont difficiles mais que leur évaluation est juste. Je pense que ceci est aussi un facteur important qui stimule à l'étude au moins une partie des étudiants.

Dans la description de mes méthodes, il n'y a pas de nouveautés. Peut-être pourrait-on me reprocher mon attitude réservée vis-à-vis des techniques audio-visuelles et la trouver démodée. Si mon enseignement est considéré comme efficace, c'est peut-être le résultat d'un peu plus que de ces méthodes. Je pense que les facteurs qui suivent sont très importants:

Le travail consciencieux, assidu et long que je fais pendant la préparation de mon enseignement est peut-être plus important pour les résultats que la méthode de présentation finale.

J'étudie et j'apprends constamment; je présente la matière aux étudiants comme je l'ai apprise et comme je l'apprendrais moi-même le plus facilement. Probablement cette approche les aide à apprendre.

Il faut aussi considérer que la dent présente des problèmes biologiques tout à fait fascinants à qui commence à la comprendre. Il est plus facile d'enseigner une matière aussi intéressante que de transmettre des informations sur des choses plutôt banales.

Peut-être aussi mon attitude envers les étudiants aide à l'enseignement. Je considère les étudiants comme mes collègues; c'est un plaisir de leur expliquer nos problèmes et de voir comment ils s'améliorent au cours de l'année scolaire.

L'appréciation des étudiants signalée dans cette enquête et leurs succès sont parmi les plus grandes satisfactions de ma carrière.

Zdenek Mézl

Zdenek Mézl est docteur en médecine (M.D.) de l'Université de Prague, Tchécoslovaquie, et docteur en chirurgie dentaire (D.D.S.) de l'Université de l'Alberta. Il était professeur de stomatologie à l'Université de Prague, et de 1957 à 1973 professeur à la Faculté de chirurgie dentaire de l'Université de Montréal. Il est maintenant professeur émérite.

Il a à son crédit plus de soixante-dix articles scientifiques, surtout sur la pathologie dentaire et buccale, et deux livres sur la pathologie du périodonte. Ses publications sont en cinq langues différentes.

Le docteur Mézl était un homme de connaissances exceptionnelles, selon ses anciens élèves, un être d'une surprenante rigueur intellectuelle, dégagé, un homme de science. "Il était au courant des dernières découvertes et s'adonnait lui-même avec ardeur à la recherche." La préparation de ses cours était minutieuse, "avec un art particulier d'insister sur les points qui étaient essentiels en eux-mêmes pour la compréhension des phénomènes à étudier plus tard."

"Son enseignement était abondamment illustré et nous permettait de visualiser les cas pour mieux les comprendre. . . . Il s'assurait lui-même que tous avaient bien compris le contenu de son exposé." "Il était toujours disponible, quittant l'université quand les étudiants sont partis." Il suit chaque élève en donnant des travaux, en faisant des examens périodiques et en corrigeant personnellement tous ces travaux dans le but de saisir pourquoi tel point n'est pas compris, il en avertit l'étudiant et voit à corriger sa façon d'enseigner ce point s'il y a lieu.

"Extrêmement exigeant pour lui-même," a temoigné un diplômé," "il l'était encore plus pour nous" . . . "le docteur Mézl avait de la noblesse, mais il n'était pas prétentieux" . . . "il était un homme humain, intègre, qui savait apprécier l'effort au travail."

Involving Students

Margaret E. Cockshutt

To examine and analyse one's teaching aims and methods, and describe them to others is not easy. In some instances I have consciously followed the methods of excellent teachers I encountered as a student. For the most part my own methods have developed almost unconsciously over a period of years, and I have evolved them slowly and painfully, by trial and error, without the benefit of courses in educational methodology. Undoubtedly there will be ideas and procedures described in this paper which will seem simple and obvious to some readers, and other methods which may seem wrong to others.

I present my own analysis and personal ideas here as honestly as I can, in the hope that my ideas and methods may be useful to some university teachers, and that I may learn more from the other papers in this volume.[1]

In order to demonstrate some of the teaching problems I face, and the ways in which I attempt to solve them, it is necessary to describe briefly the Faculty of Library Science and the nature of its student body.

The School of Library Science, University of Toronto

In 1969–70 the University of Toronto School of Library Science (as the Faculty of Library Science was then named) offered two degrees, the Bachelor of Library Science (B.L.S.) as the first professional degree, and the Master of Library Science (M.L.S.) as an advanced degree. On the recommendation of the Council of the School of Library Science, the Senate of the University of Toronto replaced the B.L.S. program in 1970–71 with a new two-year program leading to the M.L.S. as the first professional degree.

The graduates' reports on which this study of university teaching was based were in response to their evaluation of teaching in the B.L.S. courses. While my own teaching responsibilities and methods have inevitably changed with the new M.L.S. program and the passage of time, I have written this paper to discuss the B.L.S. courses and methods on which the respondents' reports were based. All the remarks in this paper apply to the B.L.S. program as it existed in 1969–70, but many of the comments on my aims and methods are still applicable in the new M.L.S. program.

The B.L.S. program offered the first year of professional education in library science to graduates of approved universities. This means that students entered the program with B.A., B.Sc., or B.Comm. degrees; M.A., M.Ed., M.Sc., M.S.W., or Ph.D. degrees. There was a wide variety of subject specialities, and the degrees were obtained from many different universities in many countries. This broad spectrum of subjects and degrees is still characteristic of the present M.L.S. program.

Many students at the Faculty of Library Science come directly from obtaining their undergraduate degrees; others may not have studied formally for twenty years. They range in age from under 21 to over 50 years. Housewives have waited until their children have grown up; men have worked in other fields for twenty years and then have decided to enter a second profession; teachers have waited for many years before they decided that they wished to specialize in school librarianship, rather than in a subject specialty. Some students have worked briefly in a library; a few have worked in a library, at nonprofessional tasks, for over ten years; about 49 per cent have never worked in a library; some confess that they never used a library while they were students. The variety of subject backgrounds and capacities for independent study presents still further problems.

The tremendous diversity of the student body in terms of age, education and experience is almost overwhelming for the instructor in the first term where the basic material is presented. I find that I tend to bore those students who have had extensive library experience, and mystify those who have had none. All I can do is aim at a middle level of subject and professional experience, try to touch on the more complex related problems for those with extensive experience, and offer considerable individual help to those who are floundering in their capacity to understand the subject or to regain studying techniques.

The B.L.S. subjects at the School of Library Science were divided into compulsory core subjects and elective subjects. Among other courses I taught a compulsory course in Cataloguing and Classification. As it was a compulsory course, I recognized that some students would like this subject and would choose to practise professionally in this area, and some students would dislike it and would endure it only because the course was required. The Council of the School had made this a required course in the belief that all librarians, in all types of libraries, needed an understanding of the basic concepts it included. Therefore I tried to make the concepts intelligible and meaningful, even if not enjoyable, to all students.

Cataloguing and Classification

In professional education the student must understand the underlying theory, and learn enough about professional practice to function as a beginning professional after he graduates. The course in Cataloguing and Classification dealt with the theory and practice of organizing information in libraries. We discussed the underlying concepts and the methods of construction of bibliographical records. Here the individual library was seen as a system of files, such as card catalogues, printed catalogues and bibliographies, magnetic tapes, and all the secondary records which depend on the original bibliographical organization of information.

In such an introductory course there must be an examination of the physical organization of a variety of physical media (for example, books, periodicals, films, filmstrips, phonograph records, manuscripts, and microfilms) into subject arrangements which will be most helpful to users of the individual library. Thus we must consider the physical arrangement in a library to permit a user to find related materials shelved in close proximity.

Together with the physical arrangement we must consider the subject analysis of the intellectual content of each item and the organization of the results in a variety of ways. The depth of the analysis may range from considering the broad subject content of a book as a whole to an exhaustive subject examination of one paragraph of a technical report. This is extremely difficult for each individual professor and student because of the subject limitations of their previous education. In spite of our individual subject weaknesses we must explore the concept of subject arrangements using bibliographical apparatus, cope with such technical problems as the semantic and syntactic problems of language, and create a structure of intelligible networks of subject relationships.

Today, of course, no library exists in bibliographical isolation. We must examine the theory and practice of bibliographical interdependence, with networks linking one library with another, exchanging both information and the means for organizing the information.

Within the traditional areas of cataloguing and classification, concepts and methods are changing at a frightening rate. It is no longer possible to teach a student practices and precepts which will last him for his professional lifetime, or even for the next ten years. There are no fixed solutions which he can learn and apply. In teaching Cataloguing and Classification I therefore presented, as best I could, a course which emphasized theories and the methods of identifying problems, and helped him to work out his own solutions to those problems, using the bibliographical aids which were currently available. He must recognize the deficiences of the current organizational tools and be able to think creatively about new solutions.

In teaching courses I have the help of my colleagues throughout the Faculty of Library Science. I have learned much from my colleagues in other areas of the Faculty and from practising librarians in discussing ideas in other areas which have implications for my own work, in modifying my prejudices and in developing my own theories and methods. This exchange of ideas with my academic and professional colleagues broadens my own horizons and is a source of great enrichment to me as a teacher.

The staff in Cataloguing and Classification consisted of professors, lecturers, and teaching assistants. We met weekly to exchange ideas, and to discuss problems in our field, the content of our class presentations, the laboratory problems we should set, and various methodologies which we might use in our lectures. These weekly meetings are still of immense help to me. I have learned in them about detailed subject fields in which my own knowledge is very limited, about the practices in various libraries in solving difficult problems, and I have profited greatly by the creativity of my colleagues in working out new teaching methods. As a result of our meetings we identify areas of agreement and disagreement about subject content, and try to reach a consensus or agree to present the complex issues and conflicting opinions while we maintain the principle of academic freedom.

Formal Classroom Presentations

Cataloguing and Classification met for three hours each week. In addition, the students were expected to work on weekly laboratory problems. They might do the work whenever they pleased on their own time, for example at nights or on weekends, but formal laboratory sessions were scheduled on the timetable when the student could get help from the teaching assistants if he wished.

In a typical teaching week I expect to spend about two classroom hours of an introductory course in the presentation of material. Inevitably I do much of this through "interrupted lectures" coupled with more informal group discussion. I regard it as my obligation here to present the material as logically and intelligibly as I can. To do this each year at the first-year level, particularly during the first term, is apt to be repetitious and dull for the professor, and therefore boring for the student, because the interesting changes and developments take place at a more advanced level. Therefore I try to read heavily in my subject area, and to incorporate some new material each year even in the introductory lectures. I know that when I fall victim to the pressures of committee work and academic vagaries, my reading and subsequent inclusion of new material fail, and I recognize that I do my beginning students a disservice here.

In preparation for each lecture I also critically analyse my previous content and methods of presentation in the hope of improving upon them. My aim is to make the intellectual patterns recognizable and understandable. I find I can do this best in my own classes by presenting the material in small steps, relating the steps in as logical a sequence as possible. To express the whole problem in meaningful concepts, I try to present it in terms of the purpose of the library as a whole and in terms of the student's own experience, since most of the students have been exposed to a library as a user. In selecting some material for inclusion and rejecting other material, I try to include material which will present and illustrate general theories and methods, and to reject small details which detract from the broad intellectual pattern and which I expect the student to investigate for himself.

In selecting content for inclusion in the session, and in considering the methods by which I shall present the material, I also try as far as possible to anticipate problems. To a large extent this is done by using past experience, but I have worked out a variety of ways by which I try to anticipate student difficulties.

In thinking about my lectures, I try to read and think about ten days or two weeks ahead of the actual presentation. Sometimes this enables me to recognize that a necessary preliminary concept has not been understood, so that I may present it again in a better way or develop it more fully before the basic need for it really arises. I try to remember back to my own student days to realize how I should have reacted to content and methodology, but here I am largely dependent on the students to teach me about teaching.

In each class I try to be sensitive to the group reaction, consciously expressed by questions and feedback or unconsciously reflected in the collective mood of the students. If I am able to find an explanation for the class failure to grasp a concept, I re-present it at once using another illustration or method. I also make an immediate note for myself in my folder of lecture notes, so that I may recall next year that this concept was not successfully presented, and add any analysis of the reasons for the failure and suggestions for a better presentation.

In these days of academic change there is considerable protest from the students against the formal lecture method. I have much sympathy with this protest, because I believe thinking and learning are best done by individuals, or by informal student groups, not by a formal rigid lecture presentation. Within the space and staff constraints of the School of Library Science, the lecture method was inevitable much of the time. In my formal lectures I tried to get around this problem of rigidity in various ways.

I know that I communicate best with individuals rather than groups.

I lecture best not by looking blankly at a class of nameless faces, but by talking personally to individuals in the class. I present an idea by talking to one individual, and then direct another concept or example or question to another student. Within the formal lecture framework I try to develop a classroom climate where there will still be a free exchange of ideas, questions, answers, and disagreements. Even in the traditional lecture method I work very hard to learn to call each student by name, and to discuss with him and react to him in the class as an individual.

I also try to gain the student's attention and interest in every way I can. In answer to questions, I prefer to use catchy humorous examples, rather than serious textbook illustrations, as I find he is more likely to recognize and remember the problem if it is presented in a new way rather than a stereotyped way. Questions present great difficulty to the instructor because the student may express them badly. Before I answer a question, I analyse it on two levels: the level of the words themselves, which may appear as a very superficial question; and the underlying implications of the question, which may raise a deep and important problem, but which the student may not have recognized himself. In fairness to the student, I must recognize both the surface question and the important deeper problem, and answer him on both levels. This is a teaching problem which I recognize, but with which I do not always grapple successfully. For the instructor to cope with these questions successfully is extremely important for the student, because only in this way does he learn to recognize and ask the important questions, rather than merely the surface questions. It is a part of the process by which he learns to analyse problems.

I also try as much as possible to use duplicated handout sheets, or transparencies, or an overhead projector, or any appropriate audio-visual media, so that the student can concentrate on understanding intellectual patterns and examples rather than on mindless note-taking.

In the third hour of the teaching week I usually discuss the problems the students have encountered in doing the laboratory exercises, and in discussing the broader issues and implications which arise from these difficulties.

In creating the laboratory problems, my colleagues and I try to develop meaningful problems where the theories can be applied in practice. The student may solve one problem in a vacuum, or he may tackle a complex problem where many concepts and conflicting solutions must be seen as interrelated parts of an organizational whole.

When we discuss these laboratory problems, I have a variety of objectives. Inevitably I have recognized subject content which I have failed to explain adequately to the majority of the class, and so I must do some remedial teaching. Mostly I try to experiment in finding meaningful ways of involving students in their own learning processes, in their presentation of the laboratory problems, and in the resulting discussion of the usefulness and success of the solutions. This is difficult in a class of 35 or 40 students; it is almost impossible in a large class.

It may be helpful to see some concrete examples of ways in which I try to involve the students in developing their own problem-solving methodologies. I have had students present each problem individually or as members of a team working out a common solution to each problem. I have had one student present a problem as a form of problem identification and analysis, and another comment critically on the usefulness of the solution. I have had all the students concentrate on one or two problems, so that the whole class participates in the discussion of a limited number of problems. In all these discussions I learn from the students. I learn about areas in the whole field of knowledge which I must discuss with them in subject analysis. I learn about previous working experiences they have had, related to library science, to which I have not been exposed, and I learn indirectly about the whole problem of communication, teaching methods, and our experiences in learning together.

Not all my experiments have been successful. Some students will rise to the occasion; others will miss the point completely. Some students will pay attention to comments from me, but will ignore presentations by their fellow students. However I believe I must go on experimenting, working together with the students to help them find their own methods of identifying, discussing, and solving problems, even within the constraints of a too-large discussion group. As members of a profession they must have learned to go on learning, thinking analytically and creatively. If I have not helped them to work out their own methodologies here, I shall have failed them as a teacher. Of course the student may have failed himself. My job is to help him learn to learn, but this is only possible if he himself wants to learn. The responsibility for success or failure thus falls on us both.

Informal Contacts

Most university teaching is done during the formally scheduled classroom hours. As I remember back to my own student days, I realize that I learned most from the work that I did by myself, from my discussions with my fellow students, and from informal unscheduled discussions with my professors.

As a professor I can do little to ensure student-to-student discussions except through providing problems on which students can think and work together, and through our joint discussions of problems and ideas in scheduled or unscheduled meetings.

I must make it possible for any student to discuss an academic problem with me informally and individually. I try to do this by scheduling office hours, and at other times by operating as much as possible on an "open-door" policy. In the resulting discussions, my aim is to work with the student entirely as an individual. He does not come to me as a member of a class group. He comes as a person with his own level of experience, his own understandings and misunderstandings, his own capabilities and weaknesses. My job is to try to identify where he is in a level of understanding, where he has gone off on a wrong tangent, why he cannot understand, how to present the material to him in a more meaningful way. Sometimes my obligation is to help him identify the area of his mistake, and then send him away to work out the solution again for himself. In all of this our consultation as student and professor must be completely individual, and all the discussions and explanations must relate directly to his own needs and difficulties.

As a teacher I find this informal consultation demanding, exhausting, and usually rewarding. Sometimes I ask the questions or discuss the problems clumsily, and then the student goes away and does not return. Usually I find this contact an opportunity for us to meet, discuss, and learn together—not only about Cataloguing and Classification—but as two people in a university where learning is the objective of us all.

As a professor in a professional school, I have an obligation to the profession as well as to the university. If I did not believe in the importance of librarianship as a profession, I should not be teaching in the Faculty of Library Science. It is therefore part of my task to instill in the student a respect for the profession and a recognition of the place of libraries in society and in education. I believe that all libraries exist only to serve people in their varying needs, and I know that this personal belief in service gives a focus to my teaching aims and colours my teaching methods.

The functions of a university professor are traditionally regarded as teaching, research, and publication. Certainly these three activities exist together as a triangle and cannot be separated, for each grows out of and enriches the other two. I have come to realize that teaching is the most important part of the triangle for me. I believe that teaching students is a valid activity in itself, although I recognize that my teaching is enriched by my other academic activities. Teaching allows me to analyse problems, to try to think creatively about their solutions, and to work with students to help them analyse and create and learn for themselves. Always as a teacher I shall have instances where I fail to communicate with another human being, but where I succeed, university teaching becomes vastly rewarding in itself.

MARGARET COCKSHUTT

A native of Brantford, Ontario, Margaret Cockshutt took a Bachelor of Arts degree in English language and literature at the University of Toronto, then qualified as a Bachelor and later as a Master of Library

Science at the same university. She joined the staff of the Faculty of Library Science there in 1949 as librarian, later transferred to full-time teaching, and has since risen to the rank of associate professor.

She has published Basic Filing Rules *(University of Toronto Press, 1961),* The Seventeenth Edition of the Dewey Decimal Classification *(Ontario Library Association, 1966), and* Sample Catalogue Cards Exemplifying the Anglo-American Cataloging Rules *(joint author, University of Toronto Press, 1968). Her articles have appeared in Canadian and American professional journals. She collaborated in research into the opportunities for professional development in Ontario academic libraries and her report on the project was published in 1971. Her current research is in classification theory and systems.*

During the period covered by graduates' reports, her main teaching field was cataloguing and classification.

According to her former students, Miss Cockshutt not only knew her subject thoroughly, but was enthusiastic about it. She presented it in carefully prepared, clear, logical lectures, illustrated by transparencies and sample catalogue cards. She could sense when the class was having difficulty with a point, and would not proceed until she felt it was understood. She was free with her time out of class too—always willing to talk to students either to help them with their studies or just to get to know them. It was evident that she was interested in and concerned about them as individuals. She learned their names early in the year.

One or another of those who had been her students described her as businesslike, thorough, demanding, lively, intelligent, generous, kind, warm, pleasant, patient, and possessed of a sense of humour—"a really remarkable combination of brains, knowledge, character and personality," according to one graduate. "It was her sense of humour, warmth, and concern for and interest in people that made her an exceptional professor," concluded another.

NOTE

1. My thanks are due to Professor Katherine H. Packer for her helpful suggestions and comments.

Analysis and Discussion

Edward F. Sheffield

This final chapter begins with an attempt at summarizing the areas of agreement among the twenty-three professors whose essays precede. Then follows a brief report on graduates' comments concerning the good teaching they had experienced. In conclusion the editor offers observations on the information resulting from the project and some suggestions about implications for the improvement of university teaching.

Areas of Agreement: A Summary

Of the twenty-three contributors to this book, half were born in Canada, six in continental Europe (four in Czechoslovakia and one each in Greece and Germany), three in the United States, two in England, and one in South Africa. With one exception they are long-time residents of Canada. Among them there are three women. Four teach in French. Almost all are relatively senior in professorial rank, and of or beyond middle age. Fifteen have doctorates; eight have lower qualifications. Ten earned their highest degree in Canada, nine in the United States, three in Britain, and one in Europe.

For most of them, teaching is but one of several roles played. They serve or have served in administrative positions in their universities—as departmental chairman in most cases, as dean in half a dozen instances, and as vice-president in three. They are actively engaged in research and writing, and they are experienced in the application of their knowledge—in scholarship, research, or practice, often outside the university setting. At least half of them are or have been workers (usually office-holders) in their professional associations. At least half have records of fruitful public or community service—as consultants, members of commissions of inquiry, contributors to conferences (local and international), short-term or part-time employees of government agencies, workers in welfare bodies and political associations.

No proper classification of their personalities is possible, but from their essays, the comments made by their former students, and the impressions gained by the editor when meeting them, it appears that they range over most of the continuum from extravert to introvert, with a tendency toward the former. Most are egotists. All are human.

One of the points on which the essay-writers are generally agreed is that the teacher's most important role is to stimulate students to become active learners on their own. Here, from the essays, are some ways in which this is expressed:

> My responsibility . . . is to help the return of wonder and the holy fear of life in the inner being of the young person. (Galavaris)
>
> En chacun je ne veux qu'éveiller ses propres possibilités. (Major)
>
> Probably the most violent and aggressive act that any person can do to other persons is to invade their minds with ideas and twists of meaning which disturb the comforting security of things known and faith kept. Yet this is what I, as a teacher, am required to do. (Packer)
>
> It is my mission to "turn them on" . . . to get them to want to learn. (Aldrich)
>
> My own teaching aims may be briefly summarized thus: to impart knowledge in an understandable fashion, to arouse interest in this knowledge, to stimulate curiosity about associated areas of knowledge and to generate independent, critical thought on the part of students. (Setterfield)
>
> En leur profondeur, tous mes objectifs s'inspirent donc d'un seul et s'y réduisent: faire aimer. (L'Archevêque)
>
> Surely this must be the teacher's prime function: to strike sparks, to build fires, so that the student's own enthusiasm will carry him through those dreary stretches that exist in all learning. (Jolliffe)
>
> The job of the teacher is to provide the stimulus for the effort at understanding. (Getz)
>
> As I see it, the teacher's role in the context of the student-to-subject relationship is that of facilitating mutual attraction, of providing a suitable environment for seduction. (Waugh)
>
> Proper balance in any teaching is a tendency and capacity to impart the known and to foment in the receiving mind a desire to know —what the teacher does not yet know. (Havelka)
>
> . . . helping to liberate the minds and hearts of young men and women. (Gilson)
>
> The object . . . is to train the student to think, and to make judgments. (Summers)
>
> My job is to help him learn to learn. (Cockshutt)

There is general agreement also that there is no one way to play the teacher's role. Indeed, they view teaching as an art which defies description. It is complex, subtle, varying, and dependent more on personality, attitudes, and human relationships than on methods. Only five of the twenty-three had had formal training in pedagogy (four in teacher-training institutions, one in the army) and none remarked on the need for it. Several reported that their approach to teaching was patterned, with adaptations, on what they admired in great teachers they had known. (Does this suggest that two people who are compatible may find the same style suitable?)

> My interest in academic things in general, and science and biology in particular, stems directly from the influence of a single teacher. . . . It is relatively simple to list some obvious qualities which contributed to his success. . . . I believe his success depended additionally on a complex interplay of subtle aspects of his attitudes and personality which defies analysis. (Setterfield)
>
> By attempting to conduct these courses in a way similar to those of my own best former professors. . . . (Meyerhof)
>
> Je me rappelle très bien les qualités qui m'ont frappé chez mes propres professeurs. . . . Mon admiration pour [un de ces professeurs] demeure profonde après vingt ans . . . je lui dois sans doute pour une bonne part ma vocation d'enseignant. (Morin)
>
> I suppose all of us old enough to become subject to nostalgia may remember a teacher who made the difference. I was lucky; I had two such teachers. (Havelka)
>
> Much . . . has been assimilated silently and unconsciously, I'm sure, from the handful of exceptional teachers I have had. (Fowler)
>
> In some instances I have consciously followed the methods of excellent teachers I encountered as a student. (Cockshutt)

In their reports on how they play their catalytic role most of the professors are essentially student-oriented. With two or three exceptions, their attitudes toward students are positive. They think students are important, they like them and respect them, and they *care*. They believe that individual students learn in different ways, but are convinced that learning takes place only when the student is actively involved in the process.

> L'étudiant apprend moins par ce que je lui dis que par la mise en question de ce que je dis et de ce qu'il sait déjà. (Major)
>
> The laboratory is potentially an invaluable opportunity for a student to experience his subjects directly and to learn by doing and it should be fully exploited. (Setterfield)
>
> They [lectures] provide the opportunity for the students to participate, personally and fully, in the thinking process of the discipline. (Valenta)

By special projects and thesis work I allow students to study a particular subject of their choice more thoroughly and give them an opportunity for some creative expression. (Meyerhof)

Getting active student participation, one of my major goals. . . . (Armstrong)

I believe that education is a co-operative process demanding reciprocal investments of time and energy from all involved . . . there are or should be no passive participants in the process. (Getz)

The teacher can neither think nor act for the student, although many teachers perform their role as if they had student proxies to carry out these processes. (Fowler)

The learning experiences are planned to help the student become personally involved in the content. (Vaines)

In this type of training there is no substitute for learning by doing. (Summers)

Mostly I try to experiment in finding meaningful ways of involving students in their own learning processes. (Cockshutt)

The professors have much to say, too, about what *they* do or should do. Their competence and their interest and belief in the importance of their subject or discipline—more than that, their enthusiasm, their love for it—are basic and general. And they like to teach it.

. . . teaching is giving yourself. It can only be described as a love affair between the teacher and the students. (Galavaris)

First of all, I believe that a university teacher should show his love for his work. He should be deeply interested in what he teaches and he should openly share his enjoyment of his subject. (O'Grady)

One of the many things that makes teaching a pleasure for me is the fortunate fact that I teach geography which in itself is intrinsically interesting. (Packer)

Anyone can convey his subject, at least in part, if it is important to him, for commitment is catching. . . . How fortunate I am that I teach biology, for I definitely feel that biology is the ultimate science. Like other salesmen, my job is therefore made easier because I have a product to sell which is not only saleable, but is one with which I am proud to be associated. (Aldrich)

In my opinion many professors, although sincerely involved in education in general, are not intimately enough involved in any particular subject to really have something to teach. As a result really exciting teaching becomes impossible. (Setterfield)

. . . students will always be eager to learn from teachers who are truly interested to teach. (Valenta)

En général, je vise à atteindre le plus possible l'affectivité de ces auditeurs avec la mienne, car je crois en ce que j'enseigne, surtout, j'aime beaucoup en parler; j'aime donc aussi ceux qui veulent bien m'écouter. (L'Archevêque)

If the teacher is not possessed by an enthusiasm and evangelical zeal that literally drive him to demand that his students find truth and beauty where he himself has glimpsed them, and fascination and excitement where he has experienced them, he had best find another subject or profession. (Jolliffe)

Law is fascinating to me, and legal study an exciting pastime. Moreover, I find teaching a marvellous occupation. (Getz)

Dans l'enseignement, l'autorité a peut-être appartenu, dans le passé, à ceux qui jettaient des foudres, mais aujourd'hui, elle ne peut tenir qu'à la compétence du professeur, à l'intérêt, voire à l'enthousiasme, qu'il témoigne pour sa discipline et à la sympathie qui s'établit graduellement entre son auditoire et lui-même. (Morin)

Enthusiasm for my discipline seems an essential prerequisite. . . . I love working with students and I consider it truly worthwhile to instruct them. (Steiner)

In general, the greater the teacher's familiarity with and affection for his subject the better he will perform. . . . Good teaching is a love affair between the teacher, his subject, and his students in which each participant must be terrified of failure. (Waugh)

I know the subjects that I teach, and they are of great personal interest. (Summers)

. . . la dent présente des problèmes biologiques tout à fait fascinants à qui commence à la comprendre. . . . Il est . . . facile d'enseigner une matière aussi intéressante. (Mézl)

If I did not believe in the importance of librarianship as a profession, I should not be teaching in the Faculty of Library Science. . . . I believe that all libraries exist only to serve people in their varying needs, and I know that this personal belief in service gives a focus to my teaching aims and colours my teaching methods. (Cockshutt)

Almost without exception the professor-essayists use the lecture as the chief vehicle of their teaching, but they do not read scripts. Most distribute course outlines to aid in providing perspective and to lessen the students' need to take notes. Few use instructional aids other than the blackboard but those who do, use them extremely well. Each has developed a style and methods suited to his subject and his talents, and the variety of teaching methods used by any one professor is usually limited. As a group they are firmly of the opinion that the presence of the teacher in the classroom, communicating and interacting with the students, is essential to the educational experience.

No matter how many educational devices and tests we invent, experiments we carry out, examinations we give, papers we correct, books we publish, my contact with academic youth has convinced me that none of these can be substituted for real education based on an inner relationship between teacher and student. (Galavaris)

Quoi qu'il en soit, mes préférences vont vers une forme d'enseignement qui oscille entre le cours et le séminaire. (Major)

. . . useful as recorded lectures or filmed demonstrations may be, there is no substitute for the humane concern that a competent, dedicated person can and should bring to the learning process. For this very reason if, and when, live lecturers and traditional classrooms become obsolete, there will still be need, even greater need, for teachers. (O'Grady)

I abandoned the completely written lecture about twenty years ago. . . . On the other hand, notes for both instructor and instructed are valuable. . . . I like to use the didactic, expository approach in lecturing. (Packer)

The professorial lecture is presently the mainstay of university teaching and despite criticism I believe it will continue so. In my experience the lecture is unquestionably the best single method of imparting information and arousing interest. . . . Professorial lecturing is not without problems as a teaching method, however. Its prime weakness lies in the fact that the students remain essentially passive. . . . To counter this situation, over the years I have used a variety of classroom methods which centre on direct student participation. . . . I am convinced that most audio-visual devices are really not compatible with my teaching style. (Setterfield)

La plus grande partie de mon enseignement se fait sous la forme du cours magistral que je crois, suivant certaines conditions, plus adéquat au niveau de la première année universitaire. . . . Je réduis la lecture de mes propres notes au minimum possible: tout au plus quelques citations importantes et très choisies ou quelques références précises. . . . Je m'applique à devenir moi-même "visuel". (L'Archevêque)

The student must furnish his own "hooks and eyes of memory," but the instructor has to catalyze these linkages in the student's mind. . . . Nor do I believe that "taped" lectures by world authorities can supply more than a useful supplement to the "live" lecturer. Only he can respond intuitively to the unasked question, or to the increasing boredom or enthusiasm of the class. (Jolliffe)

Since I give courses on subjects in which I have had experience for many years and also continue to make personal contributions to research and practice, I no longer need notes for my undergraduate lectures. I prefer to speak freely and attempt to present the material in a simple and clear manner. (Meyerhof)

I have abandoned the blackboard in favour of the overhead projector. . . . Perhaps we have become too sensitive to criticism of the lecture method as an instructional device. There are places—large classes being one of them—where its use seems to be almost inevitable. (Armstrong)

D'une manière générale, le nouveau climat exige que les cours s'effectuent le plus possible sur le ton du dialogue, "les yeux dans les yeux". La lecture des notes doit être confinée aux définitions les plus ardues, aux passages qu'il convient de citer textuellement–et encore! Un cours lu est un cours mort et il vaut mieux avoir recours à la polycopie pour les textes essentiels. (Morin)

I have become convinced over the years that this [the lecture] is the least rewarding and effective method of instructional communication. . . . For large group teaching, I usually try to invent an incisive or dramatic opening gambit. . . . I use visual aids extensively, since the material I present lends itself readily to this approach. (Steiner)

In conveying factual information to students, I feel there is still a place for lecturing, provided that it is precise, brief, and logically sequenced in the course. . . . I personally like the open-forum approach or the inquiry method of presentation, particularly when it is employed immediately following a class-directed set of readings or assignments. (Fowler)

If students are not to become mere scribes, lecture notes should be reproduced whenever possible and distributed at the beginning of the term. I found a remarkable change in the classroom environment when I began to adopt this practice. (Gilson)

I believe a teacher, present in person, has a role to play in facilitating the mysterious process of learning. (Vaines)

It has been said that there are few subjects which cannot be taught better by some method other than the lecture, but if one is forced to the reluctant conclusion that he cannot avoid the lecture, the next step is to decide how to make the best of it. . . . I use the lecture method because it suits me as a person and the subjects that I teach. . . . I use one audio-visual aid consistently–the blackboard. (Summers)

Quand la matière est classifiée, il faut choisir les moyens d'enseignement les plus appropriés . . . le cours . . . les travaux pratiques . . . la télévision en circuit fermé. . . . Pour la plupart des cours, je prépare une texte. (Mézl)

In a typical teaching week I expect to spend about two classroom hours of an introductory course in the presentation of course material. Inevitably I do much of this through "interrupted lectures" coupled with more informal group discussion. (Cockshutt)

The writers tend to stress general ideas rather than details, most of them prefer structured to unstructured teaching situations, and most favour examinations, although they find effective examining difficult and are anxious to discover better ways of doing it. They make frequent references to the importance, to them as teachers, of reading and research to keep them up to date and on the creative edge of their fields.

Most of them value the feedback they get from their students—by way of examinations, questionnaires, course evaluations and the like—because they want to know what needs improvement and in what ways their approach could be changed for the better.

Finally, the chosen professors put great stress on thorough preparation for class sessions. Indeed, this may be one of the practices by which effective teachers are most easily distinguished from ineffective ones. They are dedicated, conscientious, and demanding both of themselves and their students. They work hard at teaching.

> I work extremely hard in organizing my material to the utmost detail. (Galavaris)
>
> J'ai mis parfois jusqu'à trente ou quarante heures à préparer fébrilement une heure de cours. (Major)
>
> I never, willingly, put myself in a teaching situation for which I have not prepared both substantively and mentally. (Packer)
>
> Pour ce qui est de ma préparation éloignée à l'enseignement, il suffit, je crois, de s'en reporter à mon passé professionnel. En ce qui concerne ma préparation immédiate, je tiens, chaque fois que j'entre en classe, à y avoir consacré au moins une heure. . . . Je tiens très fortement à cette préparation immédiate, même s'il s'agit d'un cours que je répète depuis un certain temps. (L'Archevêque)
>
> Liking students, respecting them, deriving enjoyment from teaching them was the first of my cardinal rules for good teaching. The second—hard work and careful preparation—is even more important, I think. There are two parts to preparation, the mastery of the subject matter, and developing the techniques of presentation. . . . Teaching is a time-consuming task, and one of the rather interesting facts that has emerged from the time sheets that I have kept over the years is that the time required to prepare for each hour in class has not diminished perceptibly. (Armstrong)
>
> I feel that, in part at least, my success is based upon a careful preparation of each lecture. (Steiner)
>
> These and other faults usually result from inadequate preparation and few things can be more insulting to students than the idea that their teacher thought so little of his responsibility that he did not make himself ready for them. (Waugh)
>
> I [have] never found a reliable way of disguising an ill-prepared lecture. . . . Incidentally, this amount of preparation time [three hours for one] is as necessary after several years of teaching experience as it is at the beginning. (Gilson)
>
> La préparation est la plus grande partie de mon travail. . . . Le travail consciencieux, assidu et long que je fais pendant la préparation de mon enseignement est peut-être plus important pour les résultats que la méthode de présentation finale. (Mézl)

There are exceptions to almost every one of the generalizations made here, there are many other points on which the essayists have a measure of agreement, and there are scores of points made only once or twice. These men and women are more alike in their attitudes than in their personalities or their ways of teaching. As has been noted, they agree that there is no one way to be an effective teacher. Rather, each professor must find his own.

By way of postscript, there is evidence that, according to graduates of their faculties, the writers of these essays, differing as they do from each other, together exhibit a pattern of teaching characteristics similar to that of the thousand professors about whom comments were compiled in this project. In other words, as a group they are representative.

Patterns of Effective Teaching[1]

The overall pattern

In addition to providing the basis on which representative professors were chosen and invited to write about how they teach, the comments made by responding graduates yielded general information on what they considered to be the characteristics of effective university teaching. All the comments by all responding graduates about all the teachers they identified as being excellent were grouped into four main categories:

- Personal qualities or attributes
- Subject mastery, scholarship, devotion to teaching
- Attitudes toward and relations with students
- Methods and procedures
    - Content and organization
    - Presentation of material

Each of these was divided and a total of 53 sub-categories established (see Chart 1). Chart 2 shows the same categories of comments but in the order of the frequency with which they were mentioned. Here are the top ten:

1. Master of his subject, competent
2. Lectures well prepared, orderly
3. Subject related to life, practical
4. Students' questions and opinions encouraged
5. Enthusiastic about his subject
6. Approachable, friendly, available
7. Concerned for students' progress, etc.
8. Had a sense of humour, amusing
9. Warm, kind, sympathetic
10. Teaching aids used effectively

This list is certainly not surprising. Similar studies in the United States, Britain, and Australia have shown almost identical patterns. It is likely, though, that this is the first such analysis of the impressions of graduates of Canadian universities. It appears that their views are like those of students elsewhere, or their professors were like professors elsewhere, or both.

Some comparisons

After outlining the overall pattern of effective teaching in all twenty-four faculties and schools in nineteen Canadian universities, further analyses were made:

- comparing faculties of arts and science with professional schools
- comparing anglophone and francophone faculties
- comparing large, medium and small universities: more than 10,000 students, 5,000 to 10,000, fewer than 5,000
- comparing fields of study: the humanities, the social sciences, the biological sciences and the physical sciences
- comparing pure and applied studies
- comparing course levels: years beyond the junior matriculation level
- comparing class size ranges: up to 30 students, 31–60, 61–120, over 120
- comparing the graduating classes of 1958, 1963, and 1968, i.e. years since graduation

Only two of these comparisons showed noteworthy differences in pattern, between francophone and anglophone faculties and among the four main fields of study: humanities, social sciences, biological sciences, and physical sciences.

Of the characteristics mentioned frequently, five were displayed by excellent teachers in both francophone and anglophone faculties:

- Lectures well prepared, orderly
- Master of his subject, competent
- Warm, kind, sympathetic
- Course organized, systematic
- Students' questions and opinions encouraged

Those mentioned markedly more often by graduates of the anglophone faculties were:

- Had a sense of humour, was amusing
- Approachable, friendly, available
- Small-group arrangements used well
- Enthusiastic about his subject
- Concerned for students' progress, etc.
- Teaching aids used effectively

In contrast, the characteristics mentioned much more often by graduates of the francophone faculties were these:

- Experienced in his field
- Subject related to life, practical

How can the differences between these two groups be explained?

Chart 1

Characteristics of Effective University Teaching
Graduates' Comments – All 24 Faculties and Schools
(arranged in order of code numbers)

Code	Categories	Sub-categories	Comments No.	Comments %
1	Personal	Dynamic, vivacious	260	2.8
2	qualities or	Dramatic	4	0.0
3	attributes	Intelligent, brilliant	110	1.2
4	A	Mature, wise	8	0.1
5		Warm, kind, sympathetic	278	3.0
6		Had a sense of humour, amusing	321	3.5
7		Humble, modest	60	0.7
8		Flexible, open-minded	53	0.6
9		Honest, sincere, genuine	101	1.1
10		Fair, impartial	43	0.5
11		Conscientious, thorough	166	1.8
12		Organized, logical, efficient	90	1.0
13		Other (including critical) comments	264	2.9
14	Subject	Master of his subject, competent	717	7.8
15	mastery,	Ever learning, up to date, inquiring	132	1.4
16	scholarship,	Experienced in his field	133	1.5
17	devotion to	Enthusiastic about his subject	385	4.2
18	teaching	Broad knowledge and interests	59	0.6
19	B	Loved teaching, gave it high priority	163	1.8
20		Other comments	14	0.2
21	Attitudes	Respect for students as persons	142	1.6
22	toward and	Concerned for students' progress, etc.	325	3.6
23	relations	Demanding of hard work, excellence	155	1.7
24	with	Sensitive to students' feelings	214	2.3
25	students	Approachable, friendly, available	372	4.1

Comments – %
1 2 3 4 5 6 7 8

26	C	Sought social contacts with students	27	0.3
27		Interested in student activities	15	0.2
28		Other (including critical) comments	45	0.5
29	Methods and	Students expected to do much on their own	145	1.6
30	procedures	Attitudes, principles stressed over facts	69	0.8
31	D	Subject related to life, practical	555	6.1
32	Course	Approach to subject critical, scientific	66	0.7
33	content and	Professor expressed own point of view	55	0.6
34	organization	Course planned at students' level	138	1.5
35		Course goals and expectations clear	42	0.5
36		Course organized, systematic	251	2.7
37		Summaries and reviews provided	28	0.3
38		Other comment on course organization	38	0.4
39		Lectures well prepared, orderly	712	7.8
40		Voice audible, well-modulated, etc.	93	1.0
41		Use of language, vocabulary, notable	83	0.9
42	Presentation	Lectures oratorical, dramatic	55	0.6
43	of material	Professor rarely used notes; informal	175	1.9
44		Main points stressed; outline provided	187	2.0
45		Professor questioned, used Socratic method	92	1.0
46		Students' questions, opinions encouraged	481	5.3
47		Teaching aids used effectively	278	3.0
48		Professor experimented with methods	45	0.5
49		Other (including critical) comments	87	1.0
50		Small-group arrangements used well	257	2.8
51		Assignments reasonable, helpful	195	2.1
52		Grading fair, innovative	253	2.8
53		Other comments on methods and procedures	10	0.1
54	Other comment		8	0.1
55	No comment		89	1.0
			9,143	100.1

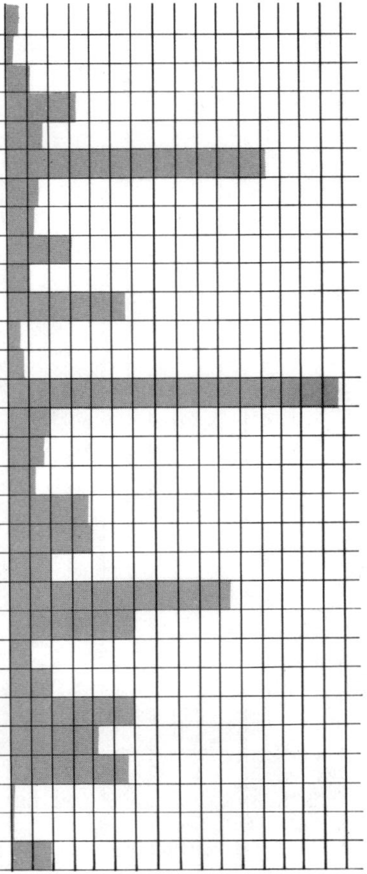

Chart 2

Characteristics of Effective University Teaching
Graduates' Comments – All 24 Faculties and Schools
(arranged in order of frequency)

Code	Category	Sub-category	Comments No.	Comments %
14	B	Master of his subject, competent	717	7.8
39	D	Lectures well prepared, orderly	712	7.8
31	D	Subject related to life, practical	555	6.1
46	D	Students' questions, opinions encouraged	481	5.3
17	B	Enthusiastic about his subject	385	4.2
25	C	Approachable, friendly, available	372	4.1
22	C	Concerned for students' progress, etc.	325	3.6
6	A	Had a sense of humour, amusing	321	3.5
5	A	Warm, kind, sympathetic	278	3.0
47	D	Teaching aids used effectively	278	3.0
13	A	Other comments on personal qualities or attributes	264	2.9
1	A	Dynamic, vivacious	260	2.8
50	D	Small-group arrangements used well	257	2.8
52	D	Grading fair, innovative	253	2.8
36	D	Course organized, systematic	251	2.7
24	C	Sensitive to students' feelings	214	2.3
51	D	Assignments reasonable, helpful	195	2.1
44	D	Main points stressed; outline provided	187	2.0
43	D	Professor rarely used notes; informal	175	1.9
11	A	Conscientious, thorough	166	1.8
19	B	Loved teaching, gave it high priority	163	1.8
23	C	Demanding of hard work, excellence	155	1.7
29	D	Students expected to do much on their own	145	1.6
21	C	Respect for students as persons	142	1.6
34	D	Course planned at students' level	138	1.5
16	B	Experienced in his field	133	1.5
15	B	Ever learning, up to date, inquiring	132	1.4
3	A	Intelligent, brilliant	110	1.2

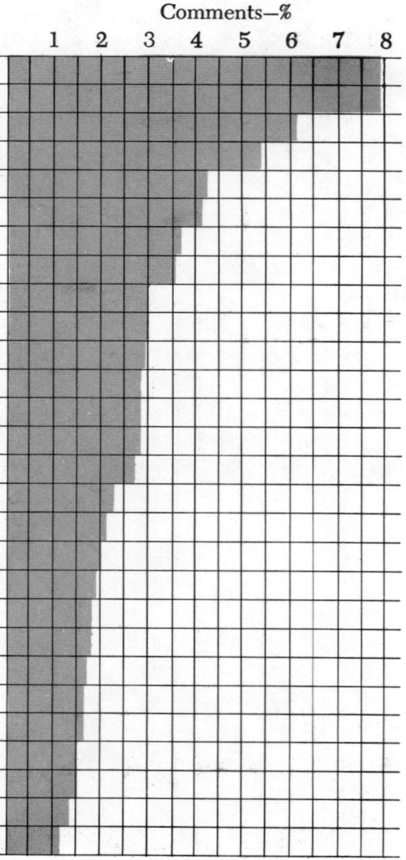

9	A	Honest, sincere, genuine	101	1.1
40	D	Voice audible, well-modulated, etc.	93	1.0
45	D	Professor questioned, used Socratic method	92	1.0
12	A	Organized, logical, efficient	90	1.0
55	–	No comment	89	1.0
49	D	Other comments on presentation of material	87	1.0
41	D	Use of language, vocabulary, notable	83	0.9
30	D	Attitudes, principles stressed over facts	69	0.8
32	D	Approach to subject critical, scientific	66	0.7
7	A	Humble, modest	60	0.7
18	B	Broad knowledge and interests	59	0.6
33	D	Professor expressed own point of view	55	0.6
42	D	Lectures oratorical, dramatic	55	0.6
8	A	Flexible, open-minded	53	0.6
28	C	Other comments on relations with students	45	0.5
48	D	Professor experimented with methods	45	0.5
10	A	Fair, impartial	43	0.5
35	D	Course goals, expectations clear	42	0.5
38	D	Other comments on course organization	38	0.4
37	D	Summaries and reviews provided	28	0.3
26	C	Sought social contacts with students	27	0.3
27	C	Interested in student activities	15	0.2
20	B	Other comments on subject mastery, etc.	14	0.2
53	D	Other comments on methods and procedures	10	0.1
4	A	Mature, wise	8	0.1
54	–	Other comment	8	0.1
2	A	Dramatic	4	0.0
			9,143	100.1

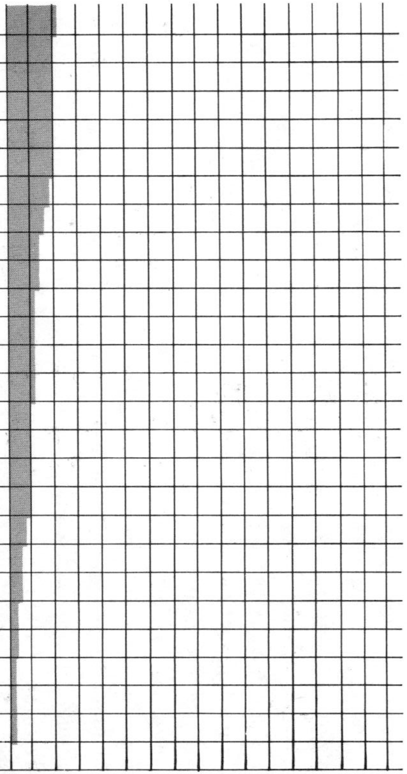

Categories: A (1–13) Personal qualities or attributes
B (14–20) Subject mastery, scholarship, devotion to teaching
C (21–28) Attitudes toward and relations with students
D (29–53) Methods and procedures

Source: Chart 1

Would it be appropriate to suggest that in the case of the francophone graduates there seems to have been more experience of distance between the lecturing professor and his students than in the case of the anglophone students? If so, was this really a difference in experience or only a difference in those parts of the experience which were thought worth mentioning? Finally, one might wonder whether the differences between the two groups are culture-linked.

When graduates named professors whom they remembered as good teachers, they indicated what courses they had taken from them. The courses named were grouped by field—humanities, social sciences, biological sciences, physical sciences.

Only three of the characteristics mentioned frequently were among the top five in all four fields:

- Master of his subject, competent
- Lectures well prepared, orderly
- Students' questions and opinions encouraged

On a number of items, though, there were contrasts. According to former students, teachers in the physical sciences scored appreciably higher than those in the other three fields on these items:

- Main points stressed, outline provided
- Course planned at students' level
- Teaching aids used effectively

In the biological sciences the differentiating items were:

- Ever learning, up to date, inquiring
- Course organized, systematic
- Lectures well prepared, orderly

There were none of note in the social sciences, but in the humanities there were these:

- Had a sense of humour, was amusing
- Enthusiastic about his subject
- Students' questions and opinions encouraged

Thus, except for the three items mentioned above as being among the top five in all fields, there seemed to be differences in the patterns of characteristics of effective teaching when comparisons were made among the humanities, the social sciences, the biological sciences, and the physical sciences as course groups or fields of study.

Another two comparisons yielded lesser differences worthy of mention—among class sizes and according to graduating year. It was found that the professors singled out in classes of more than 120 students were much more likely than those in small classes to be said to give courses which were "organized, systematic" and to "have a sense of humour, be amusing." In the smallest classes professors whose grading was "fair, innovative" were much more often noted than in larger classes.

The possibility that graduates' views of their teachers might change over the years following departure from the university, or that there might be changing styles in the appreciation of good teaching, accounts for the choice of three graduating classes at intervals of five years as participants in the study—those of 1958, 1963, and 1968. This meant that some members of the class of '58 were commenting on professors with whom they had studied as long as fifteen years earlier.

A noticeable trait of the class of '58 was that they remembered their good teachers as persons who were "demanding of hard work, excellence." Also, there was a higher proportion of comments about the warmth, kindness, and sympathy of their teachers by members of that class than by members of the two later classes. On the other hand, comments on fair or innovative grading were most common in the case of the class of '68. Were the teachers of the members of the class of '58 really warmer, kinder, and more demanding, or had a legend had time to grow? It is easier to understand the relation between fair and innovative grading and years since graduation because there is no doubt that more emphasis has been placed recently on this feature of university teaching.

It would appear that such differences as may exist between faculties of arts and science and professional schools, or between pure and applied studies, are more directly attributable to differences between fields of study. One might have expected that the patterns of effective teaching would be different in large universities from those in small institutions, but this is not noticeable. Nor does the pattern change with course level (within the undergraduate range).

In sum, this evidence suggests that, although there are a few exceptions, the general patterns of effective undergraduate teaching are basically similar in most university settings. This is not to say, of course, that teachers' personalities or methods are alike.

Other gleanings

As was mentioned in the introductory chapter, it had been expected that there would be marked agreement among the graduates of each faculty on who were the outstanding teachers in that faculty. Instead, although some professors were identified with sufficient frequency to indicate that they were among the outstanding teachers, the striking thing was the number of different professors listed. Roughly a thousand graduates responded; about a thousand different professors were named!

It is encouraging to note that the number thought to be good teachers was so large. This evidence points more significantly, however, to the fact that professors who are good teachers are only relatively good: they appeal to some students but not to others. There is compatibility between some professors and some students which is lacking with other students. No professor is likely to be thought to be a good teacher by all students in his classes. Another aspect of this relationship is shown by the fact that among the graduates' responses were many which named several effective teachers and described them as a group, attributing the same characteristics to all of them. Does this suggest that the student is receptive primarily to one pattern of teacher and teaching, and finds excellent only those professors who fit it? One graduate put it this way: "The professor's effectiveness is a function of the student's ability to identify with him."

Also raised is the possibility that some teachers are good for some *times* as well as for some *students*. There was some evidence that particular professors were named much more frequently by the class of '58 than by the class of '68, and the reverse was true in other cases.

It was interesting to note the frequency with which graduates in professional schools named professors in faculties of arts and science—professors from whom they had taken courses which were part of their curriculum but were not taught by the professional school's own faculty.

Another observation was that graduates often did not know how to spell the names of the professors they wished to list, and even more often could not remember, or never knew, their given names or initials. On the matter of names, it was not at all uncommon for graduates to refer to their former professors by their nicknames (a habit practised by undergraduates when talking to each other about a professor, but seldom when talking to the professor himself—until after the graduation ceremony).

Graduates of a particular faculty tended to draw on a vocabulary peculiar to that faculty to describe their former teachers. In some but not all such cases this probably was because an identifiable approach to teaching was common in the faculty—the case method in the Faculty of Law at UBC, for example, and nondirectiveness in the Rogerian sense in the Faculté des sciences de l'éducation at Laval.

Still another impression gained from reading the graduates' responses was that the identified teachers were not, on the whole, extraordinary. By contrast with other teachers met, however, they were thought to be effective. One can imagine some of the horrors which might have been recounted if graduates had been asked to name and comment on the *least* effective teachers they had known! As it was, even some of those remembered as good teachers had faults which were recorded—faults in personality, attitude, or method.

Some Conclusions, Observations, and Suggestions

This project was undertaken in the hope that it might contribute to the improvement of university teaching. Two dozen professors, identified by their former students as excellent teachers, have tried to explain what they believe about teaching undergraduates and how they go about it. A thousand graduates have indicated what they consider to be the elements of the good teaching they experienced. What generalizations can be made about the findings? What kinds of actions seem to be indicated in order to encourage improvement?

The results include a list of characteristics of effective university teaching which, for most readers, will have contained no surprises; the solid virtues are endorsed. It is significant, however, that the list was compiled on the basis of what former *students* said were the things that matter. The professors' essays, in turn, reveal that some highly respected Canadian academics think teaching is important and they work hard at it—in a great variety of ways. To be more specific, there follow a number of statements suggesting the principal conclusions which can be drawn from the exercise, together with some comments and suggestions.

- *As people, professors who are effective teachers differ greatly from one another. None is perfect, none a paragon.*
- *Good teachers are competent in and enthusiastic about their fields.*
- *They have respect for students; they think students are important; they care about their students.*
- *However much individual professors differ in their personalities, their styles and their methods, the resulting general patterns of effective teaching are essentially similar in all settings.*
- *There is no one way to be an effective teacher.*
- *Attitudes toward students and teaching are more important than methods and techniques.*

Assuming competence in and enthusiasm for his field and a positive attitude toward students, it is probable that almost any professor can be an effective teacher, in his own way, if he really wants to.

Competence is the result of study, research, and field experience, and is likely to be accompanied by enthusiasm or at least keen interest. Positive attitudes toward students depend on one's approach to human relations. Little is known about how such attitudes are formed; less about how they may be changed. It appears, though, that professors' attitudes toward students are strongly influenced by those of their colleagues. If a genuine interest in students and in teaching is exhibited by respected members of the professoriate, others may follow suit. Obviously, this matter of attitude requires investigation. Can it be discovered or sensed or measured? Can it be cultivated? How helpful it would be if a prospective professor's attitude toward students, and hence to a considerable extent his potential as a teacher, could be known or predicted when he is being considered for appointment!

- *Teaching is effective only when learning is effective; what the student does is the important thing.*
- *Professors tend to think that they, as teachers, are essential to students' learning.*
- *Their role is to stimulate, encourage and help students to learn.*

Many university teachers need to be reminded that what they tell students—by way of lectures, for example—is useful only to the extent that the students are actively learning as they listen, or are motivated to follow the leads offered. This is why problems and questions are often more conducive to learning than information and answers. An understanding of the psychology of learning—the processes involved and the conditions which favour it—should be an aid to a professor. Here, too, more knowledge is needed. The psychology of child learning has been explored, and much is known about adult learning. Do university students learn as children do, or as adults do? Or are they in some respects different in this?

- *Most professors rely largely on the lecture, and this is likely to continue to be so.*
- *The variety of teaching methods and instructional aids used by any one professor is usually limited.*

The lecture will survive because the costs of small-group and individual teaching are so much greater than those for large classes, and because it is a familiar and convenient vehicle for teaching. Attention should be given, therefore, to improvement of its use. Other methods and aids are relatively little used because they are unfamiliar or inconvenient. Experience of other methods would widen a professor's range of choice, although each in developing his own style is likely to adopt only a small number of those available. In this connection, it is relevant to repeat the observation that attitudes toward students and teaching are more important than methods and techniques.

- *Successful teaching requires thorough preparation and much hard work.*
- *Teaching effectiveness is increased by field experience and research.*

Here is raised the crucial question of priorities. How is a professor to divide his time and effort? For most, the competing activities are teaching, research, writing, administration, public service. The requirements of his department will limit a professor's choice among these activities. Within such limits, however, his personal preferences will influence the distribution of his time. But perhaps most influential will be the extent to which each type of activity is rewarded—in terms of rank, salary, and professional recognition. A major challenge to the university system is to discover how to reward teaching in proportion to the effort put into it. Then teaching could compete on equal terms. Then professors with the desire to emphasize teaching would have the additional motivation to give it their preferred priority.

- *Some professors are effective teachers for some students but not for others.*
- *Most professors seek evidence of the success of their teaching and welcome student comment on how it could be improved.*
- *Teaching ability and performance are difficult to evaluate.*

The element of compatibility which exists between a student and a professor who is, for him, an effective teacher suggests that students should be as free as possible in their choice of teachers. They should not be arbitrarily assigned to course sections, for example, or it should be possible for a student to change a section or course after he has become acquainted with the professor if he finds he has made a wrong choice. The fact that teachers are relatively rather than absolutely effective or ineffective suggests also that course and teacher evaluation schemes should be sophisticated enough to take account of this. Indeed, such evaluations by students are so worthwhile that they merit careful and responsible development and use. This is all the more important because professors are not good judges of each other's teaching prowess—for the same reason that no one or two students (remember the compatibility factor) can make a fair judgment of a professor, and for the added reason that, at best, professors observe the equivalent of film clips of each other teaching, while students take part, as it were, in feature-length movies.

What is known about the characteristics of effective university teaching has relevance for the preparation of new entrants (in the graduate schools), for selection among candidates for appointment, for in-service improvement of teaching, and for the provision of appropriate rewards. In recent years, especially in the United States, there has been much discussion of the role of the graduate school in the preparation of university teachers, and some experiments have been attempted. There has been much less attention to the process of selection for teaching. The importance of modifying the reward system is recognized and here too there are some experiments under way. Current interest is probably greatest with respect to in-service facilities and programs for the improvement of teaching. Some universities have units concerned with research on teaching methods, some have what might be called pedagogical service units—providing assistance, on request, to professors wanting to try new approaches to their teaching tasks—and some combine the two. Activities of these kinds are to be found in Australia, the U.S.S.R., Sweden, Denmark, Poland, West Germany, the Netherlands, Britain, the U.S.A., and recently in a few Canadian universities, notably McGill, Laval, and Montréal.

Whatever further developments there are of this sort, one should remember that professors, like students, learn only when they are active participants in the process, and only when they want to. Imposed programs of teacher improvement are not likely to work, but professors themselves may initiate them if they feel it is worth their while. Two areas of study seem most likely to be appropriate: how students learn and how teachers can help them learn—and students might well be invited to assist.

Most of these problems are touched on in the references which follow.

NOTE

1. A more detailed and technical report of the analyses and findings summarized in this section is to be found in Edward F. Sheffield, "Characteristics of Effective Teaching in Canadian Universities–An Analysis Based on the Testimony of a Thousand Graduates," *Stoa: The Canadian Journal of Higher Education*, IV, 1 (1974), 7–29.

An Annotated Bibliography

ABERCROMBIE, M. L. J., *Aims and Techniques of Group Teaching.* 2nd ed. London: Society for Research into Higher Education, 1971. Pp. 58. 1st ed. 1970.

This, the second publication of the Society's Working Party on Teaching Methods, discusses groups which are in face-to-face contact and in which the teacher withdraws from the central role. "The group system aims to emancipate the student from the authority-dependency relationship, and to help him to develop intellectual independence and maturity through interaction with peers" (p. 5). The lecture, the tutorial, and the group are compared and there are outlines of syndicate work and "free" or "associative" group discussion, the latter being the author's chief interest.

———, "The Work of a University Education Research Unit," *Universities Quarterly,* XXII, 2 (March 1968), 182–96.

When a new curriculum was introduced at the Bartlett School of Architecture of the University of London in the early sixties, an education research unit was incorporated in it "to monitor these innovations and to investigate and improve architectural education generally. From the beginning," Mrs. Abercrombie continues, "it was intended that the unit should be an agent as well as an observer of change, that much of its work should be intimately involved with the processes it was studying, one of its aims being to facilitate and catalyze the educational endeavours of the staff and students of the school."

ALBERTA, COMMISSION ON EDUCATIONAL PLANNING (Walter H. Worth, commissioner), *A Choice of Futures: Report of the Commission.* Edmonton: Queen's Printer, 1972. Pp. 325.

This swinging, psychedelic, provocative, that is to say unconventional, report discusses education at all levels, in school and out, but with emphases on higher (meaning post-secondary) and further (meaning adult) education.

There are several parts concerned with the teaching/learning process in higher education, notably the section entitled "Teaching Strategies in Higher Education" (pp. 202–204) and a subsection on higher and further education in the section on "Professional Teachers" (pp. 240–41). The former opens with these words: "Nowhere in our system of schooling will the development of responsive learning environments be more traumatic than in higher education" (p. 202). Traumatic for the professors, is the meaning. The Commission charges that "university teaching methods, particularly in undergraduate studies, are disagreeably uniform and tedious" (p. 202). Alternatives are suggested. The second of the two parts cited has an equally challenging or abrasive opening: "In a buyer's market it seems reasonable to expect that Alberta's institutions for higher and further education will soon be staffed by persons of demonstrated ability to promote student learning and to teach effectively. But without intervention this is unlikely to happen" (p. 240). It is suggested that graduate students should be able to choose between courses in research methodology and "courses about learning and teaching" (p. 241).

ALEXANDER, LAWRENCE T. AND STEPHEN L. YELON, eds., *Instructional Development Agencies in Higher Education*. East Lansing, Mich.: Michigan State University, Educational Development Program, Learning Service, 1972. Pp. 128.

In May 1971 a conference on instructional development agencies in higher education was held at Michigan State University. This book includes a report of the discussions and extended notes, in detail and in summary form, on the structure and activities of the sixteen agencies represented. Two of these are Canadian: McGill University's Centre for Learning and Development, established in 1969, and the even newer Atlantic Institute of Education which was hoping to assist universities in its region to initiate programs for the improvement of their teaching. The others, all established in the sixties, were in American universities. Data on fourteen of these agencies indicated that the provision of consultation services and short courses and workshops for university departments and faculty members was given highest priority, followed by research and development projects with respect to curriculum and instruction, and the teaching of undergraduate and graduate students about aspects of teaching and learning. One report revealed that in 1971 there were twenty-two American medical schools with instructional development units, and another twenty hoping to establish such units.

Association of Colleges for Further and Higher Education and Association of Principals of Technical Institutions, *Staff Development in Further Education*. Report of a joint ACFHE/APTI Working Party. London: ACFHE, 1973. Pp. 39.

The staff with which this report is concerned is the teachers in colleges of further education, including polytechnics, in Britain. Drawing on the experience of personal management in industry, the stated aims are: "To improve current performance and remedy existing weaknesses; To prepare staff for changing duties and responsibilities, and to encourage them to use new methods and techniques in their present posts; To prepare teachers for advancement either in their own college or in the education service generally; To enhance job satisfaction." The strongest recommendations of the Working

Party are that every college should have a staff development policy and that a senior member of its staff should be named staff development officer to act as an advisor to those interested in taking advantage of the program.

Australian Vice-Chancellors' Committee, *University Centres for Higher Education Research and Development.* A Report Prepared for the A.V.C.C. Sub-committee on Educational Research and Development. Canberra: Australian Vice-Chancellors' Committee, 1973. Pp. 16.

The directors of six established centres describe the origins, organization and activities of those centres, and offer guidelines for the establishment of similar projects in other universities. The centres represented are those of the University of New South Wales, the University of Western Australia, Monash University, the University of Melbourne, Macquarie University, and the University of Queensland.

BARZUN, JACQUES, *Teacher in America.* Garden City, New York: Doubleday Anchor Books, 1954. Pp. 280. First published in 1945, by Little, Brown & Company.

As a result of a series of visits to American colleges, to explain Columbia's new curriculum in General Education, Jacques Barzun wrote this book—in five weeks. It is a highly personalized and opinionful commentary on teaching and the late-war university scene. Two quotations suggest its flavour:

> Consequently, the whole aim of good teaching is to turn the young learner, by nature a little copycat, into an independent, self-propelling creature, who cannot merely learn but study—that is, work as his own boss to the limit of his powers. This is to turn pupils into students, and it can be done on any rung of the ladder of learning. (p. 24)

and

> Given a mastered subject and a person committed heart and soul to teaching it, a class accustomed to think, attend, and be led; the result will be, under God, as near to the discourse of men and angels as it is fit to go. (p. 45)

BEARD, RUTH, *Teaching and Learning in Higher Education.* 2nd ed. Harmondsworth, England: Penguin Books, 1972. Pp. 253. First published in 1970.

When she wrote and revised this book, Ruth Beard was director of the University Teaching Methods Unit of the Department of Higher Education, University of London Institute of Education. She introduces it in these words:

> . . . this book is concerned with much more than teaching techniques or 'teaching tips'. It stresses, in the first place, the need to redefine the purposes of higher education and course objectives and to relate these with methods in teaching and assessment. Secondly, the kinds of learning which occur in higher education are discussed at some length for, despite the paucity of research, existing evidence should at least convince teachers of the need to vary their methods. Thirdly, teaching techniques are discussed, drawing on findings from inquiries and researches as well as innovations in teaching which have proved successful; and, finally, the limitations of methods of assessment are considered at some length and their value is

> discussed in relation to various objectives in teaching and learning. In these ways it is hoped that the reader will not only discover new teaching techniques to improve his students' learning, and ways of evaluating their performance and his own, but will also become more sensitive to deficiences in the organization of courses which give rise to discontent by reducing the experience of learning from one which is exciting, illuminating and a sound preparation for living to one of cramming facts and figures for examinations. (pp. 8–9)

After discussing the planning of courses and curricula, and before dealing with objectives in specific fields, she explains: "In the ensuing chapters . . . there are few directives for teachers to follow but information is provided, together with examples of innovations and experiments, to enable them to draw their own conclusions and to modify their teaching more knowledgeably" (p. 35). Other chapters are on the psychology of learning, advantages and disadvantages of the lecturing method, teaching small groups, practical and laboratory teaching, instruction without teachers, independent study, and evaluation of learning and teaching. This is a sophisticated contribution, evidently aimed more at the practising teacher than at the beginner.

BEARD, RUTH M. AND DONALD A. BLIGH, *Research into Teaching Methods in Higher Education.* 3rd ed. London: Society for Research into Higher Education, 1971. Pp. 104.

Like its predecessors, the first of which was published in 1968, this edition summarizes the findings of British research into the processes of learning, and methods of teaching which are conducive to learning, in institutions of higher education. Many gaps are noted, but available evidence is impressive and useful. The notes are grouped under these main headings: Aims and objectives; economy and efficiency; recall and retention of information; skills and abilities; teaching for change of attitudes; and evaluation of students, teachers, and teaching methods. There is a brief section describing courses and services for university teachers but these are outlined more fully in *Training of University Teachers* by Harriet Greenaway (London: Society for Research into Higher Education, 1971). Scores of references are listed and there is an index.

BEARD, RUTH M., F. G. HEALEY AND P. J. HOLLOWAY, *Objectives in Higher Education.* London: Society for Research into Higher Education, 1970. Pp. 75. First published in 1968.

Beard first makes the case for analysing course objectives, then reviews some of the relevant aspects of the psychology of learning. In the second chapter Healey and Holloway summarize, compare, and assess the "classical" objectives of university teaching, notably as stated by Newman and Ortega y Gasset on the "liberal' side and Thomas Huxley, Herbert Spencer and Karl Jaspers on the "utilitarian" side. At one point they observe: "On the whole Newman's view seems to have held sway up to the present day in all *discussions* about university education, but it is the utilitarian one which has been used as a basis for *action*, both by successive governments and by academic planners, especially those in charge of the distribution of funds" (p. 33). Beard returns with a psychologist's approach to defining objectives, including an outline of Bloom's taxonomies of cognitive and affective objectives and discussion of the relation between objectives and teaching methods. Her final chapter examines the process of evaluation, first of student achievement (again in relation to objectives) and then of teaching. This twice-reprinted report is the first fruit of a Working Party on Teaching Methods in higher education set up in 1966 by the Society for Research into Higher Education. Others have followed and still more are in prospect.

BLIGH, DONALD A., *What's the Use of Lectures?* 2nd ed. New Barnet, Herts: D. A. and B. Bligh, 1972. Pp. 216. First published in 1971.

Bligh's response to the question is that they are useful for conveying information but not to promote thought or to change attitudes. Drawing on the psychology of learning in general and on experiments in teaching at the higher education level, he outlines the factors affecting the acquisition of information, and lecture techniques which apply these factors most effectively. But research covers only part of what is "known" and he does not hesitate to rely on "common sense" and his own experience for additional explanations and suggestions. The title of the book is a bit misleading because there is much discussion also of alternatives to the lecture, especially of methods which may be used with the lecture. Of prime importance, Bligh stresses, is the care with which a lecturer prepares for class but he points out that " 'What are the students going to do?' is a more crucial question for the lecturer than 'What am I going to do?' " The book itself is laid out like a carefully prepared series of lectures.

BONNEAU, LOUIS-PHILIPPE AND J. A. CORRY, *Quest for the Optimum: Research Policy in the Universities of Canada.* The Report of a Commission to Study the Rationalisation of University Research. Ottawa: Association of Universities and Colleges of Canada, Vol. I, 1972. Pp. 207. Vol. II, 1973. Pp. 67. (Also published in French: *Poursuivre l'Optimum.*)

The Commissioners are concerned with research, but they begin by asserting that "The first priority for the university is its teaching" (I, 20). They distinguish between frontier research and reflective inquiry and argue that a minority of teachers should engage in the former; the majority should be busy with the latter because it supports teaching more directly. In a section on "Research and Teaching," Bonneau and Corry express their view that university teachers should be rewarded for effective teaching and reflective inquiry, without feeling pressed to engage in frontier research. They go on to propose that "every staff member should be asked to state, in descending order of importance and in what proportions, what he wishes to be judged on . . . : frontier research and teaching, teaching and reflective inquiry, committee work and administrative duties" (I, 56), and that he should be so judged.

BORGER, ROBERT AND A. E. M. SEABORNE, *The Psychology of Learning.* Harmondsworth, England: Penguin Books, 1966. Pp. 249.

There are many books available on the psychology of learning. This will serve as an example which happens to be easily available.

Britain, University Grants Committee, *Report of the Committee on University Teaching Methods* (Sir Edward Hale, chairman). London: HMSO, 1964. Pp. 173.

The Committee reports on its survey of the methods by which undergraduates in British universities are taught, comments on the methods most used and on others which could be, reveals how little teacher training university teachers have had, and how great is the need for research into teaching methods. "We do not favour any prolonged course of training," concludes the Report, "but we think present arrangements unduly haphazard." Another conclusion is that "the need for operational research and experiment in university teaching" is "pressing" (p. 118).

BROUDY, HARRY S. AND JOHN R. PALMER, *Exemplars of Teaching Method.* Chicago: Rand McNally & Company, 1965. Pp. 172.

This book "concentrates . . . on teaching method as it was exhibited in the work of a few noted teachers," including the Rhetoricians, Socrates, Alcuin, Abelard, Ascham and the Jesuits, Comenius, Pestalozzi, Froebel, Herbart, and Kilpatrick.

Carnegie Commission on Higher Education, *The Fourth Revolution: Instructional Technology in Higher Education.* A Report and Recommendations. New York: McGraw-Hill, 1972. Pp. 106.

The first revolution was the introduction of schools for the education of the young, writing was the second, and printing the third. This, the fourth, has been slow to exert the influence of which it is capable. The Commission reviews the kinds of instructional technology now in use, assesses current penetration and suggests directions for new efforts. The impacts on faculty and students are discussed, and costs are considered. According to the Commission, the greatest prospects are for cable TV, videocassettes, computer-assisted instruction, and learning kits to be used with audiovisual independent study units.

CENTRA, JOHN A., *Strategies for Improving College Teaching. Prepared by the ERIC Clearinghouse on Higher Education.* Report No. 8. Washington, D.C.: American Association for Higher Education, 1972. Pp. 51.

In this brief review the author presents some of the findings of research on teaching and learning, discusses self-analysis, student ratings and institutional programs as approaches to teacher improvement, and concludes with a short chapter on the impact of technology on teaching.

COHEN, S. W., "Teaching and Learning in Australian Universities," *Australian Journal of Higher Education*, I, 2 (November 1962), 75–88.

As early as 1962 it was possible to list a number of enterprises in Australian universities—a tertiary education option in the Diploma in Education course at the University of Western Australia, and plans for a similar venture which was to start at the University of New England in 1964 (it did); short, intensive courses for university teachers at Queensland and Sydney, and short courses plus consulting services and programs of research into teaching and learning at Melbourne and New South Wales.

DUBIN, ROBERT AND THOMAS C. TAVEGGIA, *The Teaching-Learning Paradox: A Comparative Analysis of College Teaching Methods.* Eugene, Oregon: University of Oregon, Center for the Advanced Study of Educational Administration, 1968. Pp. 78.

"This is a polemical tract," say the authors. And this is their theme:

> We are able to state decisively that no particular method of college instruction is measurably to be preferred over another, when evaluated by student examination performances. We may also conclude that replication of the 91 studies examined in detail in this survey would not produce conclusions different from ours.
>
> Any future research on comparative teaching methods at the college level must move in new directions. We have suggested that a fruitful direction of further analysis will be to examine directly the links between teaching and learning for a student group of adults or near adults. (p. 10)

EBLE, KENNETH E., *Career Development of the Effective College Teacher.* [Salt Lake City, Utah]: Project to Improve College Teaching, 1971. Pp. 135. Distributed by American Association of University Professors, One Dupont Circle, Washington, D.C.

This booklet was the second produced to further the Project to Improve College Teaching, the first being the one entitled *The Recognition and Evaluation of Teaching.* Professor Eble reviews programs and possibilities for the preparation of graduate students for teaching, for the orientation of the beginning teacher to the craft, for career development in the middle years, and for sympathetic attention to the problems of those nearing retirement. Perhaps best developed is the chapter devoted to beginning teachers, for whom Eble advocates a program of grants to enable them to improve their teaching effectiveness. There is a useful chapter too on the reward system, pointing out ways in which it might be altered to give recognition to good teaching, and one on leadership which is about ways of getting faculty development systems going on the campuses.

———, *Professors as Teachers.* San Francisco: Jossey-Bass, 1972. Pp. 202.

The final report of the Project to Improve College Teaching sponsored from 1969 to 1971 by the American Association of University Professors and the Association of American Colleges. It reflects the findings of several commissioned studies and a number of conferences arranged by the Project, but most of all Professor Eble's thoughts and conclusions resulting from the many visits he made to campuses throughout the U.S.A. First he describes college teaching as he found it—conventional. Then he discusses a variety of relevant problems and makes proposals: evaluating teaching (the best chapter), what students want, learning to teach, faculty development, rewards of teaching, the teaching environment, and whether teaching is obsolete. He favours student evaluation of teaching, conscious preparation of graduate students for teaching their subjects, systematic though informal in-service staff development programs, the recognition of good teaching in promotion procedures, and improvement of the conditions in and under which teaching and learning take place. He concludes that teaching is far from obsolete. Rather, "teaching matters and . . . the seventies offer great opportunities for teachers" (p. 75).

———, *The Recognition and Evaluation of Teaching.* Salt Lake City, Utah: Project to Improve College Teaching, 1970. Pp. 111. Distributed by American Association of University Professors, One Dupont Circle, Washington, D.C.

The Project to Improve College Teaching was sponsored jointly, 1969–71, by the American Association of University Professors and the Association of American Colleges, and Kenneth Eble was its director. This report is based on an extensive review of the (American) literature on course and teacher evaluation, on extensive visits to U.S. campuses, and on the proceedings of a conference on evaluation held in April 1970. It offers information and wise comment on most aspects of evaluation and concludes with an excellent bibliography.

ESTRIN, HERMAN A. AND DELMER M. GOODE, eds., *College and University Teaching*. Dubuque, Iowa: Wm. C. Brown Company, 1964. Pp. 628.

A selection of 122 articles which appeared in *Improving College and University Teaching* during that journal's first decade. There are four main parts: The Professor's Professional Role, College Students, Curriculum and Method in College Teaching, and Evaluation and Improvement in College Teaching.

FALK, BARBARA, "The Melbourne Approach to Teacher Training for University Staff," *The Australian University*, VIII, 1 (May 1970), 57–66.

Mrs. Falk, Reader-in-Charge at the Centre for the Study of Higher Education at the University of Melbourne, describes the program which began in the academic year 1969 as "a short induction programme followed by continuous opportunity for development of teaching skills rather than a lengthy initial training which certifies teaching ability for a lifetime" (p. 60). It began with a preterm week and continued with fortnightly meetings throughout the academic year, and included individual tuition, and observation and discussion of classes. In addition, the Centre responds to requests for consultation from departments with respect to problems or projects. "The Centre is not conceived as telling colleagues in other faculties how they should teach but rather as a group of experts in learning and teaching contributing to the investigation of specific problems and the implementing of findings in various faculties" (p. 63).

FALK, BARBARA AND KWONG LEE DOW, *The Assessment of University Teaching*. London: Society for Research into Higher Education, 1971. Pp. 47.

The authors, colleagues in the Centre for the Study of Higher Education, University of Melbourne, explain their goal as follows:

> In this monograph, although fairly extensive reference is made to theoretical studies and empirical investigations considered by us to be relevant and important, our concern is more immediate and practical. What can be done with what we already know to perform the necessary tasks of appointing and promoting staff? What can be done to improve teaching in universities? (p. iv)

They observe that research and publication is judged in spite of the difficulty of arriving at objective assessment and argue that teaching must be too, however imperfectly. They note that colleagues can see the results of research but know less at first hand about how their fellows teach. Students are the ones with first-hand evidence of that and, although their evaluations are subject to shortcomings, their views should be part of the process of assessment. There are chapters devoted to criteria of effective teaching, the relevance of student attainment, the use of student evaluation, assessment of teaching by colleagues and, finally, a rationale for decision-making. They conclude:

> In the end, comparison between the teaching performance and potential of individual academics is dependent on human judgement. This judgement will be more valid and more reliable if it is based on careful collection and survey of available data including the data contributed by other persons' judgements of the hard facts and considerations of their subjective assessments. (p. 32)

A sample questionnaire used at Melbourne to get feedback from students is appended, as is a select bibliography.

FENSHAM, P. J., "Methods and Programmes for the Improvement of University Teaching," *The Australian University*, IX, 4 (December 1971), 251–69.

A few months after the publication of MacKenzie *et al.*, *Teaching and Learning* (1970), there was a five-day seminar on methods and programs for the improvement of university teaching arranged by Unesco and the International Association of Universities at the University of Amsterdam. This is a report of the seminar by a participant from Monash University. There is little detail of the substance of the discussions but interesting reference is made to the development of "university education units"—at Michigan State University, McGill University, and the University of London, at several Australian universities, and in the USSR.

FLOOD PAGE, COLIN, *Technical Aids to Teaching in Higher Education*. London: Society for Research into Higher Education, 1971. Pp. 52.

This, the third of the publications of the SRHE Working Party on Teaching Methods, emphasizes what research has shown to be the effect on learning of various instructional aids. There are but brief descriptions of the pieces of equipment and their operation. The main sections of the report are devoted to still pictures, moving pictures (films and television), recorded sounds, programmed learning and teaching machines, multi-media systems and computers.

In his summary the author makes these wise observations:

> . . . teachers are prepared to try out new things, e.g. slides and overhead projectors, if they do not disturb the previous pattern of teaching, do not cost much money, are easy to handle, do a given job at least as well as whatever they replace, and are not likely to need a lot of maintenance and technical care. The teacher's traditional ally is a piece of chalk. (p. 33)
>
> . . . the student studies in approximately the same way, whether the material is presented in the form of a lecture, conventional text-book, list of readings, or programmed text-book. (p. 40)

FRANCIS, JOHN BRUCE, "Relevance in Tertiary Instruction: A Psychological Interpretation," *Higher Education*, II, 3 (August 1973), 325–41.

Defining relevance as "the student's name for 'goodness-of-fit' in teacher-student interaction," Francis argues that effective teaching must take into account the ways in which students learn. He points out that today's students are different from yesterday's and the old medium (print) may not serve. "Students who demand relevance," he says, "are asking for 'meaningful' content which is appropriate to their developmental level and which is conveyed by media to which they naturally respond."

GAFF, JERRY G. AND ROBERT C. WILSON, "The Teaching Environment," *AAUP Bulletin*, LVII, 9 (Winter 1971), 475–93.

A discussion of three "aspects of their environments" mentioned by faculty as "having significant impact on teaching: (1) institutional policies and practices concerning teachers, (2) the nature of the student body, and (3) the character of faculty colleagues" (p. 476). In their elaboration of the first of these, the authors say: "The single most important factor in the success or failure of any attempt to improve college teaching is the motivation of the faculty. . . . Motivation . . . is the product of specific institutional policies and practices" (p. 476). Chief of these is the reward structure: ". . . there must be a *visible structure of rewards* for such efforts" (p. 476). As a corollary, "If the reward structure is to place more emphasis on teaching effectiveness and if, as seems likely, faculty performance is to come under more searching review, the need to evaluate teaching reliably becomes crucial" (p. 478). Though interesting, the discussion of the other two aspects of the working environment is less directly related to the improvement of teaching.

GAGNÉ. FRANÇOYS, *33,000 étudiants évaluent la pédagogie au niveau collégial: Analyse des résultats généreaux de l'exploitation du test PERPE en novembre 1970*. Document 1071–04. Montréal: PERPE, 1971. Pp. 75.

In the autumn of 1970, 1,057 teachers in 23 CEGEPs (collèges d'enseignement général et professionnel) in Quebec got from 33,092 students an evaluation of the teaching they were receiving. The rating instrument, PERPE (Perceptions Étudiantes de la Relation Professeur-Étudiants), yielded a measure of the students' satisfaction or dissatisfaction with respect to 61 items in six main groupings. Highlights of the analysis were that 1) students generally expected teachers to use the lecture method and were satisfied with the fact that the teachers did just that, although they would have preferred some variations in it; 2) teachers were not sufficiently student-oriented in their attitudes; 3) they were not as available, either for academic or nonacademic contacts, as students expected them to be.

GAGNÉ, FRANÇOYS ET MARIE CHABOT, "PERPE, une conception neuve du perfectionnement pédagogique," *Prospectives*, VI, 3 (juin 1970), 160–81.

Describes a test, PERPE (Perceptions Etudiants de la Relation Professeur-Etudiants), by which teachers in the CEGEPs (collèges d'enseignement général et professionnel) of Quebec can discover, confidentially, from their students what their teaching strengths and weaknesses are. An English version of the test is available as SPOT (Students' Perceptions of Teachers). The instrument is thought by the developer (Gagné) to be appropriate for use at the university level as well. A popularized report on the project appeared in *Education Québec*, I, 13 (24 mars 1971), 4–8: "PERPE: Une évaluation scientifique de l'enseignement au collégial," by Jean-Claude Crépeau.

GOLDSCHMID, BARBARA AND MARCEL L. GOLDSCHMID, *Individualizing Instruction in Higher Education: A Review*. Montreal: McGill University, Centre for Learning and Development, 1972. Pp. 53. Also published in *Higher Education*, III, 1 (February 1974), 1–24.

A digest of a variety of approaches, most of them adaptations of programmed or modular instruction. Others include computer-assisted instruction, the audio-tutorial, contingency contracting, the Keller Plan, individually prescribed instruction, and instructional options. There is an extensive bibliography.

GOLDSCHMID, BARBARA AND MARCEL L. GOLDSCHMID, *Modular Instruction in Higer Education: A Review*. Montreal: McGill University, Centre for Learning and Development, 1972. Pp. 51. Also published, in abbreviated form, in *Higher Education*, II, 1 (February 1973), 15–32.

In attempts to individualize instruction, many experiments have led to development of courses broken down into small parts which can be followed and mastered by students working independently of each other and of instructors. Modules, therefore, are curriculum packages intended for self-study. In this review of recent literature the Goldschmids outline the idea, the process, and some heartening results.

GOOD, HAROLD M. AND BERNARD TROTTER, eds., *Frontiers in Course Development: System and Collaboration in University Teaching*. Report of the Conference on Teaching University Biological Sciences, Jackson's Point, Ontario, May, 1971. [Toronto: Council of Ontario Universities, 1971.] Pp. 121.

The report of an experiment in course development of the kind recommended by Bernard Trotter in *Television and Technology in University Teaching* (1970). With the help of David G. Hawkridge, Director of the Institute of Educational Technology, The Open University, a hundred Ontario university teachers of biology spend four days together attempting, with only partial success, to use the systems approach in planning courses and modules in their subject. Of course there was discussion of instructional method too. One participant is quoted as saying, after the conference, "In twenty-two years of teaching this was the first time I gave my full attention for a sustained period to thoughts about teaching."

GREENAWAY, HARRIET, *Training of University Teachers: A survey of its provision in universities in the United Kingdom*. London: Society for Research into Higher Education, 1971. Pp. 32.

Early in 1971 a questionnaire survey of programs for the training of their teachers was conducted among the universities of Britain. All but five of the fifty institutions surveyed had some sort of scheme in operation. The mode was a one-week course, especially but not exclusively for new lecturers, conducted prior to the beginning of the academic session in September. Most programs began in 1969 or 1970, much of the impetus being given by a letter sent by the University Grants Committee to the universities in 1969. In connection with its recommendations on academic salaries the Prices and Incomes Board had made specific reference to the probationary period for new appointments. On this point the UGC gave the following advice to universities:

> The normal period of probation should be three years from initial appointment, with a possible extension (at a university's discretion) to four years. It would be for each university to decide its own method of judging whether or not a teacher had successfully completed probation.
>
> If probation is to serve its true purpose, entrants to university teaching

must be given full opportunities to develop appropriate skills and to demonstrate their suitability and competence before a decision is taken whether to confirm them in appointment. The Committee attach importance to the development by each university of appropriate arrangements (where these do not already exist) for systematic training in the early period of appointment.

(Quoted in University Grants Committee, *Annual Survey, Academic Year 1968–1969*, Cmnd. 4261, January 1970, p. 8)

In its *Annual Survey, Academic Year 1969–1970* the Committee underscored this advice: "The Committee are anxious that further progress should be made in the universities to arrange for the training of university teachers" (Cmnd. 4593, February 1971, p. 35).

HEISS, ANN M., "Preparing College Teachers," in G. Kerry Smith, ed., *The Troubled Campus: Current Issues in Higher Education, 1970* (San Francisco: Jossey-Bass Inc., 1970), 165–78.

Drawing on her study, *Challenges to Graduate Schools* (San Francisco: Jossey-Bass, 1970), Dr. Heiss observes: "Not until the teacher-scholar gains status commensurate to that of the researcher-scholar will the seduction of the faculty into research diminish and the status and preparation of college teachers receive attention" (p. 169). Her main theme is this: "In response to the criticism leveled against college and university teaching, and in view of the radical changes in teaching strategies and technology, the graduate school should reaffirm its responsibility as the teacher of teachers by offering carefully designed programs of teacher preparation for doctoral students who plan to enter academic careers" (p 170).

HENDERSON, NORMAN K., *University Teaching*. Hong Kong: Hong Kong University Press, 1969. Pp. 170. Also available from Oxford University Press.

The author, a graduate of London and Melbourne, is Professor and Head of the Department of Education of the University of Hong Kong. After a brief introduction to the idea and functions of the university, he discusses those topics which are likely to be of assistance to "those who intend to teach at the tertiary level." Chapters are provided on lecturing procedures, the university classroom: its arrangement and organization, discussion group techniques, practical sessions, audio-visual aids and programmed learning, how to help students in their study problems, and examining and evaluating students' work. Almost every possibility is anticipated and appropriate behaviour or procedure prescribed. Some reference is made to relevant research.

HEXTER, J. H., "Publish or Perish–A Defense," *The Public Interest*, no. 17 (Fall 1969), 60–77.

A spirited argument that "in the great universities" advancement should be based solely on scholarly publications.

HIGHET, GILBERT, *The Art of Teaching*. New York: Vintage Books, (n.d.). Pp. 259. First published in 1950, by Alfred A. Knopf.

"This is a book on the methods of teaching . . . suggestions drawn from practice," says the author in his preface. "It is called *The Art of Teaching* because I believe that teaching is an art, not a science" (p. vii). Then he outlines its contents:

> The book begins by considering the character and abilities which make a good professional teacher, and then goes on to examine his methods. After that, it branches out further. One of the forces which have helped to make our own civilization is certainly the influence of famous teachers; therefore the most powerful teachers of the past are examined. First, the Greek intellectuals; then Socrates, Plato, Aristotle; then Jesus of Nazareth; then the teachers of the Renaissance; the Jesuits next; and the best nineteenth-century and twentieth-century teachers; and finally the fathers of great men, who taught their sons how to be great. Last of all, our survey turns to look at teaching in everyday life, as it is done by ordinary parents to their children, by husbands and wives to each other, by doctors, priests, psychiatrists, politicians, propagandists, and even by artists and authors who do not know that they are teaching the public. It ends with a declaration of the heavy but encouraging responsibility which rests on us all whenever we attempt to teach our fellow-men. (p. viii)

HILDEBRAND, MILTON, "How to Recommend Promotion for a Mediocre Teacher Without Actually Lying," *Experiment and Innovation: New Directions in Education at the University of California*, IV, 1 (May 1971), 1–21. Also published in the *Journal of Higher Education*, XLIII, 1 (January 1972), 44–62.

A preview of research on effective university teaching and its evaluation undertaken at the University of California, Davis, by Milton Hildebrand and Robert C. Wilson, a full report of which was later published as a monograph by the Center for Research and Development in Higher Education, University of California, Berkeley (see the following entry). The chief results are the identification of characteristics which distinguish best from worst teachers and development of a strong case for student evaluations of teachers as contributions to the improvement of teaching and the evidence for academic promotion.

HILDEBRAND, MILTON, ROBERT C. WILSON AND EVELYN R. DIENST, *Evaluating University Teaching*. Berkeley, California: Center for Research and Development in Higher Education, 1971. Pp. 52.

Here are the results of a three-year study at the University of California, Davis, which had two aims. One was to define and describe effective teaching, the other "to find more valid, reliable and effective means of incorporating the evaluation of teaching into advancement procedures." The authors go on to state, significantly, "We believe this to be the most important single requirement for the improvement of university teaching; the incentive thereby provided will encourage instructors to devote the study, time, and effort necessary to do their best, and the status of teaching will increase" (p. 1). Scales for rating teaching were developed which discriminated between best and worst teachers, as identified both by their students and their colleagues (who were in substantial agreement). The authors suggest how such a scheme can be introduced at a university, stressing ratings by students, supplemented by ratings by colleagues.

Improving College and University Teaching. Delmer M. Goode, ed., Oregon State University Press, Corvallis, Oregon. Quarterly. 1953–.

Each number contains a large number of brief articles, most of them by U.S. academics. In recent years each issue has been planned around a theme. Examples are: Climate and Processes of Teaching and Learning (Autumn 1968); Professor and Profession (Autumn 1969); Teaching Goals and Strategy (Spring 1970); Professors and Students (Summer and Autumn 1970).

Instructional Science. An International Journal. Elsevier Publishing Company, Amsterdam. Quarterly. 1972–.

Of the twenty-two articles appearing in the first six issues of this journal, about one in four is likely to be of special interest to teachers in higher education. Examples are: 'Style and Effectiveness in Education and Training: A Model for Organising Teaching and Learning" by Ivor K. Davies, "Student Personality Characteristics and Optimal College Learning Conditions: An Extensive Search for Trait-by-Treatment Interaction Effects" by Lewis R. Goldberg, "Behavioural Objectives—A Critical Review" by Michael MacDonald-Ross, and "The Design and Evaluation of Science Courses at the Open University" by Anthony R. Kaye.

JOYCE, C. R. B. AND L. HUDSON, "Student Style and Teacher Style: an Experimental Study," *British Journal of Medical Education*, II, 1 (March 1968), 28–31.

In two successive years, students of statistics at the London Hospital Medical College and their four teachers classified themselves and each other with respect to cognitive style as tending toward convergence or divergence (see J. W. Getzels and P. W. Jackson, *Creativity and Intelligence*, New York: Wiley, 1962). It was found that students tended to get higher grades when taught by teachers with the same cognitive style. There were exceptions, but the patterns, including the pattern of exceptions, were consistent from one year to the next. The authors observe that the study "suggests a way of making better use of those teachers who are available for a given course; even those whose overall performance is less successful than that of their colleagues will be more useful to some students than to others" (p. 31).

KATZ, F. M., D. J. MAGIN AND P. S. ARBIB, *Role Divergence in Universities.* Monograph No. 1. Kensington, N.S.W.: University of New South Wales, Tertiary Education Research Centre, 1969. Pp. 46.

This monograph presents interim findings of research on "The impact of organizational demands on role behaviour of university staff and students" and includes three papers: "Defining the objectives of university education—differences between staff and students," "The role of the lecturer," and "Staff and student perceptions of the university." It is revealed, for example, that students' goals are much more vocational than staffs' goals for students, and that staff differ more between themselves than with students on the objectives of university education and the role of lecturer. It is suggested that the role conflicts which exist in universities may reduce their effectiveness and explain, in part, the unrest by which they are characterized.

KNAPPER, CHRIS, "Improving Teaching Effectiveness," *CAUT Bulletin*, XXI, 1 (October 1972), 9–11.

An informal first report to the Canadian Association of University Teachers by the chairman of its Committee on Professional Orientation. He observes that the need for improvement in university teaching is widely recognized but there are few effective programs for doing something about it. Among those which do exist he mentions several in the U.S.A., Britain, Australia, and Canada. His own opinion is "that the key concepts are those of feedback, self-insight and exploration on the part of the individual faculty member" (p. 10).

KNAPPER, CHRIS, BRUCE MCFARLANE AND JOSEPH SCANLON, "Student Evaluation—An Aspect of Teaching Effectiveness," *CAUT Bulletin*, XXI, 2 (December 1972), 26–29, 34. (Also in French in the same issue: "L'évaluation de l'enseignement par les étudiants," pp. 30–34.)

A report of the Professional Orientation Committee to the Council of the Canadian Association of University Teachers, one which was approved in principle by the Council in April 1972. It reviews the literature on student evaluation of teaching and concludes that "there is evidence that evaluation forms are an extremely useful tool to provide feedback for faculty, and there is even some indication that faculty who use them regularly show an improvement in their teaching performance" (p. 29). The Committee offers eight recommendations concerning ways in which evaluation should be undertaken in order to assure validity and fairness.

LADD, DWIGHT R., *Change in Educational Policy: Self-Studies in Selected Colleges and Universities.* A general report prepared for the Carnegie Commission on Higher Education. New York: McGraw-Hill, 1970. Pp. 231.

Includes, among others, a chapter on the Macpherson report at the University of Toronto and another discussing the several proposals for the improvement of classroom teaching. The latter concludes: ". . . the studies all come back to greater rewards as the only apparent way to improve the quality of teaching. But . . . none . . . has proposed really effective ways for evaluating teaching" (p. 162).

Laval, Université, Service de pédagogie universitaire, *Série documents.* Québec: Université Laval.

The first four in the series, published in late 1972 and early 1973, are:

1. Plante, Robert, *Comment 114 professeurs voient les problèmes de pédagogie à l'Université Laval.* Le rapport d'une enquête du Service de pédagogie universitaire. Résumé.
2. Girard, Richard, *Nature des objectifs pédagogiques et bibliographie commentée.*
3. Massachusetts Institute of Technology, translated by Guy Godin, *L'equipe professeur-étudiants.*
4. Brunelle, Jean, Claire Turcotte et Gilles Dussault, *Les formules pédagogiques.*

LAYTON, DAVID, ed., *University Teaching in Transition.* Edinburgh: Oliver & Boyd, 1968. Pp. 161.

The editor explains that "Most of the contributions were originally prepared as a basis for seminar discussion and practical activity in various courses on teaching methods held during recent years in the University of Leeds" (p.

viii). Seventeen authors contribute essays which are in six groups. There is one on the aims of university teaching, by B. A. Fletcher. It is followed by three on teaching large groups, five on teaching small groups, five on aids to teaching and learning, one on examinations and marking, and one on a student point of view. In it Mervyn Saunders points the finger: "What then are the causes of inadequate teaching as they appear to students? The first and most blatant one is that the academic staff of universities do not appear to view their teaching role as a vital one" (p. 150). "At the heart of the problem," he suggests, "is not lack of training in teaching methods nor the need for time for research but the attitude the lecturer adopts towards his teaching and his students" (p. 150).

LECLERC, MARIEL ET SUZANNE DUMAS, *Cent quatorze professeurs parlent de l'enseignement à l'Université.* Québec: Université Laval, 1972. Pp. 180.

In order to make an inventory of the state of teaching and the views of professors at Laval, 114 of those known to be interested in pedagogical problems were interviewed. Their comments are summarized under such headings as objectives, teaching methods, assessment of students, and course evaluation. A chapter is devoted to the professors' hopes and another to brief reports on some successful experiments in teaching. It was concluded that a university pedagogical service should be established. (It was.)

LEE, CALVIN B. T., ed., *Improving College Teaching.* Washington, D.C.: American Council on Education, 1967. Pp. 407.

Papers presented to the 1966 annual meeting of the American Council on Education and articles which appeared in the summer 1966 issue of the *Educational Record* (the ACE quarterly). In his foreword, Logan Wilson points out that it "is not intended primarily for subject matter specialists and classroom teachers, though many could profit from reading it, but for academic administrators having an indirect, yet no less real responsibility for teaching as a basic institutional endeavour" (p. ix).

LEE DOW, KWONG, "The Assessment of University Teaching," *The Australian University*, VIII, 1 (May 1970), 67–76.

While acknowledging the difficulty of establishing criteria of good teaching and the complexity of the activity, Mr. Lee Dow argues that the same is true of research. He suggests, therefore, that a "modest goal would be to assess teaching to a comparable level of precision, or imprecision, with that at which research capacities and activities are estimated" (p. 75). He advocates the accumulation of evidence of teaching ability from a variety of sources. "This would mean that assessment of a person's teaching would be made by the head of department, by colleagues, and by students in conjunction" (p. 75).

MACKENZIE, NORMAN, MICHAEL ERAUT AND HYWEL C. JONES, *Teaching and Learning: An Introduction to New Methods and Resources in Higher Education.* Paris: Unesco and the International Association of Universities, 1970. Pp. 209. (Also published in French: *Art d'enseigner et art d'apprendre.*)

"This inquiry . . . has been carried out under the Joint Unesco-International Association of Universities Research Programme in Higher Education." Norman MacKenzie is Director of the Centre for Educational Technology, University of Sussex, and Messrs. Eraut and Jones are colleagues of his there. They state their intent as follows:

> Our task has therefore been to indicate ways in which institutions of higher education, afflicted by all the stresses of transition, can begin to reconsider their methods of teaching and learning, not to offer neat or immediate remedies. For though potential remedies exist, none has been tried long enough, on a large enough scale, or evaluated with sufficient rigour to justify any sweeping claim that one method or another is necessarily more effective, cheaper, more convenient or even academically desirable. The situation is so complex, and the potential remedies are at such an early stage of development that caution is required as well as optimism. The best that can be done, in terms of our brief, is to set problems of teaching and learning within the wider context of the changing university, to indicate the nature of the emerging repertoire of resources which bear on the extension and improvement of the learning process, to comment on the conceptual changes that are occurring, and to note some of their implications for the organization and management of learning resources. (p. 21)

Among the virtues of this book is that it draws not only on most of what has been written on the subject (chiefly in the United States), but also on experience in many countries. And it is judicious. New resources for learning, including "the media," are introduced, but in a balanced way. More stress is placed on systematic approaches to teaching and learning, especially on the clarification of objectives and on course development.

McGill University, Centre for Learning and Development, *Learning and Development.* Monthly during the academic year. 1969–. Published in both English and French.

During its first three years, this newsletter, usually comprising six pages, featured articles of which these are examples: Lecturing: Time for a Change?; Instructional Options: Adapting the Large University Course to Individual Differences; Training the Graduate Student Teacher; Research on University Teaching: A Perspective; Consequences of Learning; The Learning Cell: An Instructional Innovation; Towards a System of Course Evaluation; International Seminar on Methods and Programmes for the Improvement of University Teaching; The Dynamics of the First Class; Some Solutions to the Problems of Teaching Laboratories; Experiential Learning; Modular Instruction in Higher Education; Goals, Aims and Objectives. A column on innovations at McGill and elsewhere is a regular feature.

———, *McGill Conference on University Teaching and Learning*, Part B: "Recent Experiments in Teaching at McGill University." Montreal: The University, 1971. Pp. 193.

Here are twenty-four papers, presented by forty McGill staff members, on research and experiment in their courses. Half a dozen describe varieties of small-group and individualized instruction, of which perhaps the most interesting is one on "modular course design." Another half dozen present computer-based instruction projects. There are three reports of the use of audio-visual media, four experiments which are described as project-oriented (notably "community design workshops") and five which are one of a kind. Departments or faculties represented include French, mathematics, management, religious studies, chemistry, linguistics, biology, political science, engineering (mining, electrical and chemical), philosophy, psychology, education, English, entomology, architecture, physics, and the Centre for Learning and Development (CLD). Much of the experimentation going on at McGill has been facilitated by the CLD, which was set up in 1969, and encouraged by the availability of grants for this purpose from the University's Educational Development Fund. Some of the innovations reported were cast as research projects, with appropriate methodolgy, controls, and evaluation. Some were exeriments without that kind of sophistication. Some proved or were thought to be successful, some were frankly said to have failed. All are evidence of the concern and effort of the staff members involved, and of institutional interest in the improvement of teaching.

MCKEACHIE, WILBERT J., *Research on College Teaching: A Review.* Report 6. Washington, D.C.: ERIC Clearinghouse on Higher Education, 1970. Pp. 18.

In the *Handbook of Research on Teaching* edited by N. L. Gage in 1963, there is a chapter by McKeachie on "Research on Teaching at the College and University Level." In this report he brings his review of that research up to date, covering the period 1924 to 1970. "Research on college teaching has been marked by non-significant differences," he observes, but goes on to say: "We now have some reasonably well supported answers to such basic questions about college teaching as: 'Does size of class affect teaching effectiveness?' 'Is lecture as effective as discussion?' 'Do the new media improve teaching effectiveness?' This paper reviews that research" (p. 1). The review is confined, however, to research reported in the U.S.A.

———, "Research on Teaching at the College and University Level," in N. L. Gage, ed., *Handbook of Research on Teaching* (Chicago: Rand McNally & Company, 1963), 1118–72.

After a brief review of research on learning principles relevant to teaching methods, there is an extensive section on research on teaching methods of many sorts, then short sections on student characteristics related to effective teaching and the role of faculty attitudes. The article concludes with a long list of references.

———, *Teaching Tips: A Guidebook for the Beginning College Teacher.* 6th ed. Lexington, Mass.: D. C. Heath and Company, 1969. Pp. 280. First published in 1951.

The modest aim and informal style of this oft-reprinted guide by the Chairman of the Deparment of Psychology of the University of Michigan are clearly indicated in the first paragraph: "This is not a textbook in the Educational Psychology of College Teaching. It is merely a compilation of useful (occasionally mechanical) tricks of the trade which I, as a teacher, have found useful in running classes" (p. 1). There are chapters on preparing for a course, meeting a class for the first time, lecturing, organizing effective discussion, and other methods, term papers, examinations, grading, maintaining order, the psychology of learning, student ratings of faculty, and "improving your teaching." Each offers advice and refers to relevant research findings.

MCLEISH, JOHN A. B., *The Advancement of Professional Education in Canada.* The Report of the Professional Education Project (Kellogg Foundation–Ontario Institute for Studies in Education). Toronto: [Ontario Institute for Studies in Education], 1973. Pp. 59.

This is the Executive Vice-Chairman's report of a three-year project (1969–72) "designed to facilitate constructive change in curricula and in the teaching/learning processes in professional faculties throughout Canada." His chief recommendation is "for universities to develop regionally or on their own campuses learning centres for consultation . . . available to the professional faculties" (p. 26).

Manitoba, *Report of the Task Force on Post-Secondary Education in Manitoba* (Michael Oliver, chairman). Winnipeg: Queen's Printer, 1973. Pp. 228.

One of the ten chapters of this *Report* is devoted to learning and teaching. Among the recommendations on this topic are these: that each university and community college should have an Educational Development Fund to support teaching experiments, that there be a provincial Centre for Educational Development, that college teachers be given in-service training in pedagogy, that courses in teaching be available on a voluntary basis to university faculty members and be required for graduate students acting as teaching assistants, that methods of assessing student achievement be reviewed, and that there be systematic evaluation of teaching–by students.

MATHIS, B. CLAUDE AND WILLIAM C. MCGAGHIE, eds., *Profiles in College Teaching: Models at Northwestern.* Evanston, Ill.: Northwestern University, The Center for the Teaching Professions, 1972. Pp. 181.

Here are fourteen essays on methods of organizing the teaching/learning experience, written by teachers at Northwestern who were "selected because of their commitment to and performance in the classroom." Four are set in the field of engineering, four in the school of education, three in the communication arts, and one each in psychology, sociology, and medicine. The emphasis is on experiment and innovation, and among them the contributors reveal a wide range of course designs and teaching styles or models. The most common thread running through the essays is encouragement of learning through purposeful activities.

MEUWESE, W., "Teaching Methods and the Training of Managers," *Higher Education*, II, 3 (August 1973), 377–84.

Here is the author's own abstract of the article: "Various models of the teaching-learning process are subjected to analysis. Doubt is cast on the relative effectiveness of conventional college teaching methods which have not been based on a systematic application of what is known about the learning process. Three principles of learning are outlined, and the value of the systems approach to course design is emphasized and discussed as an example of the application of this approach. Finally, the implications for management training are examined."

MEYER, G. R., "Some Developments in the Improvement of Teaching and Learning in Universities and Colleges in the United States," *Vestes, The Australian Universities' Review*, XI, 1 (April 1968), 3–11.

The programs of different types, some institutional, some interinstitutional, described by Dr. Meyer are the Center for Research in Learning and Teaching at the University of Michigan, the Committee on Institutional Co-operation serving eleven large mid-western universities, EDUCOM (the Inter-University Communications Council), the ERIC (Educational Research Information Centre) clearinghouses, the Center for Research and Development in Higher Education at the University of California, Berkeley, and the commissions on college education of the National Science Foundation. The data were gathered in 1966.

MICHAELSEN, JACOB B., "How to Get the Faculty to Teach," in Lyman A. Glenny and George B. Weatherby, eds., *Statewide Planning for Postsecondary Education: Issues and Design* (Boulder, Colorado: Western Interstate Commission for Higher Education, 1971), 87–102.

The problem, says Prof. Michaelsen, is to provide appropriate incentives. He describes the plan in operation at the University of California at Santa Cruz, a plan characterized by "performance budgeting together with co-ordination, planning, and major allocation decisions at the center, and decentralized management of programs with both rewards and penalties depending on performance" (p. 93).

Michigan, University of, Center for Research on Learning and Teaching, *Memo to the Faculty*. Four times a year. 1963–.

This series of leaflets about university teaching was begun as a service to members of the University of Michigan teaching staff. Off-campus subscriptions have been accepted, however, and the *Memo* has become widely known, especially throughout the United States. As examples, here are three recent titles: No. 43 (December 1970), "Learning Theory and the Teacher: III. Defining Instructional Objectives"; No. 44 (May 1971), "Research on College Teaching"; No. 46 (October 1971), "Grading/Evaluation."

MILTON, OHMER AND EDWARD JOSEPH SHOBEN, JR., eds., *Learning and the Professors*. Athens, Ohio: Ohio University Press, 1968. Pp. 216.

The editors have selected articles which they thought would stimulate "informed and disciplined thought, followed by responsible and imaginative action, about instructional issues. The proper leaders here, in our eyes," they state, "are the professors themselves" (p. xi). Here is the much-quoted article on "The Flight from Teaching" written by John W. Gardner in 1963. Here too are essays by Logan Wilson, Sidney L. Pressey, Ruth E. Eckert and Daniel C. Neale, Paul L. Dressel and Irvin J. Lehmann, Laurence Siegal ("The Contributions and Implications of Recent Research related to Improving Teaching and Learning"), and others. In conclusion, say the editors,

> . . . we feel impelled to propose that this collection of recent provocative articles (some of them original to the volume) be used as a base or a common point of departure for a variety of meetings and seminars among faculties—and not infrequently with student participants—toward the end of improving our arrangements for learning and teaching in American higher education. (p. xvi)

Montréal, Université de, *Le Bulletin du Service pédagogique*. Chaque mois pendant l'année académique. 1974–.

Successor to *Le Service pédagogique vous informe*, the *Bulletin* is described by its editors as "un périodique d'information pédagogique publié à l'intention des professeurs et des cadres académiques de l'Université de Montréal."

MORRIS, WILLIAM H., ed., *Effective College Teaching: The Quest for Relevance*. Washington, D.C.: American Council on Education, 1970. Pp. 162. Published for the American Association for Higher Education.

"This book is a selection of chapters from a larger collection prepared as a study of college teaching with special reference to the disciplines" (pp. vii–viii). It begins with a general discussion of the psychology of learning and methods of teaching, by Stanford C. Erickson, Director, Center for Research on Learning and Teaching, University of Michigan, continues with essays by different authors on teaching in different fields and concludes with contributions by Lewis Mayhew of Stanford and Harold Hodgkinson of the Center for Research and Development in Higher Education, University of California at Berkeley, on the teaching profession and the organization of the university.

MURRAY, HARRY G., *A Guide to Teaching Evaluation*. Toronto: Ontario Confederation of University Faculty Associations, 1973. Pp. 30.

On the assumption that Ontario universities will, increasingly, make use of student ratings of teacher effectiveness, the Ontario Confederation of University Faculty Associations commissioned Professor Murray (Psychology, University of Western Ontario) to outline the uses, issues, research findings, and practices which should be considered when such a program of evaluation is introduced. The result is appropriately called a guide; it is not an argument —except for informed action as opposed to amateurism practised in isolation.

MUSELLA, DONALD F., "A Model for Improving College Teaching," *Improving College and University Teaching*, XIX, 3 (Summer 1971), 198–200.

Dr. Musella, of the Department of Educational Administration, Ontario Institute for Studies in Education, presents a plan for a faculty-sponsored program of pre-service and in-service "education" for college teachers. On classroom teaching he makes the important point that evaluation for the purpose of improvement should be distinct from evaluation for the purpose of promotion, etc. He favours student evaluation, peer evaluation and, especially, self-evaluation.

NERUP, JØRN, OLE B. THOMSEN AND RENE VEJLSGAARD, "Teaching the Teacher to Teach: Results of 3 experiments," *Danish Medical Bulletin*, XIX, 6 (1972), 198–201.

At the University of Copenhagen two experimental courses in university pedagogics were run for doctors (fourteen in the first and seventeen in the second) and one for chemists (numbering fifteen) in 1968 and 1969. Each covered 44–46 hours of formal training, spread over two to three months, supplemented by private study. Evaluation at the end of the courses indicated that those who had taken part found the experience relevant to their teaching problems, and in 1970 interviews with the former participants revealed that most of them had used at least some of what they had learned in the course.

Nuffield Foundation Group for Research and Innovation in Higher Education (Nuffield Lodge, Regents Park, London NW1), *Newsletter*. Occasional.

In 1972 this Group visited a large number of British universities, seeking evidence of innovations, principally in curriculum and teaching. The first two newsletters contained reports on these visits. Then in 1973 the Group arranged a series of meetings to discuss its findings. These resulted in the identification and delineation of some common problem areas in which it was hoped that research might be done. *Newsletter* No. 3 (October 1973) reports on this stage of the inquiry, with particular reference to these topics: the context of innovation, student assessment, practicals and projects, interdisciplinarity, broader education, independence in learning, academic structure, and course development. Other newsletters were to follow.

Ontario, Commission on Post-Secondary Education in Ontario (chairman, Douglas T. Wright, succeeded by D. O. Davis), *The Learning Society*. Toronto: Ministry of Government Services, 1972. Pp. 263. (Also published in French: *La société s'épanouit.*)

Although the Commission devoted only two paragraphs and one formal recommendation to teaching in institutions of higher education, it is interesting to note its stance. We agree, say the Commissioners, "that post-secondary educational institutions should be encouraged to undertake some form of orientation for new instructors." Specifically, they recommend that "Graduate faculties and schools should provide students preparing for teaching careers in post-secondary institutions with opportunities to gain supervised practical teaching experience as an integral part of their program" (Recommendation 69).

Ontario Universities Program for Instructional Development (Harold M. Good, director), *Priorities '74 Report*. Workshop on Instructional Development, November 18–21, 1973, Guild Inn, Scarborough, Ontario. Kingston: Ontario Universities Program for Instructional Development, c/o Queen's University, 1974. Pp. 45.

A three-day workshop, attended by about 70 staff and students of Ontario universities, attempted to suggest priorities for the Program in 1974. (The Program, sponsored by the Ontario Committee on University Affairs and the Council of Ontario Universities, began in 1973.) The workshop report consists of the reports prepared by its eight sub-groups. In No. 1 (December 1973) of the OUPID *Newsletter* the findings are summarized. They identified needs for (1) a better system of rewarding excellent teaching, (2) more precise enunciation of objectives at all levels, (3) more critical evaluation of students, teachers and programs, (4) more varied formats for presentation of programs, (5) more attention to the contribution which universities could make to the "open sector," and (6) an instructional development committee or centre on each campus.

PETERSON, HOUSTON, ed., *Great Teachers Portrayed by Those Who Studied under Them*. New York: Vintage Books (n.d.). Pp. 351. First published in 1946 by Rutgers University Press.

Here Helen Keller tells of her teacher, Anne Mansfield Sullivan; John Stuart

Mill writes of his father, James Mill; Leverett Wilson Spring offers an account (pubished in 1888) of Mark Hopkins. There are essays on Woodrow Wilson, John Dewey, Jean Louis Rodolphe Agassiz, William James, and others—twenty-two in all.

PORTER, ARTHUR, *Towards a Community University: A Study of Learning at Western. Report of the Academic Commissioner to the Senate of the University of Western Ontario*. London, Ontario: The University, 1971. Pp. 235.

Dr. Arthur Porter, Professor of Industrial Engineering at the University of Toronto, was given leave to spend two years as *the* Academic Commissioner "to make a serious, thorough and significant study of the structure and interrelationship of the academic programs" of the University of Western Ontario. One of the seven areas to which he turned his attention is represented in the report by a chapter entitled "The Learning Environments." In it he discusses the characteristics of learning environments, the organization of resources, the evaluation of learning, the evaluation of teaching, the improvement of teaching, academic counselling, and teaching and research. He favours a multiple approach to the evaluation of teaching, including feedback from students. "Teaching," he observes, "thrives when respected and rewarded" (p. 87). He proposes that the University should provide a week-long orientation to teaching methodology for new staff, courses in pedagogy for doctoral candidates who plan to teach, and a centre for teaching and learning of the sort found at McGill University. It should encourage team teaching, and give tangible recognition and reward for good teaching.

POWELL, LEN S., *Lecturing*. London: Sir Isaac Pitman and Sons Ltd., 1973. Pp. 141.

In spite of all the criticism of lectures, most university teachers go on lecturing. So most could profit by this simple how-to-do-it book which treats lecturing as an art and explains how it can be made a fine art, whether in the classroom or on the public platform. On the basic question of objectives, Powell says that "a speaker should ask . . ., 'What do I want to *do* to my listeners', not, 'What do I want to *tell* them?' He should accept the responsibility of choosing how he wants to change people" (p. 8).

Queen's University at Kingston, *Report of the Principal's Committee on Teaching and Learning* (G. A. Harrower, chairman). Kingston, Ontario: The University, 1969. Pp. 83.

Like the Macpherson Report of the University of Toronto, which preceded it, this Report is concerned chiefly with curricular structures. But it, too, has a chapter on "Instruction and Evaluation." The most unusual suggestion is that 'an effort be made to bring the benefits of small group organization to all students by means of Student Learning Groups. We propose that these groups would consist of about ten students who have at least three courses in common. Each group would have a leader, either a graduate student or a staff member" (p. 38). Another recommendation is "that Faculty seminars concerned with problems and methods of teaching at the university level be held at least annually" (p. 44).

ROGERS, CARL R., *Freedom to Learn.* Columbus, Ohio: Charles E. Merrill Publishing Company, 1969. Pp. 358.

The high priest of "client-centered therapy" and "student-centered learning" develops his thoughts on what he now terms experiential learning. According to his definition, it "has a quality of personal involvement . . . is self initiated . . . pervasive . . . is evaluated by the learner . . . [and] its essence is meaning" (p. 5). Included is a chapter on his own way of dealing with students in a graduate course of which his experience was recent: "My Way of Facilitating a Class." Later he makes a statement which is wholly in character: "Teaching, in my estimation, is a vastly over-rated function" (p. 103). And then he goes on to explain: "I see *the facilitation of learning* as the *aim* of education" (p. 105).

ROID, GALE H., "Towards a System of Course Evaluation," *Learning and Development,* II, 6 (February/March 1971), 1–5.

Discusses evaluation as a means to improvement of teaching, and argues that questionnaires should be only part of an evaluation system.

SHEFFIELD, EDWARD F., "Approaches (Mostly Elsewhere) to the Improvement of Teaching in Higher Education," *Improving College and University Teaching,* XXI, 1 (Winter 1973), 5–9.

Though some reference is made to programs in the United States and Canada, most of those described are outside of North America—notably in Australia, Britain, the Netherlands, the Federal Republic of Germany, Denmark, Sweden and the Soviet Union.

———, "Characteristics of Effective Teaching in Canadian Universities—An Analysis Based on the Testimony of a Thousand Graduates," *Stoa: The Canadian Journal of Higher Education,* IV, 1 (1974), 7–29.

A detailed report of the study of which the results are summarized in this book, pp. 206–14.

SMITH, G. KERRY, ed., *New Teaching, New Learning: Current Issues in Higher Education 1971.* San Francisco: Jossey-Bass, 1971. Pp. 261.

Papers presented to the 1971 National Conference on Higher Education of the American Association for Higher Education. Only the first of the book's six parts is related directly to the teaching process. Two of the papers in that section are of particular interest: "Faculty Values and Improving Teaching" by Jerry G. Gaff and Robert C. Wilson, and "Assessment and Reward Systems" by Harold L. Hodgkinson. The former is based in part on the authors' study of the teaching environment (see Gaff and Wilson, above). In addition, they draw attention to another study in which faculty members revealed that, contrary to the popular notion, the majority of them value teaching highly, even more highly than research. In his paper, Hodgkinson argues that "universities should allow for the direct observation of classroom teaching by one's colleagues" (p. 52). "Classroom observation by professional colleagues has its pitfalls," he continues, "but I believe it must be used, in conjunction with student and administrator assessment procedures, if a legitimate assessment is to be made of a teacher's performance" (pp. 53–54).

SMITHERS, ALAN, "Training University Teachers," *The Times Higher Education Supplement*, 22.9.72, p. 14.

In 1972 the University Grants Committee of Britain allocated £130,000 in support of research projects concerned with the training of teaching and administrative staff in the universities. This led Dr. Smithers to comment on the attempts which had been and were being made to provide such training. Most British universities offer something like a one-week course for new lecturers. Not enough, and misguided, says Smithers: "Altogether the whole thing looks puny." In his view, "Insofar as the aim of giving practical training to university teachers can be stated it is probably to help them discover their capabilities and develop their own distinctive teaching styles." He concludes that the major problem is: "how can we best organize our universities to produce the conditions in which students can learn to learn for themselves, and what part should teachers play in this?"

Society for Research into Higher Education, *Motivation: Non-Cognitive Aspects of Student Performance*. Papers presented at the eighth annual conference of the Society for Research into Higher Education 1972, edited by Colin Flood Page and Jill Gibson. London: The Society, 1973. Pp. 118.

Although most of the contributors started their reports by pointing out that motivation is an ill-defined concept and that one cannot separate cognitive and noncognitive aspects of student performance, they went on to offer the results of studies which throw new light on the complexity of the factors related to the success and failure of university students.

SOCKLOFF, ALAN L., ed., *Proceedings of the First Invitational Conference on Faculty Effectiveness as Evaluated by Students*. Philadelphia: Temple University, Measurement and Research Center, [1973]. Pp. 252.

The ten papers which formed the basis of discussion at this April 1973 conference present a relatively discouraging picture. The editor understates the case when he observes that "it is clear that some significant improvements are needed in this field."

SULLIVAN, ARTHUR M., "Psychology and Teaching," *Canadian Journal of Behavioural Science*, VI, 1 (January 1974), 1–29.

In this presidential address presented to the Canadian Psychological Association in 1973, Professor Sullivan (Memorial University of Newfoundland) describes a long-term experiment with modular (he calls it "structured") instruction in psychology and mathematics. It was more successful in the former than in the latter, leading him to conclude that "the specific method of instruction which is most effective depends on the nature of the subject matter and the characteristics of the learners." With respect to research directed toward the attainment of effective instruction he urges that it "include systematic information concerning ability and personality characteristics of students . . . measure attainment precisely and with commonly used measuring instruments . . . be carried out in a real life learning situation and . . . continue for an extended period of time, at least several years."

THIELENS, WAGNER, JR., "Teacher-Student Interaction, Higher Education: Student Viewpoint," in Lee C. Deighton, ed., *Encyclopedia of Education* (New York: Macmillan and Free Press, 1971), 9:54–63.

A review of American research on the college classroom, with particular reference to "communication between an instructor and his students." A thorough bibliography is appended.

THOMSON, DAVID L., "The College-Teaching Problem: An Experiment," *School and Society*, LXXVI (1952), 55–56; reprinted in the *C.A.U.T. Bulletin*, VI, 2 (April 1958), 13–17.

Description of a three-week in-service program for Canadian university teachers, sponsored by the National Conference of Canadian Universities and offered twice, in 1950 and 1951. It was reported to have been a success, but was not continued.

Toronto, University of, *Undergraduate Instruction in Arts and Science: Report of the Presidential Advisory Committee on Undergraduate Instruction in the Faculty of Arts and Science* (C. B. Macpherson, chairman). Toronto: The University, 1967. Pp. 149.

Although the chief outcome of this study has been a new curriculum in arts and science at the University of Toronto, the report does include a chapter on "Teaching and Learning." In it is offered a list of six "possible or expected functions of lectures" of which five are judged desirable, the sixth undesirable. The Committee recommended a reduction in the number of lectures per week in each course—with some success. Also discussed were examinations, tutorials, discussion classes, and laboratories. In order to improve the quality of teaching the means proposed include:

(a) making available throughout the Faculty more systematic help on how to go about undergraduate teaching than is now available or customary in most departments;

(b) establishing a known policy whereby excellence, or lack of it, in teaching, counts more than it is now thought to count in appointments and promotions; and

(c) (as a means to b) establishing a more systematic appraisal of each faculty member's excellence (or lack of it) in undergraduate teaching. (p. 40)

TOUGH, ALLEN M., *Learning without a Teacher: A Study of Tasks and Assistance during Adult Self-Teaching Projects*. Educational Research Series No. 3. Toronto: Ontario Institute for Studies in Education, 1967. Pp. 92.

Allen Tough is now an associate professor in the Department of Adult Education of OISE, and this is a condensed version of the Ph.D. thesis he presented to the University of Chicago in 1965. The relevance of this report for the universities is not only because of the number of "independent study" programs to be found as curricular innovations, but because the process of learning without a teacher is so much like successful learning with one.

TRENT, JAMES W. AND ARTHUR M. COHEN, "Research on Teaching in Higher Education," in Robert M. W. Travers, ed., *Second Handbook of Research on Teaching* (Chicago: Rand McNally & Company, 1973), 997–1071.

In the words of the authors, "This report considers the literature of the decade [of the 1960s] pertinent to the teaching-learning function in higher education under five main headings: 1) teaching environments; 2) student characteristics and the learning process; 3) teaching technology and methods; 4) teaching recruitment, training and resources; and 5) evaluation of teaching." The third of these five areas is in part an updating of the review of "Research on Teaching at the College and University Level" prepared by W. J. McKeachie (*q.v.*) for the first *Handbook of Research on Teaching*, edited by N. L. Gage and published in 1963. The article concludes with a bibliography of about 400 items.

TROTTER, BERNARD, *Television and Technology in University Teaching.* A report to the Committee on University Affairs, and the Committee of Presidents of Universities of Ontario. Toronto: Published jointly by the two Committees, 1970. Pp. 84. Available from Information Branch, Ontario Ministry of Colleges and Universities, Toronto *or* the Council of Ontario Universities, Toronto.

An enlightened discussion of the instructional process and the uses of television. A new kind of university is proposed for Ontario—one adapting the basic ideas and methods of Britain's Open University. Also recommended is a Centre for Instructional Development to serve the universities of Ontario, a scheme which, in modified form, was launched in 1973 as the Ontario Universities Program for Instructional Development (*q.v.*).

World Health Organization, *The Training of Medical Teachers in Pedagogy.* Report on a Seminar convened by the Regional Office for Europe of the World Health Organization, San Remo, 18–22 April 1972. Copenhagen: World Health Organization, Regional Office for Europe, 1972. Pp. 65. (Also published in French and Russian.)

"The Seminar brought together a number of medical educators and organizers of courses for medical teachers from 22 European countries who, for a period of five days, considered the elements and organization of teacher training programmes and courses in the medical field, emphasizing the pedagogical aspects." The agenda was built around a series of questions and problems relevant to the teaching of medicine and drew heavily on the experience of the University of Copenhagen. One annex to the report is an outline of the basic course in educational methods for teachers at the Faculty of Medicine of that University.

Appendix

Letters requesting assistance in the project

UNIVERSITY OF TORONTO
TORONTO, ONTARIO, CANADA

Innis College, May 1969.

Dear University Graduate:

This request for assistance in a research project is being addressed to a representative sample of men and women who graduated from Canadian universities in 1958, 1963 and 1968.

As the first step in an investigation of the characteristics of effective teaching in university, I am asking recent graduates to help identify professors (of whatever rank, including lecturers and instructors) who, in their view, are excellent teachers. Of the teachers so identified, a score or more will be invited to write essays on the teaching of undergraduate students, reflecting their own beliefs and practices. These essays and a digest of the views of the graduates who have responded to this request will be published.

It would be greatly appreciated if you would take the 10 or 15 minutes required to complete the attached simple questionnaire, and then send it to me in the enclosed envelope.

If you care to add your name and address, I shall be glad to keep you informed of the results.

Yours sincerely,

E. F. Sheffield

Edward F. Sheffield,
Professor of Higher Education.

EFS:jac.
Enc.

Innis College, juin 1969

Cher diplômé,

J'ai l'intention de faire l'étude des caractéristiques de l'enseignement efficace au niveau universitaire et j'invite un groupe représentatif d'hommes et de femmes, qui ont obtenu leur diplôme dans une université canadienne en 1958, 1963 et 1968, à me prêter leur concours à cette fin.

Comme première démarche dans mon enquête, je demande aux diplômés de date récente de me désigner ceux de leurs professeurs (de quelque rang que ce soit) qu'ils jugent excellents. Parmi ces professeurs, j'en inviterai au moins une vingtaine à m'exposer par écrit leurs opinions sur l'enseignement au niveau pré-grade et les méthodes qu'ils mettent en pratique. Je ferai ensuite publier les exposés des professeurs ainsi que le résumé des opinions des diplômés qui auront répondu à mon invitation.

Je vous serais très obligé, si vous vouliez bien consacrer de 10 à 15 minutes pour répondre au questionnaire ci-joint et me le retourner dans l'enveloppe ci-incluse. Si vous y inscrivez votre nom et votre adresse, il me fera plaisir de vous mettre au courant des résultats de mon enquête.

Vous remerciant à l'avance de toute collaboration que vous pourrez m'accorder, je vous prie d'agréer l'expression de mes sentiments les meilleurs.

E. F. Sheffield

Edward F. Sheffield,
Professeur de l'enseignement supérieur

Pièces jointes

Questionnaire on the Characteristics of Effective University Teaching

Please complete and return to:

Edward F. Sheffield,
Professor of Higher Education,
University of Toronto,
Toronto 181, Ontario.

1. Your university (i.e. the one from which you took a bachelor's or first professional degree in 1958, 1963 or 1968): ....

2. Degree earned (e.g. B.A., M.D.) .... 3. Year: 19 ......

4. Please name one or more university teachers from whom you took courses leading to the degree named in item 2 above whose teaching you considered to be especially effective. In each case, give his/her name and indicate the course(s) you took from him/her.

	Name	*Field*	*Course (approximation of title)*	*Year (level)*	*Approx. class size*
e.g.	R. D. Lawrence	History	Greek and Roman	III	20
(1)	....	....	....	....	....
(2)	....	....	....	....	....
(3)	....	....	....	....	....

5. In 200 words, more or less, describe the characteristics, qualities, methods, procedures, etc. which, in your view, identify each of these as an excellent teacher. Please describe each separately, numbering your descriptions to match the numbers in item 4 above. (Use the back of this sheet.)

6. Your name and address (optional):

....

....

List of universities and faculties whose graduates are being invited to assist in the study

University	*Faculty or School*
University of Alberta	Education
University of British Columbia	Home Economics; Law
Carleton University	Science
Dalhousie University	Medicine
Université Laval	Sciences de l'administration (Commerce); Sciences de l'éducation (Pédagogie, Orientation)
University of Manitoba	Agriculture
McGill University	Arts
McMaster University	Physical Education
Memorial University of Newfoundland	Science
Université de Montréal	Chirurgie dentaire; Droit
University of New Brunswick	Science
Nova Scotia Technical College	Engineering
Université d'Ottawa	Arts (programmes destinés aux francophones)
Queen's University at Kingston	Engineering
St. Dunstan's University	Arts
University of Saskatchewan	Pharmacy
Sir George Williams University	Commerce
University of Toronto	Library science; Medicine
University of Western Ontario	Arts (honours only); Nursing

Questionnaire sur les caractéristiques de l'enseignement efficace au niveau universitaire

A remplir et à retourner à:

Edward F. Sheffield,
Professeur de l'enseignement supérieur,
Université de Toronto,
Toronto 181 (Ontario).

1. Nom de l'université où vous avez obtenu votre baccalauréat ou votre premier grade professionnel en 1958, 1963 ou 1968 ....

....

2. Diplôme obtenu (ex. B.A., LL.L.): .... 3. Année: 19 ......

4. Veuillez nommer celui ou ceux de vos professeurs dont vous avez suivi des cours conduisant au grade mentionné à l'article 2 ci-dessus dont l'enseignement vous a paru particulièrement efficace. Outre le nom, veuillez indiquer le (ou les) cours qu'il vous a enseigné(s).

	Nom	*Discipline*	*Cours (titre approximatif)*	*Année (niveau)*	*Nombre approx. des étudiants en classe*
Exemple:	R. D. Dupont	Histoire	Grecque et romaine	3e	20
(1)	....	....	....	....	....
(2)	....	....	....	....	....
(3)	....	....	....	....	....

5. En 200 mots environ exposez les caractéristiques (qualités, méthodes ou procédés) qui vous portent à regarder comme excellent chacun des professeurs nommés ci-dessus. Veuillez traiter chacun d'eux séparément en leur attribuant le même numéro qu'à l'article 4. (Utiliser le verso de la présente feuille.)

6. Vos nom et adresse (mention facultative):

....

....

....

Liste des universités et des facultés dont les diplômés sont invités à participer à l'enquête

Université	*Faculté ou Ecole*
University of Alberta	Education
University of British Columbia	Home Economics; Law
Carleton University	Science
Dalhousie University	Medicine
Université Laval	Sciences de l'administration (Commerce); Sciences de l'éducation (Pédagogie, Orientation)
University of Manitoba	Agriculture
McGill University	Arts
McMaster University	Physical Education
Memorial University of Newfoundland	Science
Université de Montréal	Chirurgie dentaire; Droit
University of New Brunswick	Science
Nova Scotia Technical College	Engineering
Université d'Ottawa	Arts (programmes destinés aux francophones)
Queen's University at Kingston	Engineering
St. Dunstan's University	Arts
University of Saskatchewan	Pharmacy
Sir George Williams University	Commerce
University of Toronto	Library science; Medicine
University of Western Ontario	Arts (honours only); Nursing